JAMES CONNOLLY

SELECTED POLITICAL WRITINGS

JAMES CONNOLLY

SELECTED POLITICAL WRITINGS

Edited and Introduced by

OWEN DUDLEY EDWARDS

Lecturer in History at Edinburgh University

and

BERNARD RANSOM

Edinburgh University

GROVE PRESS, INC.

NEW YORK

Library of Congress Catalog Number: 73-21014

ISBN: 0-394-17874-2
Grove Press ISBN: 0-8021-0021-X

First Evergreen Edition

Manufactured in the United States of America

Distributed by Random House, Inc., New York

GENERAL EDITOR'S PREFACE

It is often claimed nowadays that terms like Left and Right have ceased to mean very much. This is not true: the distinction endures, in as sharp a form as ever, between those who, on the one hand, accept as given the framework, if not all the features, of capitalist society; and those who, on the other, are concerned with and work for the establishment of a socialist alternative to the here and now. This, ultimately, is what the Left is about.

But the Left is itself endlessly fragmented over matters great as well as small. It always has been. But it is probably true that the Left has never been more divided than now. This is not surprising. For the great certitudes represented by the traditional mass movements of the Left—social democracy and orthodox communism—have, for different reasons, long ceased to be acceptable to the generations which came to political consciousness in the 'fifties and 'sixties. This is why those years have, for so much of the Left, been marked by extreme confusion, division and search.

Such a situation has many negative aspects. But it would be wrong to think of it as altogether negative. For the confusions, the divisions and the uncertainties betoken also a very healthy rejection of easy answers to complex problems; and no one on the Left who thinks at all seriously can now doubt that the creation of what could properly be called a socialist society is a very complex enterprise indeed.

It is precisely the awareness of its complexity which has led, in recent years, to a rediscovery—the term is not too strong—of a revolutionary literature, much of which had earlier been all but submerged in a great ideological freeze. None of this literature provides 'answers' to the questions which are posed by the socialist project. But what is best in it does at least suggest how the questions have been approached and tackled by successive generations of men and movements of the Left.

In the last decade or so, a fair amount of this heritage of the revolutionary Left has become more easily available than before. But much of it, as far as the English reader is concerned, remains too little known, and for one reason or another difficult to get at. 'Writings of the Left' is intended to fill the gaps. Each of the volumes in this series will deal, by way of selected texts, either with the work of individual thinkers; or with particular episodes in the history of the Left; or with specific themes in socialist thought. These volumes will speak, not in the voice of the Left (there is no such voice) but in the many different voices of the Left, and on matters which remain central to socialist theory and practice.

RALPH MILIBAND

CONTENTS

To the memory of

OWEN SHEEHY-SKEFFINGTON

Irishman, Socialist, defender of liberty

noble son of noble father

EDITORIAL NOTE

Most of the texts in this volume have been taken from what appear to have been Connolly's personal copies of his published writings, amended by him or under his direction. These subsequently passed into the keeping of the late William O'Brien, who bequeathed them to the National Library of Ireland, having previously made them available to Desmond Ryan for his three-volume selection of Connolly's writings. The O'Brien collection has enabled us to identify certain writings not hitherto ascribed to Connolly; other writers in Connolly's papers are also occasionally identified, such as E. W. Stewart, Francis Sheehy-Skeffington and other important figures in Connolly's circle. Our debt to the Director of the National Library of Ireland, Dr Patrick Henchy, is very great indeed: his kindness, his interest and his advice have been of the greatest benefit. We must also record our thanks to his staff, a special word being due to Mr James Scully, who took the greatest of pains to obtain essential material.

The MacErlean letters and Connolly's replies were obtained through the courtesy of the British Museum Newspaper Library at Colindale. Chapter 27 was reproduced from the collection housed in the Edinburgh Public Library. Thanks are due to the officials of both institutions. The essential bibliographical information both for the quest for the documents and for their presentation owes much to the researches of Dr Antje Sommer, who is preparing a study of Connolly. We are deeply grateful to her.

Several friends have played a part in the making of this book. Elaine Greene suggested it and vigorously kept us at it. Conor Cruise O'Brien discussed Connolly's attitude to Ulster Protestantism in most helpful detail. Patrick Lynch raised some telling points on Connolly's ideas on religion. Douglas Riach drew our attention to critical points in Connolly's view of Irish history. George Shepperson opened up some suggestive lines of investigation on left-wing attitudes to racial questions at the turn of the century. Victor Kiernan raised some very stimulating points on a number of problems. We are grateful to Dr Gourie Nag for her constructive criticism during the preparation of the introduction. Mr Dudley Edwards has to thank his wife, his mother-in-law, and Maureen Modlish, who ensured that his children's efforts to improve the book were kept down to a minimum.

A special word of thanks is due to Alf Mac Lochlainn, Keeper of Printed Books in the National Library of Ireland, who was absolutely tireless in capturing vital sources, advising on their worth, placing them in context with comparable work, and making suggestion after suggestion to shorten the road and improve the product. Thanks are also due to Ralph Miliband, our General Editor, who made some very helpful suggestions with respect to the Introduction.

In presenting these writings we have corrected obvious printer's errors and standardized minor typographical details. Titles of books and journals are printed in different styles in the original texts: we have standardized these throughout. Long quotations that are broken off from the main text have similarly been treated consistently. We have deleted typographical decorations, such as the asterisks separating paragraphs that were a distinctive feature of Connolly's pieces in *The Harp*, and standardized headings. Spelling has been left unaltered even where inconsistent, and American spelling is retained in those pieces originally published in the U.S.A. Punctuation is also unaltered except in cases of obvious error. Numbered footnotes are editorial, lettered ones are Connolly's. Chapter titles are Connolly's, except for nos. 11, 12 and all those in Part VII. We have indicated in the table of Contents which texts were first published as books or pamphlets by the use of small capitals.

James Connolly's work as his own anthologizer has been exceedingly helpful. Again and again our choice has been influenced by the recognition that he selected certain writings for permanent preservation, or for special reissue. His clues establishing continuity between certain of his essays and their sequels have again been a guideline; thus in Part V, Chapters 15, 16 and 17 fall together because of his emphasis on their inter-connection. We would like to think that, apart from *Labour in Irish History* and *The Reconquest of Ireland*, his choice of his writings would correspond to most of what is here. And in certain instances we know it would.

O.D.E.
B.C.R.

INTRODUCTION

James Connolly, possibly the most significant contributor to left-wing political theory to be produced by the British Isles in the past hundred years, was born at 107 Cowgate, an Edinburgh slum, on June 5th, 1868. His parents were Irish Roman Catholic immigrants to Scotland; both appear to have been of rural origin, forming part of that great mass of agricultural labourers who migrated from the Irish countryside to the growing industrial centres of the British Isles and North America, with consequent change of occupation but not of class. James Connolly worked as printers' 'devil', baker's boy, British soldier, and carter, and did various other menial jobs, before emigrating to Dublin in 1896 to become paid organizer for the Dublin Socialist Society.

His parents were unusual in being literate, and young Connolly educated himself to become an omnivorous reader of economic and socialist literature, history in general, and in some smaller degree, the arts; he also became proficient both as speaker and reader of several languages. His early writings, produced while he was working among Irish ghetto-dwellers in Scotland, exhibit a belief that the key to socialist evangelization among them lay in propaganda firmly rooted in an Irish historical background. His theoretical bent was primarily Marxian and, from 1889 to 1896, he was a vigorous activist in the Scottish Socialist Federation. Despite its name, this was mainly a local Edinburgh body, and was a product of the split which had occurred in the British Social-Democratic Federation in 1884. The Edinburgh section of the Federation eschewed the factious concerns of its metropolitan leaders, and constituted itself as an autonomous 'Scottish Socialist Federation'. (In other provincial centres S.D.F. members divided, either following William Morris, Belfort Bax and the Marx-Aveling family group into the new 'anti-Parliamentary' Socialist League, which held to a policy of pure propagandist activity to the exclusion of any electoral effort; or remaining with the 'opportunist' S.D.F. rump, and Henry Hyndman's practice of making electoral alliances and compromises with 'capitalist' political parties. However, the capture of the Socialist League by anarchist elements in 1890–91 left its Marxist adherents with little choice other than to rejoin the S.D.F.) The Scottish Socialist Federation maintained an independent existence until September 1895; it then affiliated to the S.D.F. and became the Edinburgh branch of that organization.

In S.S.F. study groups Connolly received a solid grounding in socialist theory, and developed his own critical powers in an atmosphere relatively free from the personal and tactical animosities which then divided British Marxists at large. Here too he gained his first experience of the hustings, being twice an S.S.F.-sponsored candidate in the Edinburgh local elections of 1894 and 1895.

On his arrival in Dublin, in May 1896, he commenced what was to be his major commitment for the remaining twenty years of his life: the codification of Marxian theory and the practical work of organization among the working-class Irish in Ireland and overseas. In his first Dublin year he founded the Irish Socialist Republican Party, which had as its object the 'establishment of an Irish Socialist Republic based upon the public ownership by the Irish people of the land and instruments of production, distribution and exchange'. Despite its separatist and nationalist orientation, the party's immediate policies owed much to the programme of the S.D.F., notably to Henry Hyndman's manifesto of 1883, *Socialism Made Plain*. The I.S.R.P. demanded the implementation through 'work by political means' of railway and canal nationalization; the abolition of private banks in favour of state banks 'issuing loans at cost'; rural depots for the non-profit-making loan of the most technologically advanced agricultural machinery; graduated income tax on all incomes over £400 p.a. to provide pensions for the old, widowed, infirm and orphaned; a 48-hour working week with an established minimum wage; free child maintenance; 'gradual extension of the principle of public ownership and supply to all the necessaries of life'; national schools under public control, and managed via popularly elected boards; free education 'up to the highest university grades'; and universal suffrage. Conquest of political power 'in Parliament [i.e. Westminster] and on all public bodies in Ireland' was stressed as 'the readiest and most effective means' for attaining the desired goals. For these ends the party founded, and Connolly edited, a weekly journal, *The Workers' Republic*, in 1898; it was obliged to suspend publication from time to time and to appear at longer intervals later in its career, but did not cease publication until 1903. By then the I.S.R.P., after a vigorous career of small membership but respectable notoriety and influence, had become moribund, and Connolly left Dublin for the U.S.A. in September 1903.

Connolly had briefly visited North America in the last months of 1902, and had been well received by Daniel De Leon, leader of the (Marxist) Socialist Labor Party of America. However, when resident in the U.S.A. Connolly found official S.L.P. policy little to his taste on a number of important issues. In De Leon's view trade-union agitation for 'palliative' concessions was a futile exercise, but he did regard labour unions as useful, if subordinate, auxiliaries in the class struggle. The task of the industrial organization was to back up the social-democratic party's victory at the polls, being ready to call a general strike should the bourgeois establishment refuse to recognize the decision of the ballot. Following this schema the S.L.P. created its own union organization, which was designed to husband energies that might otherwise be distracted by non-progressive short-term goals. This was the diminutive S.L.P. client union, the 'Socialist Trade & Labor Alliance'. Connolly was unhappy with this rejection of the day-to-day industrial struggle for improved remuneration and conditions of labour. It is important to remember his background as a trade unionist in this context: he had been a leader of the Dublin United Labourers before his emigration.

As a practising Roman Catholic, Connolly also clashed with De Leon on the issues of monogamy and religion. The S.L.P. leadership regarded the monogamic family as an obsolescent institution, and was disposed to view religious faith and Materialist philosophy as mutually exclusive systems of belief. Connolly defended both his faith and the institution of marriage; like Karl Marx, Connolly was, after all, a family man. This episode is instructive in placing Connolly firmly on the side of Irish cultural norms. Apart from his own commitment on the matter, he was a thinker and activist of realistic character, employing acceptable cultural attitudes in the area he proposed to evangelize instead of cultivating a self-gratifying but foredoomed enmity to all traditionalism. Connolly again clashed with De Leon over the issue of national associations within the S.L.P. De Leon opposed the formation of such groups as chauvinistic vagaries; all members were supposed to unite on a truly internationalist basis in the S.L.P. proper. Connolly founded the Irish Socialist Federation as a vehicle for propaganda among the Irish-American working class. Working within his own ethnic group, he asserted the republicanism prevalent in it while attacking its filio-pietism and chauvinism. To Daniel De Leon, who thought in superlatives, all nationalism was chauvinism. Real chauvinism found a much more dangerous enemy in Connolly, who, as a nationalist, could more readily perceive what the dynamics of chauvinism were. Connolly's vigorous opposition to Irish chauvinism is worth stressing, given that a fair degree of chauvinism was evident in the thought of rightist socialists of his day such as Robert Blatchford and H. M. Hyndman of England. Irish-Americans compensated for their loss of Ireland with a naive, self-glorifying and often racist ethnocentricity. Connolly's attacks on Irish chauvinism were nowhere more biting than in his American writings; they were to be an essential feature of his monthly magazine *The Harp*, published in New York from January 1908 to November 1909, and in Dublin in the first half of 1910. De Leon, fearful of Connolly's influence against him among Irish and Italian workers, and indeed in the American working-class movement at large, denounced him as 'an agent of the Jesuits'.

As a result of these conflicts, Connolly and De Leon's party were to diverge in 1907; by this time, however, the differences between the two men had taken on more profound undertones with the injection of the syndicalist issue into the dispute. In 1905, a syndicalist trade union, the Industrial Workers of the World, had been founded at Chicago, with the aim of organizing all workers into 'One Big Union' (O.B.U.). Almost every shade of anarchist, Marxist and labour opinion was represented at the founding congress, including delegates from the S.L.P. Daniel De Leon's attempt to work out an 'entente' with syndicalist modes of thought is crucial for an understanding of Connolly's further ideological development. Syndicalism had its origins in the anarchism that was so forcefully represented in the First International by Bakunin. Although Marx and Engels regarded anarchism as a typical product of pre-industrial society—and therefore as a foredoomed form of protest once a genuine proletariat had emerged—it did not in fact disappear entirely, but accommodated itself to the labour movement. The resultant 'syndicalist' workers' unions are perhaps best typified by those independent French *syndicats* that combined to form the C.G.T. in 1902. These syndicalist organizations rejected social-democratic theories of the primacy of political action, but did in general accept the Marxist critique of capitalist economics and bourgeois society. The I.W.W. may be seen as the American counterpart of the C.G.T.: in North America, however, the preferred nomenclature was 'industrial unionism'; 'syndicalism' remained a European term.

Owing to the heterogeneity of its constituent parts, the I.W.W. as founded in 1905 was not a pure syndicalist organization, although it became so later. In this initial period, Daniel De Leon became its acknowledged ideologue, and it was at this time that he revised his view of the status of the industrial union in the class struggle. He outlined his new position in a public address entitled 'The Preamble of the I.W.W.', given in Minneapolis in July 1905. (The text of this lecture was later published by the S.L.P. under the title *Socialist Reconstruction of Society*.) In this new De Leonist scheme the industrial union (the O.B.U.) was now accorded an equal status to the party instead of being a mere appendage to it: 'socialist economics' were translated into twin elements for a joint attack upon capitalist institutions. The O.B.U. was to be the mould of the future socialist commonwealth, while the party's role was to assault the bourgeois superstructure. This latter, consisting of the legislative and executive organs of the state, was a prime target since it was the seat of the coercive power of the governing class: once the party had achieved a majority in the legislature it would then pass a statutory instrument dissolving all organs of the state. Sovereignty would then fall to the central administration of the O.B.U., and the state, as such, would be liquidated. The ballot was the party's only weapon; this enabled the workers' movement to be an open one, raised above the level of a 'mere conspiracy'. The party was also charged with the task of evangelizing the workers *en masse* through 'civilised discussion'. Meanwhile it was the task of the O.B.U. to keep watch over the party in order to prevent the temptations toward opportunism from corrupting it. The general strike was also of importance in this schema: if the ruling class should disallow or 'count out' the socialist party's victory at the polls, the O.B.U. was then to apply the 'quietus' measure of the general strike, or, more accurately, the 'general lock-out of the capitalist class'. In this way a peaceful revolution was assured.

Such was Daniel De Leon's attempt to come to terms with syndicalism; however, together with 'politics', he was expelled from the I.W.W. in the 'bummery' coup of 1908, leaving the organization to the 'pure' syndicalists. Connolly remained an organizer for the I.W.W. after his erstwhile leader's enforced defection, but it must be remembered that he was never a pure syndicalist of the cruder type. He never repudiated political action, even though he undoubtedly viewed the O.B.U. as the prime weapon of the proletariat in the class struggle. The De Leonite ideas outlined above, especially as Connolly himself expressed them in his *Socialism Made Easy*,[1] remained the basis of his future ideological development. This development was to be imaginative and synthetic rather than dogmatic: he derived much of his strength as a thinker and publicist from the fact that dogmatic debate occupied a much lower place in his scale of priorities than it did in those of many left-wingers of his time. His debate with De Leon was real, but implicit in it was the distaste of the evangelist for the dogmatist. He could, and did, wield a tough pen and tongue in intra-leftist controversy, but he seems to have kept it to a minimum, and

[1] Chapter 15, p. 243.

to have had an intense dislike of its corrosive effects. One of his reasons for remaining so long outside Ireland was a sense of disgust at the faction-fighting into which the I.S.R.P. collapsed at the end of its life, and he took pains, after his return, to build a political movement along broader and less doctrinaire lines. In essence his thought involved synthesis of his learning and ideological derivations, rather than a debilitating series of self-purgations. It is profitless to tie him to a party line. Parties he regarded as servants and not masters of the workers' struggle, and his purpose in writing was primarily stimulative rather than doctrinaire.

While Connolly was struggling to radicalize the Irish-American workers by speaking and writing, he continued his drive to provide a socialist interpretation of the Irish homeland and its history. In some degree this involved the revision and republication of historical writing he had already produced in *The Workers' Republic*; he added further material in the light of what he had learned from his American experience on a practical level, and from his exposure to American theoreticians, especially De Leon. (It is characteristic of Connolly that his political, ideological and personal quarrel with De Leon did not stunt the growth of his reception of De Leon's ideas.) But increasingly his efforts to convince Irish-Americans that the lessons of their Irish background must require acceptance of socialism led him to turn more and more to Ireland itself. The transfer of publication of *The Harp* from New York to Dublin at the beginning of 1910 symbolizes the degree to which the journal itself was becoming more and more Irish-orientated, instead of merely stressing Irish questions for their relevance to a putative Irish-American participation in the American class struggle. In the spring of 1910, Dublin socialists persuaded Connolly to reply directly to an influential set of sermons preached against socialism by a prominent Jesuit, and the resultant work, *Labour, Nationality and Religion*,[1] testifies to the degree to which Connolly, still in the U.S.A., had thought himself back, as it were, into the Irish context. In July 1910 he followed his thoughts in person; his home and that of his family were to be in Ireland for the

[1] Chapter 2, p. 61.

remainder of his life. Immediately he plunged into organizational work for the Socialist Party of Ireland, which he was to develop into a much more broadly based body than its predecessor, the I.S.R.P. Initial meetings at Belfast and Cork testified to this geographical broadening; the acquisition of intellectuals and of extreme non-violent nationalists indicated the party's capacity to make something of the cultural excitement that characterized the Ireland of 1910; it will be remembered that the Irish Renaissance was by now in full flower, and in exile Connolly had already acquired a reputation among its clashing would-be cultural dictators which he and his associates were now to exploit.

The S.P.I. was less explicit than its predecessor. Its avowed aim was 'common ownership of the means of producing and distributing our wealth'; its method was the election, either of its own members, or of 'independent working-class candidates pledged to a progressive policy of social reform'. Mr Desmond Greaves, Connolly's biographer, rightly stresses that the non-syndicalist content was due to a recognition of the need for broad aims and did not, at this time, fully represent Connolly's own views; he was nevertheless made a paid organizer.

James Larkin, now emerging as the major figure in Irish Labour agitation, headed the Irish Transport Workers' Union (later the Irish Transport and General Workers' Union), an organization which had the conscious aim of becoming 'Ireland's O.B.U.'. After the S.P.I. found itself unable to continue paying Connolly, the latter moved to Belfast, where he joined and began organizational work for the I.T.G.W.U. He became a leader of significance on the Belfast labour scene, directing a dockers' strike in 1911, and organizing women textile workers with some success. The Belfast of his day, however, was becoming increasingly dominated by a vociferous religious sectarianism. This mood was activated by the imminence of the enactment of the Irish Home Rule Bill, and divided the working class into antagonistic factions. Connolly's own straightforward expression of Irish republicanism did not greatly advance his prospects among frightened Protestant workers, whose traditions had little in common with those nationalist ones on which Connolly's socialist interpretation of Irish history was built. He did attract some Protestant support, notably through the S.P.I., whose tiny Belfast membership was strongly Protestant; but his union activity aroused a largely Catholic response. Such Protestant support as it gained was eroded as the forces of Carsonism drew away many workers through fear of a Catholic-dominated Home Rule Ireland, through escapism in the thrill of drilling and marching, or through the illusory charms of a trans-class movement in which the worker found himself theoretically (though rarely in reality) clasping hands with the landlord and the capitalist. Carson may not have realized it, but one immediate result of his movement was to break the growing working-class threat to his Ulster capitalist allies.

Connolly kept in touch, in person and through exchange of information, with developments elsewhere in Ireland; by means of publication and lecture visits he maintained his long-standing links with Scotland. He was recalled to Dublin in 1913 to play a critical part during the great lockout of Larkin's men by the industrialist William Martin Murphy: a conflict which developed into the most dramatic and most ominous of the whole chain of strikes and labour disputes that convulsed the British Isles in the period immediately before the Great War. Connolly was sentenced to three months' imprisonment for his speech at a proclaimed meeting; he was released after spending a week on hunger-strike. He became acting general secretary of the I.T.G.W.U. and editor of its journal, *The Irish Worker*; this paper had been issued since 1911, and he had been an irregular contributor in his Belfast days. Police brutality against the workers and their meetings led the I.T.G.W.U. to form its own self-defence force, the Irish Citizen Army. Carson's example of creating a private army in the north to resist any imposition of Home Rule influenced the I.C.A., as it also influenced the extreme nationalist Irish Volunteers. The latter body had come into being at this time, with the intention of defending nationalists should Carson's agitation escalate into a civil war. Guns for all three armies were to make their way into Ireland in 1914; initially they contented themselves with sticks, make-believe weapons and clubs.

Meanwhile the lock-out was broken, largely because of the failure of British Labour leadership to give the sympathetic support required to achieve victory. In 'Old Wine in New Bottles',[1] Connolly, writing in A. R. Orage's *New Age*, analysed the consequence of this British failure to support the Irish strikers with industrial action on their own part. Larkin and Connolly spoke extensively in Britain during the later stages of the lock-out and afterwards; Connolly's long-standing sense of identity with the British working class was badly strained by this episode. Accordingly, he was drawn more naturally into the waters of Irish nationalist revolt.

Despite all his work for the I.T.G.W.U., Connolly had not been idle on the political front. At Easter 1912 he was instrumental in the formation of the Independent Labour Party of Ireland – I.L.P.(I). This paralleled the Irish T.U.C.'s decision of the same year to constitute itself as a Labour Party – an electoral machine to sponsor 'pure' Labour candidates. Connolly had been active too in this venture. The I.L.P.(I) was formed in expectation of an immediate grant of Home Rule, and its programme was one for an autonomous quasi-independent Ireland. This programme was explicitly syndicalist in tone, since it defined its aims in terms of the creation of an 'industrial commonwealth'. It is worth quoting Connolly's scheme of action from the I.L.P.(I) manifesto:

> 1. *Political*: Organisation of the forces of Labour in Ireland to take political action on independent lines for securing the control of all public elective bodies, and for the mastery of all the public powers of the state, in order that such bodies and such powers should be used for the attainment of the above object [i.e. the industrial commonwealth].
>
> 2. *Industrial*: Furtherance of the Industrial Organisation of the wage-earners, with a view to securing unity of action in the industrial field as a means to the conquest of industrial power, the necessary preliminary to industrial freedom.

[1] Chapter 20, p. 312.

This programme was retained when the I.L.P.(I) later reverted to the former title of 'Socialist Party of Ireland'. Connolly was really thinking in terms of a tripartite coalition for the Irish Labour movement. The I.L.P.(I)/S.P.I. provided the working-class movement with a distinct guiding socialist cadre, complementing the activities of the purely electoral Labour Party. The unions, and particularly the I.T.G.W.U., remained as the essential industrial and financial base for the whole effort. By the time that the I.L.P.(I) manifesto had emerged, Connolly had achieved a theoretical synthesis of the various intellectual currents to which he had been exposed. Perhaps this process can be best illustrated by means of a comparison with another Marxian revolutionary nationalist: Mao Tse-tung. Both Connolly and Mao were the recipients, in the forms of 'De Leonism' and 'Leninism' respectively, of tactical schemas designed to put into practice the revolutionary implications of the Marxist critique of capitalist economic relations and philosophy of history. Both men selected from and revised these schemas in deference to their own practical and national needs. Mao's goal was a Chinese People's Republic, to be created by a populist (though Communist-led) revolt. Connolly aimed at the creation of an Irish Workers' Republic, through a democratic coup by a working class organized both politically and industrially. Mao's revision of Lenin was a nationalist and agrarian-populist one. Connolly revised De Leon employing nationalist and 'right' syndicalist criteria.

We must begin our examination of this revision with an attempt to clarify the extent to which Connolly's 'De Leonism' entailed a critique of 'pure' syndicalism. There is little doubt that Connolly anticipated the eventual suppression (or supersession) of 'politics', in accordance with the Marxian tenet regarding 'the government of men being replaced by the administration of things'. Indeed there is his own striking phrase from *Labour, Nationality and Religion*: 'government under socialism will be largely a matter of statistics'.[1] While recognizing the necessity for the revolt of the structure (economic categories) against the superstructure (political

[1] p. 107.

categories)—which he sketched out in *Socialism Made Easy*—he yet avers that 'non-political co-operative effort must infallibly succumb in the face of the opposition of the privileged classes'. If Connolly means by this that political power will have to be used for the final suppression of 'politics' then this clearly removes him as far from 'pure' syndicalism as are De Leon and V. I. Lenin. When in *Labour, Nationality and Religion* he speaks of 'a state which should be a social instrument in the hands of its men and women, where state powers would be wielded as a means by the workers', he is explicitly advocating something approaching a proletarian dictatorship not dissimilar to the vision of Lenin in his *The State and Revolution.* In the article 'Changes' of May 1914,[1] Connolly makes perhaps his most sophisticated plea for a non-doctrinaire approach to the problem of the relationship between political and industrial action. Typically, he ends with a declaration of the need for tolerance and receptivity as a basis for future activity. In 'Old Wine in New Bottles' Connolly includes a strong condemnation of the general strike, comparing it to a set-piece battle between unequal armies in which the weaker—Labour—will always lose. He much prefers the weapon of the sporadic strike: a surprise tactic which 'has won more for Labour than all the great Labour conflicts in history'. This position of course contrasts markedly with the emphasis upon the efficacy of the general strike in the mythology of 'pure' or Sorelian syndicalism. So we may say that on the issues of both the role of state power and the role of the general strike, Connolly was distinctly opposed to 'pure' syndicalist thought. If Connolly can thus be distinguished from the syndicalist ultra-left with its distaste for political action and distrust of the state, we must not forget that he was consistent in his emphasis on the primacy of the industrial organization. In *Socialism Made Easy* he speaks of the O.B.U. as a preparation 'within the framework of capitalistic society, of the working forms of the Socialist Republic'. Again he says 'the fight for the conquest of the political state is not the battle; it is only the echo of battle. The real battle is being fought out every day for the power to control industry.'

[1] Chapter 21, p. 319.

We have already examined the nature of Daniel De Leon's short-lived compromise with the I.W.W.: it will be remembered that Connolly wrote *Socialism Made Easy* in harmony with this De Leonite position. However, with De Leon's expulsion from the I.W.W. and his formation of a new 'client' O.B.U. in 1908, erstwhile De Leonites—like Connolly—who remained in the I.W.W. were obliged to redefine 'De Leonism'. To the extent that Connolly remained genuinely committed to the O.B.U. as a non-dependent unit, yet insisted also upon political action, his subsequent redefinition may be called a 'right' syndicalist revision of De Leon. It is this Marxian-syndicalist synthesis of Connolly that we must now examine. Connolly's concept of a Labour coalition—under the tutelage of the I.L.P.(I)—represented a revision of the De Leonist concept of the party as a small, doctrinally 'pure' apparatus. This broad-front concept of Connolly may be compared with Mao's revision of Lenin: his collectivist notion of 'New Democracy' was a similar development of the Bolshevik idea of the party. De Leon had remained tentative and vague about the O.B.U.'s task as the instrument of revolutionary government. Connolly developed a much more positive concept of the O.B.U. and its tasks. He regarded the sympathetic strike as a means both of spreading the O.B.U.'s influence in the general labour movement and as a means of recruitment to it. This latter idea was realized in a number of instances where small unions affiliated to the I.T.G.W.U. after receiving 'sympathetic' support.

The parallel between Connolly's single union and Lenin's single party is quite marked. Like the Bolshevik party, the O.B.U. is charged with the task of supervising the whole process of production in the post-revolutionary state:

> With the industrial union as our principle of action, branches can be formed to give expression to the need for effective supervision of the affairs of the workshop, shipyard, dock or railway.
>
> ... the concept of one Big Union embracing all, [is] the outline of the most effective form of combination for

> industrial warfare, and also for the Social Administration of the Co-operative Commonwealth of the future.[1]

The organization of the O.B.U. is to be on the lines of democratic centralism—in contradistinction to the bureaucratic centralism of the bourgeois state:

> Social Democracy ... is the application to industry ... of the fundamental principles of democracy. Such application will necessarily have to begin in the workshop, and proceed logically ... upward ... until it reaches the culminating point of national executive power ... Social Democracy must proceed from the bottom upward, whereas capitalist political society is organised from above downward ... this conception of Socialism destroys at one blow all the fears of a bureaucratic state ... [2]

Lenin's party 'of a new type' is the vanguard of the proletariat, the guardian of revolutionary consciousness and the material creator of the new order. In Connolly's scheme, these tasks will be discharged by the O.B.U.—the union 'of a new type'. When this apparatus assumes the national administration, 'politics' and the state will be suppressed: this will herald a new era, not of the dictatorship (of the vanguard) of the proletariat, but of the hegemony of the organized working class. (One might note the similarity to Mao's notion of 'People's Democratic Dictatorship'). The O.B.U. is thus the vehicle of revolutionary practice, and the agency of Connolly's own form of 'democratic dictatorship'.

The reactionary crisis which destroyed the validity of this Connolly synthesis was a dual one, comprising the fact of war and the threat of partition in Ireland. Wartime government became increasingly authoritarian, and stricter national security, under the Defence of the Realm Acts, seemed to erode democratic and civil liberties, perhaps beyond redemption. Trade-union rights were particularly undermined by the new wartime labour codes introduced under such measures as

[1] James Connolly, *The Reconquest of Ireland*, in *Labour in Ireland* (Maunsel & Co., Dublin, 1917), pp. 327–8.

[2] *Socialism Made Easy*: 'Industrial Unionism and Constructive Socialism'; see p. 273.

the Munitions of War Act. The unions were obliged to accept mandatory direction of labour, suspension of the right to strike and the forcible imposition of trades 'dilution'. In Ireland, with memories of the 1913 lockout still fresh, the problem was particularly acute. The lockout had been a reflex of the Dublin employers' reluctance to recognize the I.T.G.W.U., and, having failed to destroy the Irish O.B.U. in peacetime, they attempted to make use of the war situation to dismiss I.T.G.W.U. members. These men, ostensibly released for the colours, were replaced by female labour or by scab labour specially imported for the purpose. The O.B.U., already weakened by the events of 1913, faced piecemeal and systematic destruction.

Meanwhile, the postponement of the grant of Home Rule for the duration of hostilities presaged a quite different problem. By March 1914, intimidated by Carson's volunteer force, Asquith's government had accepted the expedient of excluding certain counties in Ulster from the provisions of the Home Rule bill. For Connolly this implied the separation, from the new Irish dominion, of the Belfast labour force—the largest and most 'advanced' section of the Irish working class. Faced with this tide of militarism and reaction, unleashed by what he regarded as a wholly imperialist war, Connolly became increasingly convinced of the need to create some counter-attack in Ireland which would throw the British war machine off balance and perhaps bring it to a halt. Initially, his ideas seem to have been non-violent strike and boycott action; as the war continued, he came to accept the idea of armed insurrection. After some hesitation he accepted alliance with the I.R.B. (Irish Republican Brotherhood), a reinvigorated, extreme revolutionary nationalist movement initially founded by the Fenians over fifty years earlier; the I.R.B. itself was largely ignorant of the plans for a rising, which were determined by its Military Council, a group of five to whom Connolly and, later, Thomas MacDonagh were added in 1916. The I.R.B. Military Council had some influence among the Irish Volunteers, whose defensive ethos was undermined in part of its ranks by MacDonagh, Patrick Pearse and other officers of secret I.R.B. membership. (The Irish

Volunteers had in fact lost nine-tenths of their membership on the issue of support for Britain in World War I; it must be remembered that the 1916 insurrection was carried out in the teeth of opposition from the great bulk of the Irish people.) Connolly openly campaigned against the war in *The Irish Worker*, which variously became *Irish Work* (December 1914), *The Worker* (December 1914–January 1915), and after a lapse returned to the name of Connolly's first newspaper, *The Workers' Republic* (May 1915–April 1916), the changes in nomenclature being largely occasioned by governmental efforts at censorship and suppression.

It was only a fraction of the Irish Citizen Army that followed Connolly, and a fraction of the Irish Volunteers that followed Pearse and MacDonagh as they commenced the Easter Week Rising on Monday, April 24th, 1916. German aid had collapsed with Sir Roger Casement's capture in Kerry on the preceding Friday, and the subsequent scuttling of the German ship bearing the meagre amount of arms allocated for the Irish diversion. Eoin MacNeill, head of the Irish Volunteers, had at last become aware of the intentions of some of his subordinates, and countermanded the manœuvres intended to bring all of his organization into the field; accordingly, little of importance happened outside Dublin in Easter Week. The insurgents had initially hoped to hold out until the conclusion of the war—itself expected at an early date—but Connolly, for one, had no illusions about the situation when he finally marched out. 'We are going out to be slaughtered,' he told an associate as he left Liberty Hall, his union headquarters, on Easter Monday. All that remained was the hope of an inspirational martyrdom, and Connolly, in charge of the Dublin insurgent forces, placed his men in defensive positions. Ironically, the hope was to be fulfilled, but it was revolutionary nationalism and not Irish socialism that was to be its beneficiary. After a week's fighting, in which Connolly was badly wounded, the insurgents surrendered unconditionally. Ireland had been placed under martial law during the hostilities, and the Military Council plus eight of its lieutenants were executed by firing squads after court-martial. Connolly's execution was delayed by his medical condition, which had become serious as a result of his wounds, and by the time he was shot, the British government was intervening to end the executions. But if any hope existed for Connolly's reprieve it was destroyed when an Irish nationalist newspaper, the *Irish Independent*, called for his death. The action of the *Independent* directly derived from the fact that it was owned by Connolly's old enemy, the leader of the Dublin employers, William Martin Murphy. On May 12th, fortified by the last rites of the Roman Catholic Church, Connolly was carried on a stretcher before a firing squad in Kilmainham Jail and set in a chair. Asked by the priest to pray for his executioners, he replied, 'I will say a prayer for all brave men who do their duty according to their lights.' We may leave the final word to the devoted pen of Desmond Greaves: 'He gripped the sides of the chair to steady himself, and held his head high waiting for the volley.'

It was in the early days of the Easter Rising that a little girl went into a newspaper shop in Edinburgh to buy a paper for her father. 'Look who's in the paper,' shouted the shopman, 'your uncle's in the paper.' She took the paper, paid for it, looked at it, and began running home desperately. 'What's the matter with you?' demanded her father as she hurtled into the house, gasping and red-faced. And when she could speak she said with terrified bewilderment, 'Oh Daddy, Daddy, look what's happened to Uncle James!'

Hauntingly the child's cry rings down the years. Look indeed what's happened to Uncle James; during the days he lived after the beginning of the Rising, the bewilderment of his associates outside Ireland was as pitiful and uncomprehending as that of his little niece, while after his death he has been claimed for so many vastly divergent causes that at times it seems unbelievable that the same man is in question. British comrades were horror-stricken. John Leslie, his old Edinburgh mentor, reproached himself bitterly for having urged Connolly to return to Ireland, during Connolly's visit to Scotland, in despondent mood, in 1911. 'They will never understand why I am here,' Connolly told his daughter Nora, of the British Socialists, when she visited him before his execution; 'they will all forget I am an Irishman.' British Socialists could not accept the notion that the Irish working class had a destiny other than that of an exotic appendage to the British working class. Where Irishmen behaved 'otherwise', in Bishop Berkeley's word, this was only to reveal their primitive inability to slough off their heritage of bourgeois (and essentially unprogressive) nationalism. The practical issue of national revolution in Ireland, raised by Connolly's martyrdom, must have seemed an extraordinary attempt to roll back history 700 years. Any who knew Connolly's writings on Irish history, such as his book *Labour in Irish History*,[1] might well have such uncertainty strengthened by Connolly's utopian treatment of an allegedly classless pre-Norman Ireland. (He rather lost sight of the slave class which served pre-Norman Irish society; St Patrick should have reminded him.) Connolly was undoubtedly acting, in 1916, in conformity with the known views of Marx, Engels and Lenin on the nationalities question, and Lenin confirmed as much by a powerful statement in support of the Rising; but on such a matter all three of them were decidedly at variance with general British attitudes. After the Great War, British Socialists did agitate the Irish question, but much more in liberal terms than with any sense of Connolly's legacy. A few Marxists, such as T. A. Jackson (who was later to write a vigorous popular Marxist historical work—*Ireland Her Own*)[2], sought to vindicate Connolly then and later, but for the most part he was forgotten as a socialist in England, and while his influence remained in Scotland it was subsumed into the general literature of socialist piety. An Irish group of Communists in Britain was to revive Connolly's name, and in so far as it was guided by the forceful and scholarly Mr Desmond Greaves it was steeped in Connolly's writings; but it seems reasonable to suggest that many of its Irish-born recruits were attracted to Connolly, initially, by his status as a republican nationalist martyr. Meanwhile, British comrades seem more anxious to acknowledge Connolly as a bridge to winning support among pious Irish nationalists rather than as a teacher. Connolly gets much the same response from the British 'New

[1] See Bibliography. [2] Cobbett Press, London and Dublin, 1946.

Left'; one has to be polite about him, because he is apparently a peculiar Irish Marxist household god, but he is hardly viewed as an inspiration to British Socialists. For the most part in Britain, as until fairly recently in Ireland, Connolly is respected rather than read. Occasionally some of his writings have achieved publication in Britain (loyal Scottish comrades reprinted *Erin's Hope*[1] and *Socialism Made Easy* in 1917) but such efforts have not generally been made beyond Mr Greaves's circle.

Where Connolly did achieve some measure of attention was in the Socialist movement outside Britain. We do not know whether Lenin had read any of Connolly's writings; it seems unlikely, although, oddly enough, he did read some of the nationalist writings of Sir Roger Casement. He was extremely well informed on Irish events, and made some profound comments on the 1913 lockout; it is clear that he, and therefore the international socialist movement which came to follow him, grasped the lesson that an advanced and highly class-conscious workers' movement had thrown its weight (or some part thereof) behind the Easter insurrection. Larkin, who went to Moscow in the 1920s, would have reinforced the point, although his undisciplined spontaneity of approach was to pose its own problems with the new bureaucracy of the U.S.S.R. It seems probable that Lenin was not aware of how sophisticated at least one theoretician of the workers engaged in the Easter Rising was, and accordingly there might have been a disposition to see Connolly as a primitive socialist; the term was to be used of him by later European Marxist writers, for example Vladimir Dedijer of Yugoslavia. Lenin himself applied the word 'premature' as opposed to 'primitive' to the Easter Rising, which in point of fact was fair enough.

All of this is to focus attention on the political writing one cannot select for this book: the message for posterity written in Connolly's death. And in Ireland, as elsewhere, this was to be the most influential legacy of Connolly. It is in Ireland that the survival of Connolly has assumed some of its most contradictory forms. It was natural that the Irish Communist movement, a tiny persecuted minority, should have welcomed him, and indeed, its use of his writings gave it some degree of

[1] Chapter 9, p. 165.

independence of thought which larger partics, lacking a Marxist national theoretician of such stature, failed to exhibit. In 1968 the Irish Communists condemned the Russian invasion of Czechoslovakia in terms much less measured than certain other Western Communist critics of that event employed. His own party, the Irish Labour Party, was for many years anxious to avoid commitment to its founder's radical social policies, and remained timorous of clerical criticism in a way that ran wholly counter to the vigorous refutations of reactionary clerical statements that Connolly himself produced. The 'New Left', notably as it emerged in the Northern Ireland crisis, studied Connolly's writings with great profit. Many of his remarks on Catholic sectarianism and petty capitalism in Ulster were to prove inspirational in the civil rights drive to destroy Catholic ghetto-mindedness. The small but influential Irish Communist Organization, whose anti-Moscow, anti-Peking stance throws it heavily back on Connolly, has reissued many of his little-known writings, with slightly sensational charges as to their previous suppression.

If we pass over the admittedly well-argued but dubiously motivated writings of the late Joseph Stalin on anti-colonialism, Connolly might be seen to stand forth as the lineal ancestor of Frantz Fanon, testifying to socialism as a faith for the victims of imperialism, and not solely or even primarily as that of the proletariat of highly advanced capitalist societies or far-flung empires. And while we associate Connolly with the integration of progressive nationalism with socialism we must remember that his life's work was done primarily not in Ireland itself but among the Irish diaspora. He saw that so formidable an ethnic group, scattered over many lands, offered a great potential for socialism; but he tried to evangelize it, not by a tyrannical refusal to allow for its special characteristics, but rather by building on the socialist possibilities of these. Hence in *Labour in Irish History* and in *The Reconquest of Ireland* he sought to build up a history of the Irish working class that would convince these scattered Irish workers of the radical dictates of their past. Necessarily he was writing under great difficulties.

Research had far to go and he wished his book to be a stimulus to further work on a neglected topic, not in any sense to be the last word on it. His desire to use nationalist feelings to win a favourable audience for socialist doctrines led him into some of the pitfalls of nationalist history. The rosy view of pre-Norman Ireland is one example; the diatribe against Daniel O'Connell is another, since Connolly had allowed himself to be hypnotized by O'Connell's undeserved posthumous obloquy in extreme nationalist eyes as being a moderate. In particular he neglected O'Connell's effort to put Ireland into the international struggle against oppression by his whole-hearted opposition to slavery; and he also remained silent on the defence of slavery by O'Connell's bitter critic, John Mitchel, whose intransigent nationalist writing Connolly quoted so favourably. His failure to assess the growth of the Belfast working class in the nineteenth century is a tragic omission, particularly in that it prevented his coming to terms with a working-class tradition that was not Irish nationalist; this marks in some ways one of his major weaknesses as an Irish socialist. Connolly appealed, essentially, to an international Irish working class of Catholic origin, although he did so in a highly anti-sectarian way. He does not seem to have attempted to agitate that other Irish diaspora, the so-called 'Scotch-Irish', however many recruits among Belfast Protestants he may have obtained in 1911 on his own terms. He bitterly opposed, and was among the first to assail, any question of partitioning Ireland; but he seems to have had some difficulties in seeing the fullest multi-ethnic implications of a 32-county republic.

Labour in Irish History and *The Reconquest of Ireland* must be noted in any comment on his writings, but their specifically Irish relevance places them slightly beyond the fullest appreciation by non-Irish readers. We have included only one chapter of the former work and nothing at all from the latter. Of his other major works, the selection given here has been chosen to illustrate Connolly's contribution on certain important topics, and some attention has been paid to the desirability of including works not readily available elsewhere. It might be said that Connolly tackled the question of propaganda work in two ways, which often interacted. He tried to establish what should be the attitude of the socialist towards certain cultural institutions in the ethnic groups to which he was addressing himself, and he looked for the best means of showing what socialism was in terms which would be acceptable to that ethnic group. It therefore seems desirable to present some of Connolly's most important comments on the relationship of socialism to Catholicism, and of socialism to Irish nationalism. In addition, some of his earlier, expository writings have been included. While Connolly represents a constantly self-educating mind, and was accordingly to lose some early rigidity, he attacked first principles more directly in his earlier years as a writer than was necessary when his movement was in full swing, and when the Irish world was convulsed by his ally Larkin.

In the Irish context, it would have made no sense to have committed socialism to a pure and simple opposition to Catholicism, even supposing that Connolly himself had been theologically opposed to that or any other religion. What was wanted was a clear statement of what the relationship of the two systems of belief should be to one another. We may interpret *Labour, Nationality and Religion* narrowly if we choose; but there is a case for viewing it, not just as an essay on socialism and Catholicism, but on the relations of socialism to religion, and to theological cult in general. It seems advisable to stress that, at certain stages, Connolly is arguing primarily from a Catholic standpoint, and secondarily in the light of socialist teaching. We may indicate the treatment of divorce and of divine Providence as apposite examples. Against Father Kane's view of human society as a divinely ordained hierarchy, Connolly advances the charge of 'rank blasphemy', since, he avers, the cleric is imputing to the hand of God responsibility for social conditions which are really the reflection of man's worst instincts. On the issue of divorce, Father Kane implies that socialism is hostile to the sacrament of marriage, saying that 'Divorce in the socialist sense means that women would be willing to stoop to be the mistresses of one man after another'. Connolly replies with a demonstration of capitalist society's explicit anti-Catholicism. Referring to the high divorce rate of 'America and its capitalist class', he maintains that it is the moral ethic of 'individualism and the cash nexus' which is responsible for the cheapening of Christian marriage, and not socialist propaganda. Connolly's attempt to defend the materialist concept of history from Father Kane's charge that it is anti-religious is masterly. In opposition to the priest's contention that Christ brought into the world a moral force for change 'hostile to economic causes', Connolly is at pains to stress the material base of Christ's mission. The Redeemer appeared precisely at 'the psychological moment' of the Jewish nation's bondage, during the period of their worst experience of economic oppression. He reminds us of the nature of early Christianity as 'a religion of slaves and labourers', and that it was the 'canting, fed classes' who intrigued for Christ's crucifixion. All of this testifies that Connolly's socialism, however dominated by the influence of Marx, drew inspiration from decidedly Christian sources also. This essay has much urgency today. Connolly's remarks on the freedom of the press, of speech, of research, of religion and of the family in the socialist state, and the assertion that capitalism has been the enemy and not the friend of such freedoms, must stand as an assertion of values no less necessary because states have since swept them aside in the name of socialism. Some few other points on the essay may be noted. Father Kane's Lenten sermons were no minor matter of an ill-informed cleric bawling a commonplace denunciation of socialism. The Society of Jesus was at this time acknowledged to be the foremost intellectual order within the Roman Catholic Church in Ireland; the sermons would have attracted hundreds, and would have been read in newspaper and pamphlet form by thousands. The whole exercise was designed to be the intellectual death-blow to socialism in the Ireland of that generation. The care with which the Irish socialists went to such lengths to get Connolly himself, in far-away America, to refute it, testifies to the urgency of the case.

It seems advisable to include Connolly's letters to the *Catholic Times* which followed the publication of his pamphlet. These have not previously been republished, apart from a few passages quoted in Desmond Ryan's *James Connolly*, and merit attention because of their vigorous distinction between the political and religious actions of church authorities. It was in some ways a point of little originality; indeed, as Connolly had himself noted in his pamphlet, it had been stated in a liberal context by the much abused Daniel O'Connell; but it exhibits a judicious use of the thin end of the wedge which Connolly was driving into a triumphalist Catholicism—then at the height of its assertiveness over all aspects of the consciences of its followers. Although popes had not followed the doctrine of papal infallibility by any effort to implement it, a vulgar belief had grown up among Christians of all denominations that any Vatican enunciation of policy was to be regarded by Catholics as infallible. Given the papal condemnation of socialism by Pope Leo XIII in his *Rerum Novarum*, there was urgency in Connolly's effort to dispose of such assumptions. In the process he became involved once more in controversy with an Irish Jesuit, this time the Rev. John MacErlean, S.J., a distinguished antiquary.

That the Kane–Connolly–MacErlean controversy took place at all conveys how emphatically democratic Connolly's socialist motivation was. These writings of his, particularly *Labour, Nationality and Religion*—his longest contribution to a specific debate—convey how much he wished to employ every possible vehicle for propaganda; his socialism was, as he saw it, to triumph in the workshop, on the political scene, in the public arena of debate, in speech, and in the press. His debates were for the conquest of the popular mind, and not for the establishment of a correct socialist party line. Even if the 1916 insurrection had succeeded, by some miracle, this process of persuasion through debate would have had to continue. Most of his colleagues were either not socialists, or only partly so, and few of the rank and file of the insurgents were socialist at all. He emerges, therefore, as a Marxian theoretician operating *in* a democratic framework, and hence *for* one. This strongly libertarian element in Connolly's socialism is evident in both *Labour, Nationality and Religion* and the wartime writings reprinted here. His remarks are no mere propaganda points, and there is a permanence both in themselves and in their author's intention. Socialism is the richer for such a sentence as this from 'Our Disappearing Liberties': 'Whatever cause seeks to flourish by stifling criticism and imprisoning thought is a hateful cause, and can only rely on the support of those natures who turn instinctively to darkness and obscurity.'[1]

As the essay 'Changes' reveals, Connolly's acceptance of syndicalism was both the product and the cause of this increasing commitment to libertarianism. His experiences in seeking to build up support for the Dublin workers in 1913–14, on syndicalist lines, deepened his distaste for figures of excessive authority, whether capital or labour. Indeed, much of his activity involved clashes with would-be dictators of socialist thought—Henry Hyndman, Daniel De Leon, and even Jim Larkin. Syndicalism represented the answer to Connolly's growing fear that the workers were being increasingly led to sleep before elections, only to be betrayed afterwards. Syndicalism also meant workers' concentration on real questions which they understood, relating as they did to their own work, instead of leading them to pin their hopes on all-powerful political leaders. The very freedom this gave enhanced respect for freedom; the limitation of power which it placed upon political leaders also strengthened that freedom.

As we have noted above, Connolly's syndicalism was decidedly American, and not European, in origin; something which he himself makes quite clear in 'Old Wine in New Bottles'; and he believed that in trying to organize sympathetic industrial response to the Dublin crisis of 1913–14 he was carrying out the principles of the I.W.W. His ultimate aim was clearly 'one Big Union' in the British Isles. This did not run counter to the logic of his insistence for a separate labour party for Ireland. In political terms the two islands might be naturally separate; in economic terms they were inseparably linked, as the fate of the Dublin strikers was to show. It is ironic that so little has been made of the Dublin lock-out in its capacity as the most singular European extension of the work of the I.W.W. We tend too readily to see the Atlantic as a barrier; as Connolly's experience underlines, it was in some respects an Irish lake. The syndicalist element in Connolly's thought has been recognized but misinterpreted. George Dangerfield's brilliant work *The Strange Death of Liberal England* readily acknowledges Connolly's significance, but does

[1] p. 344.

so in a manner which reflects, and has probably contributed to, the confusion of the issue. 'It is impossible to say at exactly what date the doctrine of Syndicalism crept out of France across the English Channel. But it is generally conceded that it made this journey at some time between 1905 and 1910, and James Connolly, the Irish labour leader, is suspected of being responsible for its arrival.'[1] The journey was in fact a longer one, being trans-Atlantic and not cross-Channel. French theoreticians were of much less importance than the practical experience of the I.W.W. Sorel, on whose writings Dangerfield lays such amusing emphasis, was of comparatively little importance in the American context, and of virtually none in the case of Connolly. Violence was his ultimate weapon, and he exercised it in a political, and not an industrial context, save in that, under extreme provocation, he organized his followers in self-defence. The creation of the Irish Citizen Army was not a response to Sorel; it was a response to police brutality. As Connolly himself said, the syndicalism he learned in the U.S.A. and helped to bring into being in the British Isles was in many ways different from its European counterpart.

The title *Selected Political Writings* might well convey a *savant* in some impressive library producing formidable works intended and destined to enrich the corpus of political thought. We must remember that Connolly's political writings were, for the most part, dashed off very quickly, perhaps in the corner of a public hall, perhaps in the corner of a room with his children playing alongside and his wife sewing. His intention in writing was to furnish weekly propaganda for immediate consumption by his working-class audience, and he had scant hope of subsequent reference to his works. He did think sufficiently highly of some of his work to take pains for its preservation and re-appearance. *Erin's Hope*, *The New Evangel*,[2] *Socialism Made Easy*, even his own anthology of the informal column 'Home Thrusts' from *The Workers' Republic*, all came

[1] MacGibbon & Kee, London, 1966, p. 190; originally published by Constable, London, 1935.

[2] Chapter 10, p. 192.

into being because of his desire that the content on which they were initially based should not have a purely ephemeral existence. He thought some of what he had written to be of value, and in his final days worried about its republication. But if we now read him with the reflective consideration which we bestow on political statements written in a more leisurely manner, it is worth thinking of his work as communication, as well as in terms of its thought. How he conveys his message, given its evangelistic content and his awareness of the ethnic peculiarities of his chosen mission-field, has its own importance in addition to what that message is. Hence this collection draws attention to the question of communication, and in some cases writings have been chosen which are primarily illustrative of his methods in that regard. Beyond that, it seems worth stressing that Connolly should not be read as mere dead prose. We should try to see ourselves in the presence of a short, stocky, moustached, vigorous, humorous man with grey eyes and a Scottish accent, a man of kindness and tranquillity despite personal hardship, but capable of becoming stern and biting; and in reading him we should try to listen to his voice, for he is talking.

OWEN DUDLEY EDWARDS
BERNARD RANSOM

PART I

PIONEER IRISH SOCIALISM

... the capitalist system is the most foreign thing in Ireland. — James Connolly, *Labour in Irish History,* foreword

1. THE FIRST IRISH SOCIALIST: A FORERUNNER OF MARX

William Thompson, partly as a result of Connolly's emphasis on his writings, has received a solid appraisal in R. K. P. Pankhurst's William Thompson (1775–1833)—Britain's Pioneer Socialist, Feminist and Co-operator[1] *as well as a brilliant assessment by Patrick Lynch, 'William Thompson and the Socialist Tradition'.*[2] *Mr Pankhurst's subtitle indicates Thompson's wide arena of activity, however sardonically Connolly might have deplored the homeland there ascribed to the subject. In this chapter, taken from* Labour in Irish History *(1910), quotations from Thompson have been retained as Connolly's publisher printed them, but significant alterations have been noted: Connolly was a moderately careful copyist, but by his manner of living necessarily a hurried one. The* Irish People *from which Connolly chooses his epigraph was the newspaper of the Irish Revolutionary Brotherhood, better known as the Irish Republican Brotherhood, still better known as the I.R.B., and best known by the name of its American sister body, the Fenians. The I.R.B. were officially opposed to the agitation of the land question, or social questions in general, before national independence in the form of separate republican status from Britain was secured, but the newspaper was obliged to find some methods of riveting attention on national aims in addition to persistently reasserting them. Of the Fenian leaders Thomas Clarke Luby (1822–1901), the probable author of the epigraph, had decidedly radical views on social questions, as had the first 'head centre' of the I.R.B., James Stephens (1824–1901), but in deference to their associates' conservatism and fears of social agitation as divisive they limited their evangelization on the point to minor observation. Connolly naturally built on such statements in his effort to build socialism on nationalist foundations, an effort which led to his own decision to join the Military Council of the revived I.R.B. in 1916—with fatal results—and which also gave the special character of both nationalist and socialist interpretation to* Labour in Irish History, *his foremost work.*

[1] Watts, London, 1954.

[2] In J. W. Boyle, ed., *Leaders and Workers* (Mercier Press, Cork, n.d. [1964]).

Anton Menger (1841–1906) can hardly be described as a biographer of Thompson, save in that his work took notice of Thompson's life. Foxwell's introduction appeared in M. E. Tanner's translation of Menger's Right to the Whole Produce of Labour: the origin and development of the theory ... *(London, 1899). Standish James O'Grady (1846–1928) wrote pleasant historical fictions, some of which were acknowledged by him to be such, respecting the 'heroic' age of Gaelic Ireland; he was frequently confused or conflated with the Gaelic antiquarian Standish Hayes O'Grady, a truly distinguished scholar (1832–1915), and Connolly may have been adding the latter's distinction to his citation of the former.* The Peasant *was a weekly journal edited by the nationalist and pro-labour William P. Ryan (1867–1942), initially as the* Irish Peasant *(1905–6), and then, following its suppression as a result of pressure from Cardinal Logue, brought out under the briefer title with the loss of financial support. By early 1909 Ryan had changed the paper's name again to* The Irish Nation and Peasant, *its actual title at the point Connolly cited it. Connolly was a close friend of Ryan: the latter's view of him is well indicated in his son Desmond's memoir of Connolly.*[1]

Of Labour in Irish History *it may be said that it represented the work of at least twelve years, and early drafts had appeared in serial form in the Edinburgh* Socialist *and his own* Workers' Republic, *as well as later in* The Harp *(1909, six years later). The chapter given here had previously appeared only in* The Harp. *It was Chapter X (pp. 106–21) in the book, which was published in Dublin in 1910 by Maunsel & Co., undoubtedly the publishers most notably associated with the Irish literary renaissance.*

> 'It is a system which in its least repulsive aspects compels thousands and tens of thousands to fret and toil, to live and die in hunger and rags and wretchedness in order that a few idle drones may revel in ease and luxury.'—*Irish People*, July 9, 1864.

For Ireland, as for every other part of Europe, the first quarter of the nineteenth century was a period of political darkness, or unbridled despotism and reaction. The fear engendered in the heart of the ruling classes by the French Revolution had

[1] Desmond Ryan, *James Connolly* (Talbot Press, Dublin, 1924).

given birth to an almost insane hatred of reform, coupled with a wolfish ferocity in hunting down even the mildest reformers. The triumph of the allied sovereigns over Napoleon was followed by a perfect saturnalia of despotism all over Europe, and every form of popular organisation was ruthlessly suppressed or driven under the surface. But driving organisations under the surface does not remove the causes of discontent, and, consequently, we find that as rapidly as reaction triumphed above ground its antagonists spread their secret conspiracies underneath. The popular discontent was further increased by the fact that the return home of the soldiers disbanded from the Napoleonic wars had a serious economic effect. It deprived the agriculturists of a market for their produce, and produced a great agricultural and industrial crisis. It threw out of employment all the ships employed in provisioning the troops, all the trades required to build, equip and repair them, all the industries engaged in making war material, and in addition to suspending the work and flooding the labour market with the men and women thus disemployed, it cast adrift scores of thousands of able-bodied soldiers and sailors to compete with the civilian workers who had fed, clothed and maintained them during the war. In Ireland, especially, the results were disastrous owing to the inordinately large proportion of Irish amongst the disbanded soldiers and sailors. Those returning home found the labour market glutted with unemployed in the cities, and in the rural districts the landlords engaged in a fierce war of extermination with their tenantry, who, having lost their war market and war prices, were unable to meet the increasing exactions of the owners of the soil. It was at this period the great Ribbon conspiracy took hold upon the Irish labourer in the rural districts, and although the full truth relative to that movement has never yet been unearthed sufficient is known to indicate that it was in effect a secret agricultural trades union of labourers and cottier farmers—a trades union which undertook in its own wild way to execute justice upon the evictor, and vengeance upon the traitor to his fellows. Also at this time Irish trade unionism, although secret and illegal, attained to its maximum of strength and compact organisation. In 1824 the chief constable of Dublin, testifying before a committee of the House of Commons, declared that the trades of Dublin were perfectly organised, and many of the employers were already beginning to complain of the 'tyranny of the Irish trades unions.' Under such circumstances it is not to be wondered at that the attention which in the eighteenth century had been given to political reforms and the philosophy thereof gave way in the nineteenth to solicitude for social amelioration.

In England, France, and Germany a crop of social philosophers sprang up, each with his scheme of a perfect social order, each with a plan by which the regeneration of society could be accomplished and poverty and all its attendant evils abolished. For the most part these theorists had no complaint to make against the beneficiaries of the social system of the day; their complaint was against the results of the social system. Indeed they in most cases believed that the governing and possessing classes would themselves voluntarily renounce their privileges and property and initiate the new order once they were convinced of its advantages. With this belief it was natural that the chief direction taken by their criticism of society should be towards an analysis of the effects of competition upon buyer and seller, and that the relation of the labourer as producer to the proprietor as appropriator of the thing produced should occupy no part of their examination. One result of this one-sided view of social relations necessarily was a complete ignoring of historical development as a factor in hastening the attainment of their ideal; since the new order was to be introduced by the governing class it followed that the stronger that class became the easier would be the transition, and, consequently, everything which would tend to weaken the social bond by accentuating class distinction, or impairing the feelings of reverence held by the labourer for his masters, would be a hindrance to progress.

Those philosophers formed socialist sects, and it is known that their followers, when they lost the inspiring genius of their leaders, degenerated into reactionaries of the most pronounced type, opposed to every forward move of labour.

The Irish are not philosophers as a rule, they proceed too rapidly from thought to action.

Hence it is not to be wondered at that the same period which produced the Utopian Socialists before alluded to in France, England, and Germany produced in Ireland an economist more thoroughly Socialist in the modern sense than any of his contemporaries—William Thompson, of Clonkeen, Roscarberry, County Cork—a Socialist who did not hesitate to direct attention to the political and social subjection of labour as the worst evil of society, nor to depict with a merciless fidelity to truth the disastrous consequences to political freedom of the presence in society of a wealthy class. Thompson was a believer in the possibility of realising Socialism by forming co-operative colonies on the lines of those advocated by Robert Owen, and to that extent may be classed as a Utopian. On the other hand he believed that such colonies must be built by the labourers themselves, and not by the governing class. He taught that the wealth of the ruling class was derived from the plunder of labour, and he advocated as a necessary preliminary to Socialism the conquest of political representation on the basis of the adult suffrage of both sexes. He did not believe in the State as a basis of Socialist society, but he insisted upon the necessity of using political weapons to destroy all class privileges founded in law, and to clear the ground of all obstacles which the governing class might desire to put in the way of the growth of Socialist communities.

Lest it may be thought that we are exaggerating the merits of Thompson's work as an original thinker, a pioneer of Socialist thought superior to any of the Utopian Socialists of the Continent, and long ante-dating Karl Marx in his insistence upon the subjection of labour as the cause of all social misery, modern crime and political dependence, as well as in his searching analysis of the true definition of capital, we will quote a passage from his most important work, published in 1824: *An Inquiry into the principles of the distribution of Wealth most conducive to Human Happiness as applied to the newly proposed System of the Voluntary Equality of Wealth*, third edition.[1]

> What, then, is the most accurate idea of capital? It is that portion of the product of labour which, whether of a permanent nature or not, is capable of being made the

[1] London, 1869, p. 178.

> instrument of profit. Such seem to be the real circumstances which mark out one portion of the products of labour as capital. On such distinctions, however, have been founded the insecurity and oppression of the productive labourer—the real parent, under the guidance of knowledge, of all wealth—and the enormous usurpation over the productive forces[1] and their fellow-creatures of those who, under the name of capitalists, or landlords, acquired the possession of those accumulated products—the yearly or permanent supply of the community. Hence the opposing claims of the capitalist and the labourer. The capitalist, getting into his hands, under the reign of insecurity and force, the consumption of many labourers for the coming year, the tools or machinery necessary to make their labour productive, and the dwellings in which they must live, turned them to the best account, and bought labour and its future products with them as cheaply as possible. The greater the profit of capital, or the more the capitalist made the labourer pay for the advance of his food, the use of the implements or machinery and the occupation of the dwelling, the less of course remained to the labourer for the acquisition of any object of desire.

Or again, see how, whilst advocating political reform as a means to an end, he depicts its inefficiency when considered as an end in itself:

> As long as the accumulated capital of society remains in one set of hands, and the productive power of creating wealth remains in another, the accumulated capital will, while the nature of man continues as at present, be made use of to counteract the natural laws of distribution, and to deprive the producers of the use of what their labour has produced. Were it possible to conceive that, under simple representative institutions, any such of the expedients of insecurity should be permitted to remain in existence as would uphold the division[2] of capital and labour, such

[1] The original reads '... productive powers ...'
[2] The original reads 'disunion'.

> representative institutions (though all the plunder of political power should cease) would be of little further benefit to the real happiness of mankind, than as affording an easy means for the development of knowledge, and the ultimate abolition of all such expedients. As long as a class of mere capitalists exists society must remain in a diseased state. Whatever plunder is saved from the hand of political power will be levied in another way under the name of profit by capitalists who, while capitalists, must be always law makers.[1]

Thompson advocated free education for all, and went into great detail to prove its feasibility, giving statistics to show that the total cost of such education could be easily borne by Ireland, without unduly increasing the burden of the producers.[2] In this he was three generations ahead of his time—the reform he then advocated being only partially realised in our day. Living in a country in which a small minority imposed a detested religion by force upon a conquered people with the result that a ferocious fanaticism disgraced both sides, he yet had courage and foresight enough to plead for secular education, and to the cry of the bigots who then as now declared that religion would die unless supported by the State, he answered:

> Not only has experience proved that religion can exist without interfering with the natural laws of distribution by violation of security, but it has increased and flourished as during centuries in Ireland and in Greece under and in spite of the forced abstraction of its own resources from its own communicants, to enrich a rival and hated priesthood, or to feed the force that enchained it.[3]

How different was the spirit of the Socialism preached by Thompson from the visionary sentimentalism of the Utopians of Continental Europe, or of Owen in his earlier days in England, with their constant appeals to the 'humanity' of the possessing classes, is further illustrated by the following

[1] Thompson, *Distribution of Wealth*, p. 449.
[2] Ibid., pp. 241ff.
[3] Ibid., p. 175.

passage which, although lengthy, we make no apology for reproducing. Because of its biting analysis of the attitude of the rich in the various stages of political society, and the lust for power which accompanies extreme wealth, the passage might have been written by a Socialist of the twentieth century:

> The unoccupied rich are without any active pursuit; an object in life is wanting to them. The means of gratifying the senses, the imagination even, of sating all wants and caprices, they possess. The pleasures of power are still to be attained. It is one of the strongest and most unavoidable propensities of those who have been brought up in indulgence to abhor restraint, to be uneasy under opposition, and therefore to desire power to remove these evils of restraint and opposition. How shall they acquire the power? First by the direct influence of their wealth, and the hopes and fears it engenders; then when these means are exhausted or to make these means more effectual they endeavour everywhere to seize on, to monopolise the powers of Government.
>
> Where despotism does not exist they endeavour to get entirely into their own hands, or in conjunction with the head of the State, or other bodies, they seize as large a portion as they can of the functions of legislation. Where despotism does not exist, or is modified, they share amongst themselves all the subordinate departments of Government; they monopolise, either directly or indirectly, the command of the armed force, the offices of judges, priests and all those executive departments which give the most power, require the least trouble, and render the largest pecuniary returns. When despotism exists the class of the excessively rich make the best terms they can with the despot, to share his power whether as partners, equals[1] or mere slaves.
>
> If his[2] situation is such as to give them a confidence in their strength, they make terms with the despot, and insist on what they call their rights; if they are weak they gladly

[1] The original reads 'agents'. [2] 'their' in the original.

crawl to the despot, and appear[1] to glory in their slavishness to him for the sake of the delegated power of making slaves to themselves of the rest of the community. Such do the historians[2] of all nations prove the tendencies of excessive wealth to be.[3]

In the English-speaking world the work of this Irish thinker is practically unknown, but on the Continent of Europe his position has long been established. Besides the work already quoted he wrote an 'Appeal of one-half of the Human Race—Women—against the Pretensions of the other half—Men—to retain them in Political and thence in Civil and Domestic Slavery,' published in London in 1825. *Labour Rewarded, the Claims of Labour and Capital Conciliated; or, How to Secure to Labour the Whole Product of its Exertions*, published in 1827, and *Practical Directions for the Speedy and Economical Establishment of Communities*, published in London in 1830, are two other known works. He also left behind the manuscript of other books on the same subject, but they have never been published, and their whereabouts is now unknown. It is told of him that he was for twenty years a vegetarian and total abstainer, and in his will left the bulk of his fortune to endow the first co-operative community to be established in Ireland, and his body for the purpose of dissection in the interests of science. His relations successfully contested the will on the ground that 'immoral objects were included in its benefit.'

His position in the development of Socialism as a science lies, in our opinion, midway between the Utopianism of the early idealists and the historical materialism of Marx. He anticipated the latter in most of his analyses of the economic system, and foresaw the part that a democratisation of politics must play in clearing the ground of the legal privileges of the professional classes. In a preface to the English translation of the work of one of his German biographers, Anton Menger, the writer, H. S. Foxwell, M.A., says of his contribution to economic science:

[1] 'affect' in the original.
[2] 'histories' in the original.
[3] Thompson, *Distribution of Wealth*, pp. 164–5.

> Thompson's fame will rest not upon his advocacy of Owenite co-operation, devoted and public spirited as that was, but upon the fact that *he was the first writer to elevate the question of the just distribution of wealth* to the supreme position it has since held in English political economy. Up to his time political economy had been rather commercial than industrial, indeed he finds it necessary to explain the very meaning of the term 'industrial,' which, he says, was from the French, no doubt adopted from Saint Simon.[1]

If we were to attempt to estimate the relative achievements of Thompson and Marx we should not hope to do justice to either by putting them in contrast, or by eulogising Thompson in order to belittle Marx, as some Continental critics of the latter seek to do. Rather we should say that the relative position of this Irish genius and of Marx are best comparable to the historical relations of the pre-Darwinian evolutionists to Darwin; as Darwin systematised all the theories of his predecessors and gave a lifetime to the accumulation of the facts required to establish his and their position, so Marx found the true line of economic thought already indicated and brought his genius and encyclopaedic knowledge and research to place it upon an unshakable foundation. Thompson brushed aside the economic fiction maintained by the orthodox economists and accepted by the Utopians that profit was made in exchange, and declared that it was due to the subjection of labour and the resultant appropriation by the capitalists and landlords of the fruits of the labour of others. He does not hesitate to include himself as a beneficiary of monopoly. He declared, in 1827, that for about twelve years he had been 'living on what is called rent, the produce of the labour of others.'[2] All the theory of the class war is but a deduction from this principle. But although Thompson recognised this class war as a fact, he

[1] Anton Menger, *The Right to the Whole Produce of Labour: the origin and development of the theory of Labour's claim to the whole product of Industry*, translated by M. E. Tanner, with an introduction and bibliography by H. S. Foxwell, M.A. (London, 1899), p. xlvii: Connolly's italics.

[2] See William Thompson, *Labor Rewarded. The Claims of Labor and Capital Conciliated – By One of the Idle Classes* (Hunt & Clarke, London, 1827), p. 1.

did not recognise it as a factor, as *the* factor in the evolution of society towards freedom. This was reserved for Marx, and in our opinion is his chief and crowning glory. While Owen and the Continental Socialists were beseeching the favour of kings, Parliaments and Congresses this Irishman was arraigning the rich, pointing out that lust of power for ever followed riches, that 'capitalists, while capitalists, would always be law makers,' but that 'as long as a class of mere capitalists exists society must remain in a diseased state.'[1] The fact that the daring Celt who preached this doctrine, arraigning alike the social and political rulers of society and society itself, also vehemently demanded the extension of the suffrage to the whole adult population is surely explanation enough why his writings found no favour with the respectable classes of society, with those same classes who so frequently lionised the leaders of the Socialist sects of his day.

In our day another great Irishman, Standish O'Grady, perhaps the greatest litterateur in Ireland, has been preaching in the pages of *The Peasant*, Dublin, 1908–9, against capitalist society, and urging the formation of co-operative communities in Ireland as an escape therefrom, and it is curiously significant of how little Irishmen know of the intellectual achievements of their race that O'Grady apparently is entirely unconscious of the work of his great forerunner in that field of endeavour. It is also curiously significant of the conquest of the Irish mind by English traditions that Irish Nationalists should often be found fighting fiercely against Socialism as 'a German idea,' although every social conception which we find in the flower in Marx we can also find in the bud in Thompson, twenty-three years before the publication of the *Communist Manifesto*, forty-three years before the issue of *Das Kapital*.

We will conclude this chapter by another citation from this Irish pioneer of revolutionary Socialism; we say of revolutionary Socialism advisedly, for all the deductions from his teachings lead irresistibly to the revolutionary action of the working class. As according to the Socialist philosophy the political demands of the working class movement must at all times depend upon the degree of development of the age and

[1] See p. 51, note 1. The full quotation given on p. 51 is accurate.

country in which it finds itself, it is apparent that Thompson's theories of action were the highest possible expression of the revolutionary thought of his age.

> The productive labourers stript of all capital, of tools, houses, and materials to make their labour productive, toil from want, from the necessity of existence, their remuneration being kept at the lowest compatible figure with the existence of industrious habits ... [1]
>
> How shall the wretchedly poor be virtuous? Who cares about them? What character have they to lose? What hold has public opinion on their action? What care they for the delicate pleasures of reputation who are tormented by the gnawings of absolute want? How should they respect the property or rights of others who have none of their own to beget a sympathy for those who suffer for their privation? How can they feel for others' woes, for others' passing light complaints, who are tormented by their own substantial miseries? The mere mention of the trivial inconveniences of others insults and excites the indignation instead of calling forth their complacent sympathies. Cut off from the decencies, the comforts, the necessaries of life, want begets ferocity. If they turn round they find many in the same situation with themselves, partaking of their feelings of isolation from kindly sympathies with the happy. They become a public to each other, a public of suffering, of discontent and ignorance; they form a public opinion of their own in contempt of the public opinion of the rich, whom, and their laws, they look upon, as the result of force alone. From whom are the wretched to learn the principle while they never see the practice of morality? Of respect for the security of others? From their superiors? From the laws? The conduct of their superiors, the operation of those laws have been one practical lesson to them of force, of restraint, of taking away without their consent, without any equivalent the fruits of their labour. Of what avail are morals or

[1] Thompson, *Distribution of Wealth*, p. 133. The word 'figure' does not appear in the original.

> principles[1] or commands, when opposed, when belied, by example? These can never supply motives of virtuous conduct. *Motives arise from things, from surrounding circumstances, not from the idleness of words and empty declamations. Words are only useful to convey and impress a knowledge of these things and circumstances. If these things*[2] *do not exist words are mere mockery.*[3]

With this bit of economic determinist philosophy—teaching that morality is a thing of social growth, the outcome of things and circumstances—we leave this earliest Irish apostle of the social revolution. Fervent Celtic enthusiasts are fond of claiming, and the researches of our days seem to bear out the claim, that Irish missionaries were the first to rekindle the lamp of learning in Europe, and dispel the intellectual darkness following the downfall of the Roman Empire; may we not also take pride in the fact that an Irishman also was the first to pierce the worse than Egyptian darkness of capitalist barbarism and point out to the toilers the conditions of their enslavement, and the essential pre-requisites of their emancipation?

[1] 'words or precepts' in the original.
[2] 'states of things' in the original.
[3] Thompson, *Distribution of Wealth*, p. 190.

PART II

LABOUR, RELIGION AND IRELAND

The Socialist question was not a religious question. It was a question to be settled in the mines and factories, not at the altar. The Socialist movement had nothing whatever to do with the next world. It was no concern of their organisation whether there was a heaven or a hell, but, if there was a heaven hereafter, it was poor preparation to live in hell here. – James Connolly, speaking in Glasgow; reported in *Forward*, October 15th, 1910

2. LABOUR, NATIONALITY AND RELIGION

BEING A DISCUSSION OF THE LENTEN DISCOURSES AGAINST SOCIALISM DELIVERED BY FATHER KANE, S.J., IN GARDINER STREET CHURCH, DUBLIN, 1910

On the origins of the work, see pp. 36–8. The text is taken from the edition of 1910, the only one published in Connolly's lifetime.

> 'Nature furnishes its wealth to all men in common. God beneficently has created all things that their enjoyment be common to all living beings, and that the earth become the common property of all ... Only unjust usurpation has created the right of private property.'—St. Ambrose

'Let the Pope and cardinals, and all the powers of the Catholic world united make the least encroachment on that (American) constitution, we will protect it with our lives. Summon a General Council (of the Church)—let that council interfere in the mode of our electing but an assistant to a turnkey of a prison—we deny its right; we reject its usurpation. Let that council lay a tax of one cent only upon our churches—we will not pay it. Yet, we are most obedient Papists—we believe that the Pope is Christ's vicar on earth, supreme visible head of the Church throughout the world, and lawful successor of St. Peter, prince of the apostles. We believe all this power is in Pope Leo XII [then reigning], and we believe that a General Council is infallible in doctrinal decisions. Yet we deny to Pope and Council united any power to interfere with one tittle of our political rights, as firmly as we deny the power of interfering with one tittle of our spiritual rights to the President and Congress. We will obey each in its proper place, we will resist any encroachment by one upon the right of the other.'—Rt. Rev. John England, Catholic Bishop of Charleston, U.S.A., 1824.

FOREWORD

Nothing is more conducive to the spread of a movement than the discussions arising out of the efforts of a capable opponent to refute its principles. Out of such discussions arises clearness of thought, and the consequent realization on the part of both sides to the controversy of the necessity of considering the movement under discussion in the light of its *essential principles*, rather than of its accidental accompaniments—the basic ideas of the movement itself rather than the ideas of the men or women who may for the moment be its principal exponents or representatives. Men perish, but principles live. Hence the recent efforts of ecclesiastics to put the Socialist movement under the ban of the Catholic Church, despite the wild and reckless nature of the statements by which the end was sought to be attained, has had a good effect in compelling Catholics to examine more earnestly their position as laymen, and the status of the clergy as such, as well as their relative duties toward each other within the Church and toward the world in general. One point of Catholic doctrine brought out as a result of such examination is the almost forgotten, and sedulously suppressed one, that the Catholic Church is theoretically a community in which the clergy are but the officers serving the laity in a common worship and service of God, and that should the clergy at any time profess or teach doctrines not in conformity with the true teachings of Catholicity it is not only the right, but it is the absolute duty of the laity to refuse such doctrines and to disobey such teaching. Indeed, it is this saving clause in Catholic doctrine which has again and again operated to protect the Church from the result of the mistaken attempts of the clergy to control the secular activities of the laity. It seems to be unavoidable, but it is entirely regrettable, that clergymen consecrated to the worship of God, and supposed to be patterned after a Redeemer who was the embodiment of service and humility, should in their relation to the laity insist upon service and humility being rendered to them instead of by them. Their Master served all Mankind in patience and suffering; they insist upon all Mankind serving them, and in all questions of the social and political relations of men they require the common laity to bow the neck in a meekness, humility and submission which the clergy scornfully reject. They have often insisted that the Church is greater than the secular authority, and acted therefore in flat defiance of the secular powers, but they have forgotten or ignored the fact that the laity are a part of the Church, and that therefore the right of rebellion against injustice so freely claimed by the Papacy and the Hierarchy is also the inalienable right of the laity. And history proves that in almost every case in which the political or social aspirations of the laity came into opposition to the will of the clergy the laity represented the best interests of the Church as a whole and of Mankind in general. Whenever the clergy succeeded in conquering political power in any country the result has been disastrous to the interests of religion and inimical to the progress of humanity. From whence we arrive at the conclusion that he serves religion best who insists upon the clergy of the Catholic Church taking their proper position as servants to the laity, and abandoning their attempt to dominate the public, as they have long dominated the private life of their fellow-Catholics.

The 1910 Lenten Discourses of Father Kane, S.J., in Gardiner Street Church, Dublin, serve to illustrate these, our contentions. The Socialists of Ireland are grateful to those who induced such a learned and eloquent orator in their capital city to attempt combating Socialism. Had it been an antagonist less worthy their satisfaction would not have been so great. But they now feel confident that when an opponent so capable, so wide in his reading, so skilled in his presentation, so admirable in his method of attack, and so eloquent in his language has said his final word upon the question, they may rest satisfied that the best case against their cause has been presented which can ever be forthcoming under similar auspices. In presenting their arguments against the position of the reverend lecturer—as against his reverend co-workers who all over the world are engaged in the same unworthy task of combating this movement for the uplifting of humanity—we desire, in the spirit of our preceding remarks, to place before our readers a brief statement of some of the many instances in which the Catholic laity have been compelled to take political action contrary to the express commands of the Pope and the Catholic Hierarchy, and in which subsequent events or the more enlightened conscience of subsequent ages have fully justified the action of the laity and condemned the action of the clergy.

Most of our readers are aware that the first Anglo-Norman invasion of Ireland, in 1169, an invasion characterised by every kind of treachery, outrage, and indiscriminate massacre of the Irish, took place under the authority of a Bull issued by his Holiness, Pope Adrian IV. Doubt has been cast upon the authenticity of the Bull, but it is certain that neither Adrian nor any of his successors in the Papal chair ever repudiated it.

Every Irish man and woman, most enlightened Englishmen, and practically every foreign nation today wish that the Irish had succeeded in preserving their independence against the English king, Henry II, but at a Synod of the Catholic Church, held in Dublin in 1177, according to Rev. P. J. Carew, Professor of Divinity in Maynooth, in his *Ecclesiastical History of Ireland*, the Legate of Pope Alexander III, 'set forth Henry's right to the sovereignity of Ireland in virtue of the Pope's authority, and inculcated the necessity of obeying him *under pain of excommunication*.' The English were not yet eight years in Ireland, the greater part of the country was still closed to them, but already the Irish were being excommunicated for refusing to become slaves.

In Ireland, as in all Catholic countries, a church was a sanctuary in which even the greatest criminal could take refuge and be free from arrest, as the civil authority could not follow upon the consecrated ground. At the Synod of 1177 the Pope, in order to help the English monarch against the Irish, abolished the right of sanctuary in Ireland, and empowered the English to strip the Irish churches, and to hunt the Irish refugees who sought shelter there. The greatest criminals of Europe were safe once they reached the walls of the church, but not an Irish patriot.

In the year 1319 Edward Bruce, brother of Robert the Bruce of Scotland, was invited into Ireland by the Irish chiefs and people to help them in their patriotic war for independence. He accepted the invitation, was joined by vast numbers of the people in arms, and together the Irish and Scotch forces swept the English out of Ulster and Connacht. The English king appealed for help to Pope John XXII, and *that Pontiff responded by at once excommunicating all the Irish who were in arms against the English.*

The Battle of the Boyne, fought July 1st, 1690, is generally regarded in Ireland as a disaster for the Irish cause—a disaster which made possible the infliction of two centuries of unspeakable degradation upon the Irish people. Yet that battle was the result of an alliance formed by Pope Innocent XI with William, Prince of Orange, against Louis, King of France. King James of England joined with King Louis to obtain help to save his own throne, and the Pope joined in the League with William to curb the power of France. When the news of the defeat of the Irish at the Boyne reached Rome the Vatican was illuminated by order of the new Pope, Alexander VIII, and special masses offered up in thanksgiving. See Von Ranke's *History of the Popes*,[1] and Murray's *Irish Revolutionary History.*

Judge Maguire, of San Francisco, California, writing of this period before the Reformation, says truly: 'Under all their Catholic majesties, from Henry II to Henry VIII (nearly 400 years), the Irish people, with the exception of five families, were outlaws. They were murdered at will, like dogs, by their English Catholic neighbours in Ireland, and there was no law to punish the murderers. Yet during all of this unparalleled reign of terror, history fails to show a single instance in which the power of the Catholic Church was ever exerted or suggested by the Pope for the protection of her faithful Irish children.'

The Irish people as a whole are proud of the fact that, according to the reported testimony of General Lee of the American army, more than half of the Continental soldiers during the War of the Revolution were from Ireland, yet during that War of Independence Bishop Troy, the Catholic Bishop of Ossory, ordered the Catholics of his diocese to 'observe a day's fast and to humble himself in prayer that they might avert the *divine wrath provoked by their American fellow-subjects who, seduced by the specious notions of liberty* and other illusive expectations of sovereignty, disclaim any dependence upon Great Britain and endeavour by force of arms to distress

[1] Translated by E. Foster; Bell & Sons, London, 1846.

their mother country.' Quite recently, in 1909, Professor Monaghan, speaking before the Federation of Catholic Societies in America, declared with the approval of the bishop and clergy that the Catholic Hierarchy of the United States would, if need be, sell the sacred vessels off the altar in defence of the American Republic. *Thus the enlightened opinion of the Catholics of our day condemns the Pastoral of the Catholic bishop of the Revolutionary period, and endorses the action of the Catholics who disregarded it.*

In 1798 an insurrection in favour of an Irish Republic took place in Ireland, assuming most formidable proportions in County Wexford. The insurrection had been planned by the Society of United Irishmen, many of whose leaders were Protestants and Freethinkers. The Catholic Hierarchy and most of the priesthood denounced the society and inculcated loyalty to the Government. The more intelligent of the Catholic masses disregarded these clerical denunciations. In the Memoirs of his life, Miles Byrne, a staunch Catholic patriot and revolutionist, who took part in the insurrection, says: 'The priests did everything in their power to stop the progress of the Association of United Irishmen, particularly poor Father John Redmond, who refused to hear the confession of any of the United Irish, and turned them away from his knees.' Speaking of Father John Murphy, he says he 'was a worthy, simple, pious man and one of those Roman Catholic priests who used the greatest exertions and exhortations to oblige the people to give up their pikes and firearms of every description.' The wisdom of the people and the foolishness of the clergy were amply demonstrated by the fact that the soldiers burned Father Murphy's house over his head, and compelled him to take the field as an insurgent. A heroic fight and a glorious martyrdom atoned for his mistake, but the soldier-like qualities he showed in the field were rendered nugatory by the fact that as a priest he had been instrumental in disarming many hundred of the men whom he afterwards commanded. As an insurgent officer he discovered that his greatest hope lay in the men who had disregarded his commands as a priest, and retained the arms with which to fight for freedom.

Dr. Troy, when Catholic Archbishop of Dublin, was, according to an incident related in the 'Viceroy's Post-Bag' by Mr. Michael MacDonagh, interrogated by the British authorities as to the duty of a priest who discovered in the confessional a plot against the Government, and answered that, 'If in confession any plot against the existing Government was disclosed to the priest, he (the priest) would be bound to give information to the Government that such plot was in agitation, taking care that nothing could in any way lead to a suspicion of the person from whom, or the means in which, the information had been obtained.' Chief Secretary Wickham, who reports this conversation with the archbishop, goes on to say, 'I then asked him whether such confession so made to the priest, particularly in the case of a crime against the State, was considered as a full atonement so as to entitle the penitent to absolution without a disclosure of such crime being first made to the police or to the Government of the country. To this the Doctor answered very distinctly that he did not consider the confession to the priest alone, under such circumstances, a sufficient atonement, *and that either the priest ought to insist on a such confession to the State or to the police being made*, or to enjoin the making of such disclosure subsequent to absolution in like manner as penance is enjoined under similar circumstances.'

There is little doubt in our mind but that Dr. Troy misrepresented Catholic doctrine, but it is noteworthy that a parish priest at Mallow, Co. Cork, ordered a member of the United Irishmen, who had sought him in the confessional, to give information to the authorities of a plot of the Royal Meath Militia to seize the artillery at that point and turn it over to the revolutionists. This priest, Father Thomas Barry, afterwards drew a pension of £100 per year from the Government for his information; his action was, and is, abhorred by the vast mass of the Irish Catholics, but was in strict accord with his duty as laid down by Archbishop Troy.

All impartial historians recognise that the Legislative Act of Union between Great Britain and Ireland was passed

By perjury and fraud
By slaves who sold
For place or gold
Their country and their God.

Yet we are informed by Mr. Plowden, a Catholic historian, that 'a very great preponderance in favour of the Union existed in the Catholic Body, *particularly in their nobility, gentry, and clergy*.' On March 1st, 1800, no less than 32 Orange lodges protested against the Act of Union, but the Catholic Hierarchy endorsed it.

Every year the members of the Irish race scattered throughout the earth celebrate the memory of Robert Emmet, and cherish him in their hearts as the highest ideal of patriot and martyr; but on the occasion of his martyrdom the Catholic Archbishops of Dublin and Armagh presented an address to the Lord Lieutenant, representative of the British Government in Ireland, denouncing Emmet in the strongest possible terms. That this action was in conformity with the position of the whole Catholic Hierarchy was evidenced in 1808 when all the Catholic bishops of Ireland met in Synod on September 14th, and passed the following resolution, as reported in Haverty's 'History of Ireland': 'That the Roman Catholic prelates pledge themselves to adhere to the rules by which they have been *hitherto uniformly guided*, viz., to recommend to his Holiness (for appointment as Irish Roman Catholic bishops) *only such persons as are of unimpeachable loyalty*.'

After Daniel O'Connell and the Catholics of Ireland had wrested Catholic Emancipation from the British Government they initiated a demand for a Repeal of the Union. Their service to Catholic Emancipation was a proof positive of their Catholic orthodoxy, but at the urgent request of the British Government Pope Gregory XVI issued a Rescript commanding the priests to abstain from attending the Repeal meetings. O'Connell said this was an illegal interference with the liberties of the clergy, declared he would 'take his religion from Rome, but not his politics,' and the Catholic opinion of our day emphatically endorses his attitude and condemns the action of the Pope.

In 1847 the Catholics among the Young Irelanders prepared a memorial to be presented to the Annual Assembly of the Bishops, defending themselves from the charge of infidelity. The Archbishop of Tuam declared he would retire if they were admitted. *They were not admitted.* Today the memory of the Young Irelanders is held close to the heart of every intelligent Irish man or woman.

During the great Irish famine of 1845–6–7–8–9 the Irish people died in hundreds of thousands of hunger, whilst there was food enough in the country to feed three times the population. When the starving peasantry was called upon to refuse to pay rent to idle landlords, and to rise in revolt against the system which was murdering them, the clergy commanded them to pay their rents, instructed them that they would lose their immortal souls should they refuse to do so, and threw all the weight of their position against the revolutionary movement for the freedom of Ireland. Mr. A. M. Sullivan, an extremely ardent Catholic, writing in 'New Ireland' says of this attitude of the clergy during that crisis that, 'Their antagonism was fatal to the movement—more surely and infallibly fatal to it, than all the powers of the British Crown.'

The Irish revolutionary movement known popularly as the Fenian Brotherhood was denounced by all the Catholic Hierarchy and most of the clergy, Bishop Moriarty of County Kerry saying that 'Hell was not hot enough nor eternity long enough to punish such miscreants.' The Fenians were represented as being enemies of religion and of morality, yet the three representatives of their cause who died upon the scaffold died with a prayer upon their lips, and Irish men and women the world over today make the anniversary of their martyrdom the occasion for a glorification and endorsement of the principles for which they died—a glorification and endorsement in which many of our clergymen participate.

In January, 1871, the Catholic Bishop of Derry denounced the Home Rule movement of Isaac Butt. To-day priests and people agree that the movement led by Isaac Butt was the mildest, most inoffensive movement ever known in Ireland.

The Irish Land League, which averted in 1879 a repetition of the famine horrors of 1847, which broke the back of Irish landlordism, and abolished the worst evils of British rule, was denounced by Archbishop M'Cabe in September, 1879, October, 1880, and October, 1881.

In 1882 the Ladies' Land League, an association of Irish ladies organised for the patriotic and benevolent purpose of raising funds for the relief of distress, of inquiring into cases of eviction, and affording relief to evicted tenants, was denounced by Archbishop M'Cabe as 'immodest and wicked.' After this attack upon the character of patriotic Irish womanhood Archbishop M'Cabe was created a Cardinal.

On May 11th, 1883, in the midst of the fight of the Irish peasantry to save themselves from landlord tyranny, his Holiness the Pope issued a Rescript *condemning disaffection to the English Government*, and also condemning the testimonial to Charles Stewart Parnell. The Irish people answered by more than doubling the subscription to the testimonial. The leader of that fight of the Irish against their ancient tyrants was Michael Davitt, to whose efforts much of the comparative security of peasant life in Ireland is due. Davitt was denied an audience by the Pope, but at his death priests and people alike united to do tribute to his character and genius.

In 1883 Dr. M'Glynn, a Catholic priest in America, was invited to deliver a lecture for the purpose of raising funds to save from starvation the starving people of the West of Ireland. The Vatican sent a telegram to Cardinal M'Closkey ordering him to 'suspend this priest M'Glynn for preaching in favour of the Irish revolution.' The telegram was signed by Cardinal Simeoni. Afterwards Father M'Glynn was subjected to the sentence of complete excommunication for preaching revolutionary doctrines upon the land question, but after some years the Vatican acknowledged its error, and revoked the sentence without requiring the victim to change his principles.

In all the examples covered by this brief and very incomplete retrospective glance into history the instincts of the reformers and revolutionists have been right, the political theories of the Vatican and the clergy unquestionably wrong. The verdict of history as unquestionably endorses the former as it condemns the latter. And intelligent Catholics everywhere accept that verdict. Insofar as true religion has triumphed in the hearts of men it has triumphed in spite of, not because of, the political activities of the priesthood. That political activity in the past, like the clerical opposition to Socialism at present, was and is an attempt to serve God and Mammon—an attempt to combine the service of Him who in His humbleness rode upon an ass, with the service of those who rode rough-shod over the hearts and souls and hopes of suffering humanity.

The Capitalist Class rose upon the ruins of Feudal Catholicism; in the countries where it gained power its first act was to decree the confiscation of the estates of the Church. Yet to-day that robber class, conceived in sin and begotten in iniquity, asks the Church to defend it, and from the Vatican downwards the clergy respond to the call. Just as the British Government in Ireland on January 21st, 1623, published a Royal Proclamation banishing all priests from Ireland, and in 1795 established a College at Maynooth for the education of priests, and found the latter course safer for British rule than the former, so the capitalist class has also learned its lesson and in the hour of danger enlists as its lieutenants and champions the priesthood it persecuted and despised in the hour of its strength. Can we not imagine some cynical supporter of the capitalist class addressing it to-day as the great Catholic orator, Richard Lalor Shiel, addressed the British Government on the occasion of the Maynooth Grant of 1845, and saying in his words:

> You are taking a step in the right direction. You must not take the Catholic clergy into your pay, but you can take the Catholic clergy under your care ... Are not lectures at Maynooth cheaper than State prosecutions? Are not professors less costly than Crown Solicitors? Is not a large standing army, and a great constabulary force more expensive than the moral police with which by the priesthood of Ireland you can be thriftily and efficaciously supplied.

CHAPTER I

It is not to be wondered at that the spirit of restless revolt which has gained such predominating influence over the nations of the world should have passed beyond the arena

> of politics to assert itself in the domain of practical economy. The causes likely to create a conflict are unmistakable. They are the marvellous discoveries of science, the colossal development of industry, the changed relations between workmen and masters, the enormous wealth of the few and the abject misery of the many, the more defiant self-reliance and the more scientific organisation of the workers, and finally a widespread depravity in moral principle and practice. The momentous seriousness of the coming crisis fills every thoughtful mind with anxiety and dread. Wise men discuss it; practical men propose schemes; platforms, Parliaments, clubs, kings, all think and talk of it. Nor is there any subject which so completely engrosses the attention of the world.—Encyclical on Labour by Pope Leo XIII, 1891.

In our analysis of the discourses against Socialism which formed the burden of the Lenten Lectures of Father Kane, S.J., we propose to cite at all times the text we are criticising, and we regret it is not practicable within our space to quote in full the entire series of lectures, and can only trust that our readers before making up their minds upon the question will procure a verbatim report of these discourses in order that they may satisfy themselves upon the correctness of our quotations. As far as it is possible without destroying the unity of our argument we shall follow the plan of the lecture itself, and attempt to answer each objection as it was formulated. But when an objection is merely stated, and no attempt made to follow it by a reasoned argument sustaining the objection we shall not waste our readers' time or our own by wandering off in an attempt to answer. One point stated by our reverend opponent, and then immediately forgotten or systematically ignored, requires to be restated here as the veritable anchor from which the argument should not be allowed to drift. Had our opponent clung to that anchor it would not have been possible for him to introduce so much extraneous matter, so much senseless speculation and foolish slander as he did introduce in the course of his long-drawn-out criticism. That point as stated by Father Kane is:

'*Once for all we must understand a Socialist to be that man, and only that man, who holds the essential principle of Socialism, i.e., that all wealth-producing power, and all that pertains to it, belongs to the ownership and control of the State.*' Thus, at the outset of his lectures, in his first discourse, the reverend gentleman makes it clear that Socialists are bound as Socialists only to the acceptance of one great principle—*the ownership and control of the wealth-producing power by the State*, and that therefore totally antagonistic interpretations of the Bible or of Prophecy and Revelation, theories of marriage, and of history, may be held by Socialists without in the slightest degree interfering with their activities as such, or with their proper classification as supporters of Socialist doctrine. If this great central truth had been made as clear as its importance justifies, and as firmly adhered to by our opponent as the Socialists themselves adhere to it, then it would not be necessary for the present writer to remind our critics of those uncomfortable facts in Irish history to which we have referred in our introduction, nor to those other facts in universal history we shall be forced to cite ere our present survey is finished.

Says our critic:

> We now come to examine its principles. One fundamental principle of Socialism is that labour alone is the cause of value, and that labour alone can give any title to ownership. This was first formulated by Saint Simon, and is generally adopted by Socialists. This principle is false. It is founded on an incomplete explanation of the origin of value. We will put it to the test later on. At present we need only remark that a thing may be of real use and therefore of real value to a man who has a right to use it, even independently of any labour spent upon it. Fruit in a forest would have real value for a hungry man, even though no human labour had been given to its growing. Another principle, one invented by Karl Marx, is what he calls the Materialistic Conception of History. It is an application of the wild philosophic dreams of the German, Hegel; it means, in plain English, that the economic, or broadly speaking, the trade conditions existing in the

> world, determine the way in which the production of wealth must work out. Now, this working out of production determines what men's social, ethical and religious opinions shall be. But the economic conditions are always in a state of evolution, and thus, after a time, they come into collision with the previous social, ethical and religious state of things. But these latter do not die without a struggle, and consequently re-act, and limit to some extent the influence of the material evolution which is going on. I have given this principle as fully as I can in a short space. It assumes that everything in the world depends absolutely and exclusively upon the mere action of mere material causes. It is a principle the only proof of which is in the begging of the question, in supposing that there is no God, no soul, no free will, nothing but mud and the forces of mud.

We are indebted to our critic for his statement of the importance of this doctrine of the Materialistic Conception of History, although we are amused at his characterisation of the doctrine itself. In the beginning of his description, ever mindful of the necessity of prejudicing his hearers, he describes it as an application of the 'wild philosophic dreams' of Hegel; in the middle it is stated that the doctrine rejects dreams as a foundation of religious belief and bases our ideas of religion upon the impression derived from material surroundings, and in the final sentence, so far from it being dreams, it is 'nothing but mud and the forces of mud.'

Let us examine briefly the true context of this doctrine. While remembering that there are many good Socialists who do not hold it, and that a belief in it is *not* an essential to Socialism, it is still accepted as the most reasonable explanation of history by the leading Socialists of this world. It teaches that the ideas of men are derived from their material surroundings, and that the forces which made and make for historical changes and human progress had and have their roots in the development of the tools men have used in their struggle for existence, using the word 'tools' in its broadest possible sense to include all the social forces of wealth-production. It teaches that since the break-up of common ownership and the clan community all human history has turned around the struggle of contending classes in society—one class striving to retain possession, first of the persons of the other class and hold them as chattel slaves, and then of the tools of the other class and hold them as wage-slaves. That all the politics of the world resolved themselves in the last analysis into a struggle for the possession of that portion of the fruits of labour which labour creates, but does not enjoy, i.e., Rent, Interest, Profit. Here let us say that no Socialist claims for Marx the discovery or original formulation of the doctrine of the Materialistic Conception of History—indeed, the brilliant Irish scholastic, Duns Scotus, taught it in the Middle Ages—but that more precise formulation of the guiding forces of history which relate to the influence of economic factors and which we call Economic Determinism has indeed Marx as its clearest expositor, although the Irish economist, William Thompson of County Cork, in 1826, had pointed it out before Marx was out of swaddling clothes.

On the first point, viz., the influence of our material surroundings upon our mental processes and conceptions, a few words should be sufficient to establish its substantial truth in the minds of all those who do not fear the light.

Down on the western coast of Ireland the fishermen use, or did until quite recently, as their sole means of sea-going, a little boat made simply of a framework covered with animal hides or tarpaulin, and known as a coracle. At one time in the history of the world such boats represented the sole means of ocean travel. Now, is it not as plain as that two and two makes four that the outlook upon life, the conceptions of Man's relation to Nature, the theories of international relations, of politics, of government, of the possibilities of life which characterise the age of the 'Lusitania,' the flying machine, and the wireless message, could not possibly have been held by even the wisest men of the age of the coracle. The brains of men were as able then and as subtle in their conceptions as they are today, in fact the philosophers of ancient Asia have never been surpassed and seldom equalled in brain power in the modern world; but the most subtle, acute and powerful mind of the ancient world could not even understand the terms of the social, political or moral problems which confront us today, and are intelligently understood by the average day labourer. We are confronted with a salient instance of this in Holy Scripture. We read the inspired revelation of prophets, judges, and saints giving the world instructions for its future guidance; we read of commands to go forth and convey the gospel to the heathen; but nowhere do we read that those inspired men knew or spoke of a continent beyond the Atlantic in which immortal souls were sitting in darkness, if souls can be said to sit. The wise men of the ancient world, the inspired men of the Holy Land, the brilliant philosophers and scholastics of mediæval Europe, were all limited by their material surroundings, could only think in terms of the world with which they were acquainted, and their ideas of what was moral or immoral were fashioned for them by the social system in which they lived. Slavery is held today to be immoral, and no chattel slaveowner would be given absolution; but when Constantine the Great accepted the Christian religion the Pope of the period received him with acclamation, and no one suggested to him the need of surrendering his slaves, of which he held thousands. Queen Elizabeth of England, 'Good Queen Bess,' engaged in slave trading and made a good profit in the venture; but no Catholic historian or pamphleteer of the period ever attacked her for that offence, although attacks for other causes were made in plenty. How is it that the point of view as to the morality of slavery has changed? It cannot be that religion is changed, for we are told that religion is the same yesterday, today, and for ever. If it is not because it has been discovered that it is cheaper to hire men and discharge them when the job is done, than it was to buy men and be compelled to feed them all the time, working or idle, sick or well, for what reason has the change in our conceptions come? Stated brutally, the fact is that slavery is immoral because it is dearer than wage labour. And so with all our other intellectual processes. They change with the change in our environment, particularly our economic or social environment.

A negro slave in the Southern States of America was told by his owner to go up and fasten the shingles on the top of the roof of his master's dwelling. 'Boss,' said he to the slaveowner, 'if I go up there and fall down and get killed you will lose that 500 dollars you paid for me; but if you send up that Irish labourer and he falls down and breaks his neck you won't even have to bury him, and can get another labourer tomorrow for two dollars a day.' The Irish labourer was sent up. Moral: Slavery is immoral because slaves cost too much.

As man has progressed in his conquest of the secrets of Nature, he has been compelled to accept as eminently natural that from which his forefathers shrank as a manifestation of the power of the supernatural; as the progress of commerce has taken wealth, and the power that goes with wealth, out of the exclusive ownership of kings and put it in the possession of capitalists and merchants, political power has acquired a new basis, and diplomatic relations from being the expression of the lust for family aggrandisement have become the servants of the need for new markets and greater profits—kings wait in the ante-chambers of usurers like Rothschild and Baring to get their consent for war or peace; Popes have for hundreds of years excommunicated those who put their money out at usury and have denied them Christian burial, but now a Pierpont Morgan, as financier of the Vatican, lends out at interest the treasures of the Popes. And man caught in the grasp of the changing economic conditions changes his intellectual conceptions to meet his changed environment. The world moves even although men stand still, and not the least of the changes have been those of the ghostly fathers of the Church towards the world and its problems. Like the girl to the kisses of her sweetheart the Church has ever to the blandishments of the world—

> 'Swearing she would ne'er consent, consented.'

Our critic proceeds:

> The third principle of Socialism is the theory of Karl Marx by which he tries to prove that all capital is robbery. He calls it the theory of Surplus Value. Value is the worth of a thing. Now, the worth of a thing may be in that it satisfies some need, as a piece of bread or a blanket; or the worth of a thing may be in that you can barter it for

something else, as if you have more bread than you want, but have not a blanket, you may give some of your bread to a man who has no bread but can spare a blanket. The first kind of value is use value, or own worth. The second kind of value is exchange value, or market worth. Instead of mere direct barter, money is used in civilized nations as an equivalent and standard for exchange value. Now, Karl Marx asserts that exchange value, *i.e.*, the worth of a thing as it may be bought or sold, arises only from the labour spent on it. He goes on to say that a workman only gets his wages according to the market value of his labour—that is to say, he is only paid for his time and toil—whereas the value of his labour, *i.e.*, the worth which results from his labour, may be far in excess of the wages which he gets. Marx calls this value or worth which results from labour over and above the wages of labour, which is equivalent to the labourer's support, Marx calls this overworth surplus value. He states that while it goes to the pocket of the employer, it is really the property of the workman, because it is the result of his labour. This surplus value is really capital, and is used by the employer to create more surplus value—that is to say, more capital. Let me put this in another way: while the value of a thing for a man's own use may depend on the thing itself, the value of a thing in the market arises only from the labour spent on it. But the labour spent on it may also have its market value in winning its wage, or it may also have its use value in producing greater value than its wage. But this use value arises from labour as well as the exchange value, and, therefore, belongs to the workman and not to the employer. All this ingenious and intricate system rests absolutely upon the one assumption that exchange value depends only on the labour spent. Now, this assumption is quite false and quite groundless. The worth of a thing in the market will depend first of all upon the nature of the thing's own worth for use. Secondly, upon the demand and other outside circumstances. And thirdly upon the labour spent. A bottle of good wine will have more exchange value than a bottle of bad wine, even though it may not have cost more labour. A pair of boots carved out of wood with long and careful toil will fetch less in the market than a simple pair of brogues. The principle that labour alone is the source of value and the only title to ownership, was adopted by the American Socialist platform in 1904, with the recommendation that the workmen of the world should gradually seize on all capital.

Now, as to the Socialist system. In the official declaration of the English Socialists we read—The object of Socialism is 'the establishment of a system of society, based upon the common ownership and democratic control of the means and instruments for producing and distributing wealth, by, and in the interest of, the whole community.

There is little to refute here that will not have readily occurred to the mind of the intelligent reader. In fact, the haste with which Father Kane left this branch of the subject evinced his knowledge of its dangerous nature. The exposition of the true nature of capital, viz., that it is stored-up, unpaid labour, forms the very basis of the Socialist criticism of modern society, and its method of wealth production; it is the fundamental idea of modern Marxist Socialism, and yet in a discourse covering four columns of small type in the *Irish Catholic* (what a misnomer!) the full criticism of this really fundamental position takes up only twelve lines. And such a criticism!

'A bottle of good wine will have more exchange value than a bottle of bad wine, even though it may not have cost more labour.' Does the reverend father not know that if good wine can be produced as cheaply as bad wine, and in as great quantity, then good wine will come down to the same price as the inferior article? And if good wine could be produced as cheaply as porter it would be sold at the same price as porter is now—heavenly thought! It is the labour embodied in the respective articles, including the labour of keeping in storage, paying rental for vaults, etc., that determines their exchange value. Wine kept in vaults for years commands higher prices than new wine, but could chemists give new wine the same flavour as is possessed by stored-up wine then the new would bring down the price of the old to a price governed by the amount of labour embodied in the new.

'A pair of boots carved out of wood with long and careful labour will fetch less in the market than a simple pair of brogues.' How illuminating! But what governs the price of the brogues? Why, the amount of labour socially necessary to produce them. The amount of labour necessary to produce an article under average social conditions governs its exchange value. 'Boots carved out of wood with long and careful labour' are not produced under average social conditions; in discussing the economic question we discuss governing conditions, not exceptions. Hence the exchange value of boots such as those instanced by Father Kane is as problematical as the moral value of his hair-splitting. If you do not believe labour cost governs the exchange value of a commodity ask a Dublin master builder to tell you what factors he takes into account when he is asked to give an estimate for building an altar. If he is a Catholic he will cast up his estimate with the same items as if he were a Protestant—that is to say, he will count the cost of labour, including the cost of labour embodied in the raw material, and he will base his estimate upon that cost. Ask any manufacturer, whether employing 2 men or 2,000, how he determines the price at which he can sell an article, and he will tell you that the cost of labour embodied in it settles that question for the market and for him. Yet it is this simple truth that Father Kane and such enemies of Socialism deny. Altars, beads, cassocks, shoes, buildings, ploughs, books—all articles upon the market, except a politician's conscience—have their exchange value, determined in like manner—by their labour cost.

The learned gentleman winds up this lecture with a sneer at Socialist proposals, and an unwilling admission of the terrible logic of our position in future politics. He says:

> The means and method of the Socialist have now to be considered. Here we have to consider their destructive and constructive methods—what and how they are to knock down, what and how they are to build up. Here,

however, we meet with an endless difference of Socialist opinions. As to the knocking down process, some Socialists are very enterprising, and appear to quite fall in with the Anarchist programme of the dagger, the firebrand and the bomb. Others prefer to work through Parliament by legal voting and by legal measures. Most of them appear from their speeches and writings to be very little troubled with scruples as to the right or wrong of means to be employed. Some fashionable and aesthetic dabblers in Socialism, amongst whom are men of culture, education and wealth—as, for instance, are some prominent members of the Fabian Society—would work very quietly and very gently; they would even contemplate offering some compensation to the owners whose property they stole, but more probably when the real crash came they would gracefully retire with their culture, their education and their money. A man who makes £25,000 a year by amusing the public is not the sort of man who is likely, when the time comes, to willingly give up all that he owns for the honour of sweeping a street crossing as a Socialist. That is only the superficial nonsense which some people pass off as Socialism. Come to the practical point. The way in which Karl Marx explains how all capital is to be confiscated is as follows. On the one hand that fierce competition which is the war of the financial world will result in the survival of a very few and very grasping capitalists. On the other hand, the army of labour will be more enlightened, better organised, and more scientifically led. It is easy to see what the enormous multitude of the proletariat—with force, votes and law on their side—can do with the few fat but helpless millionaires whose money is wanted. In any case the Socialist intends by one means or another to take private property from all those who have any. As to the constructive methods of the Socialist, we have dreams, visions, castles in the air, fairy tales in which there is much that is amusing, some things that are very sentimental, and some things that are very foul; but in all of them one element is lacking—common sense.

It is surely not necessary to point out that according to the Socialist doctrine the capitalist class are themselves doing much of the constructive work; they, pushed by their economic necessities, concentrate industries, eliminate useless labour and abolish useless plants, and prepare industry for its handling by officials elected by the workers therein. On the other hand the 'army of labour, more enlightened, better organised and more scientifically led,' banded into industrial unions patterned after the industry in which they are employed, will have prepared the workers to take possession of the productive and distributive forces on the day the incapable capitalist class are forced to surrender to a 'proletariat *with force, votes, and law* on their side.'

CHAPTER II

The Rights of Man

The Rights of Man is a doctrine popularised by the bourgeois (capitalist) philosophers of the eighteenth century, and has no place in Socialist literature. Although Father Kane is kind enough to credit Socialism with the doctrine, it is in reality the child of that capitalist class he is defending, and was first used by them as a weapon in their fight for power against the kings and hierarchy of France. Now that capitalism has attained to power and made common cause with its old enemies, royalty and hierarchy, it would fain disavow much of the teaching of its earlier days, and hence listens complacently whilst Father Kane attacks the Right of Man, and sneers at the 'mob,' as he elegantly terms the common people for whom his Master died upon the Cross. We do not propose to follow the reverend gentleman into all his excursions away from the subject, but shall content ourselves with citing and refuting those passages which have a real and permanent bearing upon the question at issue.

He begins:

> Man's right to live is also the right to take the means wherewith to live. Hence he can make use of such material means as are necessary in order that he should

live. But he cannnot make use of certain necessary means if others may use them also. Hence his right to use these means is at the same time a right to exclude others from their use. If a man has a right to eat a definite piece of bread, he has a right that no one else shall eat it. We will set this truth in another light. The right of private ownership may be considered either in the abstract, or as it is realised in concrete form. That right in the abstract means that by the very law of nature there is inherent in man a right to take hold of and apply for his own support those material means of livelihood which are not already in the right possession of another man. What those particular means are is not decided in the concrete by Nature's law. Nature gives the right to acquire, and by acquiring to own. But some partial fact is required in order to apply that abstract law to a concrete thing. The fact is naturally the occupying or taking hold of, or entering into possession of, a thing, by which practical action the abstract law of Nature becomes realised in a concrete practical fact. With this, or upon this, follows another right of man, the right to own his labour and the right to what his labour does. Furthermore, this right to exclusive personal ownership is not restricted to the means of one's daily bread from day to day; it is a right to be secure against want, when the needed means may not be at hand. The man who has tilled a field through the winter and spring has a right to hold as his own the harvest which he has earned. Hence the right of ownership is by Nature's law not merely passing, but permanent; it does not come and go at haphazard; it is stable. Hear the teaching of Pope Leo XIII in his Pontifical explanation of this point (Encyclical on Labour): 'The Socialists, working on the poor man's envy of the rich, endeavour to destroy private property, and maintain that personal property should become the common property of all. They are emphatically unjust, because they would rob the lawful possessor ... If one man hires out to another his strength or his industry, he does this in order to receive in return the means of livelihood,

> with the intention of acquiring a real right, not merely to his wage, but also to the free disposal of it. Should he invest this wage in land, it is only his wage in another form ...
>
> 'It is precisely in this power of disposal that ownership consists, whether it be question of land or other property. Socialists ... strike at the liberty of every wage-earner, for they deprive him of the liberty of disposing of his wages. Every man has, by the law of Nature, the right to possess property of his own ...
>
> 'It must be within his right to own things, not merely for the use of the moment, not merely things that perish in their use, but such things whose usefulness is permanent and stable ... Man is prior to the State, and he holds his natural rights prior to any right of the State ...
>
> 'When man spends the keenness of his mind and the strength of his body in winning the fruits of Nature, he thereby makes his own that spot of Nature's field which he tills, that spot on which he sets the seal of his own personality. It cannot but be just that that spot should be his own, free from outside intrusion ... '

If one of the boys at the National Schools could not reason more logically than that he would remain in the dunce's seat all his schooldays. Imagine a priest who defends landlordism as Father Kane and the Pope does, saying, 'The man who has tilled a field through the winter and spring has a right to hold as his own the harvest which he has earned,' and imagining that he is putting forward an argument against Socialism. Socialists do not propose to interfere with any man's right 'to hold what he has earned'; but they do emphatically insist that such a man, peasant or worker, shall not be compelled to give up the greater part, or any, of 'what he has earned,' to an idle class whose members 'toil not neither do they spin,' but who have attained their hold upon the nation's property by ruthless force, spoliation and fraud.

'Man's right to live is also the right to take the means wherewith to live.'

'His right to use these means is at the same time a right to exclude others from their use.'

That is to say that a man has the right to take the means wherewith to live, and he has also the right to prevent other men taking the means wherewith to live. The one right cancels the other. When the supply of a thing is limited, and that thing is necessary, absolutely necessary, to existence, as is land, water and the means of producing wealth, does it not follow that to allow those things to be made private property enables the owners of them to deny Man 'the right to live,' except he agrees to surrender the greater portion of the fruits of his toil to the owners? *Capitalism and Landlordism are based upon the denial to Man of his Right to Live except as a dependant upon Capitalists and Landlords; they exist by perpetually confiscating the property which the worker has in the fruits of his toil, and establish property for the capitalist by denying it to the labourer.* Why talk about the Right to Live under Capitalism? If a man had all the patriotism of a Robert Emmet or a George Washington, if he had all the genius of a Goldsmith or a Mangan, if he had all the religion of a St. Simeon Stylites or a St. Francis d'Assisi, if he belongs to the working class he has no effective Right to Live in this world unless a capitalist can see his way to make a profit out of him. Translated into actual practice these 'natural rights' of which the reverend gentleman discoursed so eloquently mean for 23,000 families in Dublin the right to live in one room per family—living, sleeping, eating and drinking and dying in the narrow compass of the four walls of one room.

'When man spends the keenness of his mind and the strength of his body in winning the fruits of Nature he thereby makes his own that spot of Nature's field which he tills,' so says his Holiness, as quoted by Father Kane. It follows then that the Irish peasantry, like the peasantry of Europe in general, are and were the real owners of the soil, and that the feudal aristocracy, the landlord class, whose proudest boast it was, and is, that they have never soiled their hands by labour, are and were thieves exacting by force tribute from the lawful owners of the soil. Yet those thieves have ever been supported by the Hierarchy in their possession of property against the peasants who had made it their own 'by spending the keenness of their mind and the strength of their body' in tilling it.

The working class of the world, by their keenness of mind

and their strength of body, have made everything in the world their own—its land, its factories, its ships, its railroads, its houses, everything on earth and sea has been consecrated by the labour of the working class, and therefore belongs to that class; and as factories, ships, railroads and buildings cannot be divided up in pieces, they must be owned in common. If land belongs to those who have tilled it, by what means, other than common ownership, shall we re-establish the right of that 75 per cent. of the Irish people who, according to Mulhall, were evicted between 1837 and 1887, or of those agricultural labourers who toil upon the land but own no one foot of it, or of all those labourers in towns and cities whose forefathers have been hunted like wild beasts from the land they had made their own, by the keenness of mind and strength of body applied to labour, and who are now compelled to herd in towns, dependent upon the greed of capitalists for the chance to exist?

Father Kane, in this portion of his address, came to curse Socialism, but his arguments serve to bless it.

> Let me bring from another world—the old Pagan world—the greatest philosopher of pure reason, as witness to the truth of the same principle. Aristotle wrote: 'Socialism wears a goodly face and affects an air of philanthropy. The moment it speaks it is eagerly listened to. It speaks of a marvellous love that shall grow out from it between man and man. This impression is emphasised when the speaker rails against the shortcomings of existing institutions, giving as the reason for all our shortcomings the fact that we are not Socialists. These evils of human life are not, however, owing to the absence of Socialism, but to the always inevitable presence of human frailty.'

This is a puzzle. The word Socialism, and the Socialist principles, were unheard of until the beginning of the nineteenth century; and Aristotle flourished in the year 384 B.C. Hence to quote Aristotle as writing about Socialism is like saying that Owen Roe O'Neil sent a telegram to the Catholic Confederation at Kilkenny in 1647, or that George Washington crossed the Delaware in a flying machine. It is an absurd anachronism.

For hundreds of years the works of Aristotle were used to combat Christianity, principally by the Arabians in the Middle Ages, and now the same works are used by a Christian priest to combat Socialism. Truly 'misfortune makes strange bedfellows'!

Father Kane says:

> We will go back to the old Greek philosopher, Aristotle, the philosopher compared to whom our Kant, Hegel, Comte, Hobbes and Locke are merely dreaming boys or blundering students. Aristotle founded his philosophy on fact, and worked it out through common sense. Our modern philosophers, with marvellous talent, evolve their principles out of their own inner consciousness, and ground their conclusions on their own mental mood.

In a criticism of Draper's 'Conflict between Religion and Science,' published by the Catholic Truth Society as the report of a lecture delivered in Cork and Limerick by the Rev. Dr. O'Riordan, the author says, 'Owing to the use which the Arabians had made of the name of Aristotle, his name had become a word of offence to Christians, so much so that even Roger Bacon said that his works should be burnt;' and further on, 'St. Thomas (Aquinas) took up the philosophy of Aristotle and, purifying it of its Pagan errors, he established Christian truth out of the reasoning of the Greek philosopher.' So that, according to Father Kane, Aristotle 'founded his philosophy on fact, and worked it out through common sense,' and according to Dr. O'Riordan this philosophy of fact and common sense was subversive of Christianity until it was 'purified of its Pagan errors.' Well, we Socialists, while second to none in our admiration for the encyclopædic knowledge of Aristotle, will carry the purifying process begun by St. Thomas Aquinas a step further. We will purify Aristotle's philosophy of the teaching he derived from the slave-world in which he lived, and make it Socialistic. Let us remind Father Kane that Aristotle's mind was so completely dominated by his economic environment that he was unable to conceive of a world in which there would be no chattel slaves, and so declared that slaves must always exist. A prophecy now falsified for hundreds of years.

We do not propose to follow the reverend gentleman in his wonderful attempt to discredit the Marxist position on Value; that has been dealt with sufficiently already in the passage upon Value in Exchange, in the criticism of the first Discourse, and the attempt to elaborate his position by our opponent in his second Discourse is about as enlightening as an attempt to square the circle generally is. It is summed up in his declaration that 'Labour alone cannot create use value, therefore Labour alone cannot constitute exchange value.' Which is equivalent to saying that Appetite and Desire are the real arbiters in civilised life and under normal conditions of the basis on which articles exchange among human beings. The appetite and desire of human beings for water and for bicycles will illustrate to the simplest mind the absurdity of our opponents' position. Water under normal conditions in a modern community will not fetch a half-penny the bucketful, but bicycles retail easily at £7 and £8 apiece. Yet our desire and appetite for water is based upon a human necessity so imperative that we would die without its satisfaction, but countless millions go through life without even straddling a bicycle. What makes so cheap the article without which we would die? The small amount of labour necessary to convey it from the mountains to our doors, of course. And what makes so costly the article that is not a necessity at all? The comparatively great amount of labour embodied in its production, of course. Then, what fixes the Exchange Value of an article in the normal, modern market? Its cost in labour, certainly.

> It is contrary to Divine Law even to covet our neighbour's field. The Church of Christ has always approved, both in principle and in practice, of private and personal property. It is utterly and irreconcilably against the teaching of the Catholic to deny man's right to hold personal property, even independently of the sanction of the State, or to brand such ownership as theft. Pope Leo XIII wrote: 'Christian democracy, by the very fact that it is Christian, must be based upon the principles of Divine Faith in its endeavours for the betterment of the masses. Hence to Christian democracy justice is sacred. It must

maintain that the right of acquiring and possessing property cannot be gainsaid, and it must safeguard the various distinctions and degrees which are indispensable in every well-ordered commonwealth. It is clear, therefore, that there is nothing common between Social and Christian democracy. They differ from each other as much as the sect of Socialism differs from the Church of Christ.'

Dear, oh dear! What heretics we must be! And yet we are in good company. Saints and pontiffs of the Catholic Church have gone before us on this road, and the wildest sayings of modern Socialist agitators are soft and conservative beside some of the doctrines which ere now have been put forth as sound Catholic teachings. Read:

> The use of all things that is found in this world ought to be common to all men. Only the most manifest iniquity makes one say to the other, 'This belongs to me, that to you.' *Hence the origin of contention among men.*—St. Clement.
>
> What thing do you call 'yours'? What thing are you able to say is yours? From whom have you received it? You speak and act like one who upon an occasion going early to the theatre and possessing himself without obstacle of the seats destined for the remainder of the public pretends to oppose their entrance in due time, and to prohibit them seating themselves, arrogating to his own sole use property that is really destined to common use. And it is precisely in this manner act the rich.—St. Basil the Great.
>
> Therefore if one wishes to make himself the master of every wealth, to possess it and to exclude his brothers even to the third or fourth part (generation), such a wretch is no more a brother but an inhuman tyrant, a cruel barbarian, or rather a ferocious beast of which the mouth is always open to devour for his personal use the food of the other companions.—St. Gregory. Nic.
>
> Nature furnishes its wealth to all men in common. God beneficently has created all things that their enjoyment be common to all living beings, and that the earth become the common possession of all. *It is Nature itself that has given*

> *birth to the right of the community, whilst it is only unjust usurpation that has created the right of private poverty.*—St. Ambrose.
>
> The earth of which they are born is common to all, and therefore the fruit that the earth brings forth belongs without distinction to all.—St. Gregory the Great.
>
> The rich man is a thief.—St. Chrysostom.

Our reverend critic proceeds:

> To enchain men with fetters of equality would be to degrade the wise, the good, the energetic, the noble amongst them, to the depths of the men who are nearest to the brute. Freedom must have fair play. Man must be free to make and mould his own life according to his own talent, his own opportunity, his own energy, his own ambition, his own merit, and his own will, according to the circumstances in which Providence has placed him. But you say is it not a pity that, owing to the mere accident of birth, a brainless and worthless creature should wear a ducal crown, while a man of mind and character is sweeping the crossing of a street? Yes, to merely human view it is a pity, just as it is a pity that one girl should be born beautiful while another girl is born ugly; just as it is a pity that one man should be born weak-minded and weak-kneed while another man is born with a treasure trove of talent and with a golden mine of sterling character; just as it is a pity that one more man, by the accident of birth, is born to be himself. There is accident all round, if you wish to call it accident. No man deserves what he gets with him when he is born into the world, and no man has deserved anything different. What you may, perhaps, call accident I call Providence. We do not choose our own lot; it is given to us. It is our duty to make the best we can of it.

The first part of this is clap-trap: the second is rank blasphemy. The clap-trap consists in the pretence that the Socialist idea of equality involves the idea that men should be reduced to one moral or intellectual level. Trade unionists are generally and rightfully in favour of a minimum wage—a wage below which no worker shall be depressed. Unscrupulous employers and ignorant journalists and politicians dealing with this demand strive to make the thoughtless believe that a minimum wage will prevent higher wages being paid for extra skill. In other words, they speak as if it were a maximum wage that was demanded. So with the Socialist idea of equality. Like the trade unionist our demand is for a level *below* which no man shall be driven, a common basis of equality of opportunity to all. That whatever promotion, distinction, reward or honour be given to or attained by a man shall not confer upon him the right to exploit, to degrade, to dominate, to rob or humiliate his fellows. And our hope and belief is that in the future sane men and women will find as much delight in, strive as eagerly for, the honour of serving their fellows as they do now for the privilege of plundering them. Men and women are at all times zealous for honour, for the esteem of their fellows; and when the hope of plunder is removed out of the field of human possibility those specially gifted ones who now exhaust their genius in an effort to rule, will as vehemently exert themselves to win the honour accorded to those who serve.

The second part is, we repeat, rankly blasphemous. The reverend gentleman, unable to answer the obvious question he supposes, attempts to draw an analogy between what he would call the 'hand of God' in shaping the faces, forms, minds and characters of His creatures, and the historical and social conditions which have created dukes and crossing-sweepers, brainless aristocrats and intelligent slum-dwellers, morally poisonous kings and Christian-minded hod-carriers, vile ladies idling in mansions and clean-souled women slaving over the washtub. The attempt is an insult to our intelligence. We, as individuals, are not personally responsible for our faces, forms or minds; these are the result of forces over which we had and have no control. But the gross injustices of our social system we are responsible for, in the degree in which we help or acquiesce in their perpetuation. In the degree in which we support them to-day we become participators in the crimes upon which they were built. And what were those crimes? Need we remind our readers of the origin of private property in Ireland? It had its root in the adulterous treason of an Irish chief; it was founded upon the betrayal of liberty, and enforced by the wholesale slaughter and enslavement of the Irish people. Must we remind our readers that if they seek for the origin of aristocratic property in Ireland they must seek for it not in the will of a beneficent Deity as this bold blasphemer alleges, nor in titles won by honest labour on the soil, but in the records of English marauders, in the stories of poisonings and treacheries told in the State Papers of the English ruling class, in the light of the burning homes of Munster in the wake of the armies of Inchiquin,[a] in the despatches of the English nobleman who boasted to Elizabeth that his army had left in Ulster 'nothing save carcases and ashes,' in the piteous tale of the imprisoned jurors of Connacht[b] who refused to perjure themselves and yield up Irish tribe lands to greedy aristocratic thieves from England, or in the log of the emigrant ships whose course across the Atlantic was marked by the floating corpses of hunted Irishmen, Irish women and Irish children.

Or shall it be necessary to recall to our readers the grim fact that the origin of great estates in England is found in the court records, which tell us that in the reign of Good Queen Bess 72,000 workers were hanged in the name of law and order, hanged as vagrants after they had been driven off the lands they had tilled; that during the Peasant Wars of Germany the nobility slaughtered so many poor peasants that one of the aristocracy eventually called a halt, saying, 'If we kill them all we shall have no one to live upon'; that in Scotland 15,000 people were evicted off one estate in the nineteenth century—the Sutherland clearances; that in fact in every European country the title deeds to aristocratic property have been written in the blood of the poor, and that the tree of capitalism has been

[a] Inchiquin was an Irish apostate in the service of the English. Taken as a hostage into England when a child he was reared up in hatred of the religion and people of his fathers. As an English general in the Irish rebellion of 1641 he became infamous for his cruelties and purposeless massacres; the march of his armies could always be traced by the fire and smoke from burning homes and villages.

[b] The English Government under Charles I appointed a 'Commission to inquire into defective titles' in Connacht. As all lands in Ireland under the ancient Celtic system were common property it followed that all Irish titles were defective under the feudal law of England. Much land fell into the hands of the English adventurers under this 'Commission', and when the Irish juries refused to be bribed or terrorised into returning verdicts to suit the Commissioners they were promptly imprisoned and their property confiscated.

watered with the tears of the toilers in every age and clime and country.

Next, wonder of wonders, our clerical friend becomes solicitous for a free press and free speech. He declares:

> In Socialism there could be no healthy public opinion, no public opinion at all except that manufactured by officialdom or that artificially cultivated by the demagogues of the mob. There could be no free expression of free opinion. The Press would be only the Press of the officials. Printing machines, publishing firms, libraries, public halls, would be the exclusive property of the State. We do not indeed advocate utter licence for the Press, but we do advocate its legitimate liberty. There would be no liberty of the Press under Socialism; no liberty even of speech, for the monster machine of officialdom would grind out all opposition—for the monster machine would be labelled, 'The Will of the People,' and 'The Will of the People' would be nothing more than the whim of the tyrant mob, the most blind and ruthless tyrant of all, because blindly led by blind leaders. Brave men fear no foe, and free men will brook no fetter. You will have thought, in your boyhood, with hot tears, of the deeds of heroes who fought and fell in defence of the freedom of their Fatherland. That enthusiasm of your boyhood will have become toned down with maturer years in its outward expression, but mature years will have made it more strong and staunch for ever, more ready to break forth with all the energy of your life and with all the sacrifice of your death in defiance of slavery. You may have rough times to face; you may have rough paths to tread, you may have hard taskmasters to urge your toil, and hard paymasters to stint your wage; you may have hard circumstances to limit your life within a narrow field; but after all your life is your own, and your home is your own, and your wage is your own, and you are free. Freedom is your birthright. Even our dilapidated modern nations allow to a man his birthright—freedom. You would fight for your birthright, freedom, against any man, against any nation, against the world; and if you could not live for your

> freedom, you would die for it. You would not sell your birthright, freedom, to Satan; and I do not think that you are likely to surrender your birthright, freedom, to the Socialist. Stand back! We are free men. Stand back, Socialist! God has given us the rights of man, to our own life, to our own property, to our own freedom. We will take our chance in the struggle of life. We may have a hard time or a good time, we may be born lucky or unlucky, but we are free men. Stand back, Socialist! God has given us our birthright, freedom, and, by the grace of God, we will hold to it in life and in death.

After you have done laughing at this hysterical outburst we will proceed to calmly discuss its central propositions. To take the latter part first, it is very amusing to hear a man, to whom a comfortable living is assured, assure us that we ought to tell the Socialist that 'we will take our chance in the struggle of life.'

He speaks of our 'birthright, freedom,' which is allowed us even by dilapidated modern nations, and that we ought not to surrender it to the Socialists. In Ireland 87 per cent. of the working class earn less than 20s. per week; in London a million of people, according to the non-Socialist investigator, Charles Booth, live below the poverty line—never getting enough to eat; in all civilisation, according to Huxley, the lot of the majority of the working class is less desirable than the lot of the mere savage; and this awful condition of the only class in society that is really indispensable is the result of the capitalist system, which mocks the workers with a theoretical freedom and an actual dependence. The freedom of the worker is freedom to sell himself into slavery to the class which controls his supply of food; he is free as the wayside traveller is free of clothes after highwaymen have robbed and stripped him. Says well the poet Shelley:

> What is Freedom? Ye can tell
> That which slavery is too well,
> For its very name has grown
> To an echo of your own.
> 'Tis to work, and have such pay,

As just keeps life, from day to day,
In your limbs as in a cell
For the tyrant's use to dwell.

How can a person, or a class, be free when its means of life are in the grasp of another? How can the working class be free when the sole chance of existence of its individual members depends upon their ability to make a profit for others?

The argument about the Freedom of the Press—a strange argument from such a source—is too absurd to need serious consideration. Truly, all means of printing will be the common property of all, and if any opposition party, any new philosophy, doctrine, science or even hair-brained scheme has enough followers to pay society for the labour of printing its publications, society will have no more right nor desire to refuse the service than a Government of the present day has to refuse the use of its libraries to the political enemies who desire to use those sources of knowledge to its undoing. It will be as possible to hire a printing machine from the community as it will be to hire a hall. Under Socialism the will of the people will be supreme, all officials will be elected from below and hold their position solely during good behaviour, and as the interests of private property, which according to St. Clement are the sole origin of contention among men, will no longer exist there will be little use of law-making machinery, and no means whereby officialdom can corrupt the people.

This will be the rule of the people at last realised. But says Father Kane, at last showing the cloven foot, 'the Will of the People would be nothing more than the whim of the tyrant mob, the most blind and ruthless tyrant of all, because blindly led by blind leaders.' Spoken like a good Tory and staunch friend of despotism! What is the political and social record of the mob in history as against the record of the other classes? There was a time, stretching for more than a thousand years, when the mob was without power or influence, when the entire power of the Governments of the world was concentrated in the hands of the kings, the nobles and the hierarchy. That was the blackest period in human history. It was the period during which human life was not regarded as being of as much value as the lives of hares and deers; it was the period when freedom of speech was unknown, when trial by jury was suppressed, when men and women were tortured to make them confess crimes before they were found guilty, when persons obnoxious to the ruling powers were arrested and kept in prison (often for a lifetime) without trial; and it was the period during which a vindictive legal code inflicted the death penalty for more than 150 offences—when a boy was hung for stealing an apple, a farmer for killing a hare on the roadside. It was during this undisturbed reign of the kings, the nobles, and the hierarchy that religious persecutions flourished, when Protestants killed Catholics, Catholics slaughtered Protestants, and both hunted Jews, when man 'made in God's image' murdered his fellow-man for daring to worship God in a way different from that of the majority; it was then that Governments answered their critics by the torture, when racks and thumbscrews pulled apart the limbs of men and women, when political and religious opponents of the State had their naked feet and legs placed in tin boots of boiling oil, their heads crushed between the jaws of a vice, their bodies stretched across a wheel while their bones were broken by blows of an iron bar, water forced down their throats until their stomachs distended and burst, and when little children toiled in mine and factory for 12, 14 and 16 hours per day. But at last, with the development of manufacturing, came the gathering together of the mob, and consequent knowledge of its numbers and power, and with the gathering together also came the possibility of acquiring education. Then the mob started upon its upward march to power—a power only to be realised in the Socialist Republic. In the course of that upward march the mob has transformed and humanised the world. It has abolished religious persecution and imposed toleration upon the bigots of all creeds; it has established the value of human life, softened the horrors of war as a preliminary to abolishing it, compelled trial by jury, abolished the death penalty for all offences save one, and in some countries abolished it for all; and to-day it is fighting to take the children from the factory and mine, and put them to school. This mob, 'the most blind and ruthless tyrant of all,' with one sweep of its grimy, toil-worn hand swept the rack, the thumbscrew, the wheel, the boots of burning oil, the torturer's vice and the stake into the oblivion of history, and they who to-day would seek to view those arguments of kings, nobles, and ecclesiastics must seek them in the lumber room of the museum.

In this civilising, humanising work the mob had at all times to meet and master the hatred and opposition of kings and nobles; and there is not in history a record of any movement for abolishing torture, preventing war, establishing popular suffrage, or shortening the hours of labour led by the Hierarchy. Against all this achievement of the mob its enemies have but one instance of abuse of power—the French Reign of Terror—and they suppress the fact that this classic instance of mob fury lasted but eight months, whereas the cold-blooded cruelty of the ruling classes which provoked it had endured for a *thousand years*.

All hail, then, to the Mob, the incarnation of Progress!

CHAPTER III
Honour of the Home

The old Pagan idea that the State is everything and owns everything, so as to leave the individual man without any right except such as is conceded to him by the State—that old Pagan idea has been adopted by the Socialist. That idea is distinctly contrary to natural law as well as to the law of Christ. That idea is absolutely antagonistic to our ideas of home. It would change our home into a mere lodging-house, where are fed and sheltered the submissive vassals of the State. Socialism has taken up that Pagan idea and pushed it even further than the Pagan. For the Pagan left the father home's master, and left the wife and child at home. Socialism would ruin the home firstly, because it would rob the father of the home, of his God-given right to be master in the citadel of his own home; secondly, because it would banish home's queen from what ought to be her kingdom; it would break the marriage bond which alone can safeguard the innocence and the stability of the home; it would make

> the wife of the home practically a tenant at will; thirdly, because it would kidnap the child.

The intelligent reader will note that the reverend critic is entirely incapable of grasping the conception of a State in which the people should rule instead of being creatures of an irresponsible power as the people were under the Pagan powers of Rome to whom he is referring. He says, 'It [Socialism] would change our home into a mere lodging-house where are fed and sheltered the *submissive vassals of the State*.' Thus it is that he cannot clear his mind of the monarchical conception of the State; a State which should be a social instrument in the hands of its men and women, where State powers would be wielded as a means *by the workers* instead of being wielded as a repressive force *against the workers* is so strange an idea to him that he simply cannot understand what it signifies. The reader who understands this, and perceives the enormous gap in this clerical reasoning, will understand also that all the terrific bogies which our critics conjure up as a necessary result of the Socialist State are—only bogies.

This attempt to develop this theory of the State plunges him into a mass of contradictions. Read:

> The first and most fundamental principle of ethics is that whereas amongst lesser creatures physical force or animal instinct impels each thing to act as is befitting its nature, to act in the actual circumstances, so as to achieve the right order of its kind and the right end of its existence, man not flung forward by unreasoning power, but led by reason's light, contemplates the order of relations that are around him, and weighing their relative necessity or importance, acts so that his action shall be in keeping with his own nature and in harmony with the right conditions in which his life is cast. Now, right and duty are the moral aspects of these fact-relations, and have their moral force according to the deeper order and more fundamental necessity of these fact-relations which are the cause of their existence and the measure of their power. The reason for man's personal rights is in his actual existence. Hence such rights are paramount above all. The reason of the family

is in the insufficiency of man alone to secure the right development of human nature. The reason of civil society is in the insufficiency of the family alone to attain that fuller perfection of human nature which is the heritage of its birth, but which it can only reach through the help of many homesteads united into one common weal. Hence, civil society is only intended by Nature to be the helper of the family, not its master; to be its safeguard, not its destroyer; to be in a right true sense its servant, but in no sense its owner. Hence, those Socialistic theories which would hand over the family and the individual to the supreme command of the State are false to reason and rebel against right. Rather it is the interest of the State itself to recognise that its welfare and its security rests upon the right, independence, and deep-rooted stability of the families of which it is the flower and the fruit.

A State that is tossed about in its social and political existence by the fluctuating tide of transient individual opinions, ambitions, actions, cannot have that healthy, hardy, deathless spirit which vivifies into the same life not merely the chance companions of a day but the successive generations of a nation.

Surely here is a Daniel come to judgment! We had to read this passage over several times to satisfy ourselves that it was not a quotation from a Socialist writer, instead of what it purports to be—a part of the discourse of the reverend gentleman himself. For it is the reasoning upon which is built that Materialist Interpretation of History the lecturer has so eloquently denounced. If the reader will turn to the first lecture he will see that the doctrine of Marx, as explained by Father Kane, teaches that the economic conditions in which man moves, governs or determines [*sic*] his conceptions of right and wrong, his social, ethical and religious opinions. Father Kane there denounced this doctrine in his most violent language. Now, in the part just quoted, he himself affirms the same doctrine. He says: 'The first and most *fundamental* principle of ethics is that ... *man* not flung forward by unreasoning power, but led by reason's light, contemplates the order of relations that are around him, and weighing their relative necessity or importance, *acts so that his action shall be in keeping with his own right nature, and in harmony with the conditions in which his life is cast.* Now, *right and duty*, are the moral aspects of these fact-relations, and *have their moral forces according to the deeper order and more fundamental necessity of those fact-relations which are the cause of their existence and the measure of their power.*' If this is not an affirmation of the Socialist doctrine that our conceptions of right and wrong, and the political and governmental systems built upon them have the 'cause of their existence and the measure of their power' in the 'fact-relation' of man and his fellow-man and not in any divine or philosophical system of mere thought, then language fails to convey any meaning. The remainder of the quotation quite as effectually cuts the ground from under the lecturer's own feet. Observe the last sentence. 'A State that is tossed about in its social and political existence by the fluctuating tide of transient individual opinions, ambitions, actions, cannot have that healthy, hardy, deathless spirit which vivifies into the same life not merely the chance companions to a day, but the successive generations of a nation.' Is not this a lifelike picture of the capitalist State and its endeavour to build a system of society which seeks a healthy national existence and social conscience in 'transient individual opinions, ambitions, and actions' instead of in an ordered co-operation of all for the common good of all? The whole passage we have quoted is essentially Socialist, and opposed to that capitalism its author defends. If the doctrine of Economic Determinism is heresy then Father Kane was preaching heresy from the pulpit.

As if conscious of his slip our critic immediately makes haste to divert attention by a lurid description of the 'Socialist doctrine of divorce.' Socialists as such have no doctrine of divorce, but a little inconsistency like that does not deter our opponents.

There is no Socialist Government in the world to-day, but almost every civilised nation has divorce laws, and the least Socialist nations and classes have the most divorces. America and its capitalist class, for example. Our clerical friends proceed upon the maxim of their sister profession, the lawyers —'When you have a bad case abuse your opponent's attorney,' and hence the constant attempt to slander Socialists upon this point. Now, what is the real truth on this matter? It is easily stated. Socialists are bound to agree upon one fundamental, and upon that only. That fundamental is, in the language of Father Kane, 'that all wealth-producing power and all that pertains to it belongs to the ownership and control of the State.' Hence, upon all other subjects there is, and will be, the widest possible diversity of opinion. Divorce is one of those non-essential, non-fundamental points upon which Socialists may and do disagree. But observe this. The law-making authority for Socialists is their national and international congresses; the law-making authority of capitalism is its Parliaments, Chambers, Congresses, Reichstags, etc. Nowhere has a National or International Congress of Socialists imposed divorce upon Socialists as something they must accept, but in almost every capitalist State the capitalist law-makers, the spokesmen and defenders of capitalism, have established divorce as a national institution. Who, then, are the chief supporters of divorce? The capitalists. And who can come fresh from the Divorce Courts, reeking with uncleanness and immorality, to consummate another marriage, and yet know that he can confidently rely upon Catholic prelates and priests to command the workers to 'order themselves reverently before their superiors,' with him as a type? The capitalist.

The divorce evil of today arises not out of Socialist teaching, but out of that capitalist system, whose morals and philosophy is based upon the idea of individualism, and the cash nexus as the sole bond in society. Such teaching destroys the sanctity of the marriage bond, and makes of love and the marriage bed things to be bought and sold. Can it be wondered at that such teaching as that which exalts the *individual* pursuit of riches as the absolutely necessary cement of society should produce a loosening of all *social* bonds, including that of marriage, and threatens to suffocate society with the stench of its own rottenness? Yet it is such capitalist ethics and practice our priests and prelates are defending, and it is of such Father Kane arises as the champion and expounder.

Certain Socialists, horrified at this rising stream of immorality, have sought to find a remedy in the proposal that marriage be regarded as a private matter over which the State shall have no authority. They do so as individuals, and many equally good Socialists believe that such an idea is flatly opposed to the Socialist philosophy; but in itself the proposal carries none of that loathsomeness the critic imputes to it. *It is an insult to the entire human race to say that husbands and wives are only kept together by law, and that women would become mistresses of one man after another if the law did not prevent them.* Yet this is what Father Kane said: 'Divorce in the Socialist sense means that woman would be willing to stoop to be the mistress of one man after another.'

A more unscrupulous slander upon womanhood was never uttered or penned. Remember that this was said in Ireland, and do you not wonder that some Irishwomen—some persons of the same sex as the slanderer's mother—did not get up and hurl the lie back in his teeth, and tell him that it was not Law which kept them virtuous, that if all marriage laws were abolished tomorrow, it would not make women 'willing to stoop to be the mistress of one man after another.' Aye, verily, the uncleanness lies not in this alleged Socialist proposal, but in the minds of those who so interpret it. The inability of Father Kane to appreciate the innate morality of womanhood, and the superiority of the morals of the women of the real people to that of the class he is defending, recalls to mind the fact that the Council of the Church held at Macon in the sixth century gravely debated the question as to whether woman had or had not a soul, and that the affirmation that she had was only carried by a small majority. Many of the early Fathers of the Church were, indeed, so bitter in their denunciation of women and of marriage that their opinions read like the expressions of madmen when examined in the cold light of the twentieth century. Origen said: 'Marriage is unholy and unclean—a means of sensual lust.' St. Jerome declared, 'Marriage is at the least a vice; all that we can do is to excuse and justify it'; and Tertullian, in his hatred of women, thundered forth boldly that which Father Kane dared only insinuate. 'Woman,' he preaches, 'thou oughtest always to walk in mourning and rags, thine eyes filled with tears of repentance to make men forget that thou hast been the destruction of the race. Woman! thou art the Gates of Hell.' Thus throughout the centuries persists the idea of the Churchmen that women can only be kept virtuous by law.

In his further quotation Father Kane is equally disingenuous. Thus:

> Listen now to one of the great German Socialist authorities, Bebel, who, in his famous book, 'Die Frau,' wrote: 'Every child that comes into the world, whether male or female, is a welcome addition to society; for society beholds in every child the continuation of itself and its own further development. It, therefore, perceives from the very outset that its duty, according to its power, is to provide for the new-born child ... It is evident that the mother herself must nurse the child as long as possible and necessary ... When the child waxes stronger, the other children await it for common amusement under public direction.' Behold their plan: All boys and girls, as soon as they are weaned, are to be taken from their parents and brought up, boys and girls together, first in State nurseries, and then, boys and girls together, in State boarding schools, but brought up without any religion whatever. Thus the child would grow up a stranger to its father and mother, without the hallowed influence of a happy home.

The reader will observe there is nothing whatever in the words quoted from Bebel which justifies the statement that the child is to be taken from the parents, or brought up a stranger to its father and mother, or without the influence of a home. There is simply the statement that it is the duty of the State to provide for the care, education and physical and mental development of the child. All the rest is merely read into the statement by the perverted malevolence of our critic. And yet this same critic had declared, as already quoted in this chapter, 'the reason of civil society is in the *insufficiency of the family alone* to attain that fuller perfection of human nature which is the heritage of its birth.' But when he comes across the Socialist proposal to supplement and help out that 'insufficiency' he forthwith makes it the occasion for the foulest slanders.

CHAPTER IV

The Suicide of a Nation

> Most scientific Socialists appear to follow Karl Marx in his theory that economic forces alone determine the evolution of all else in the world. In other words, to put the matter in a broad, blunt way, they assert that financial or business or trade conditions determine and decide the inevitable course and development of all other matters—intellectual, moral, social and religious. Marx says: 'The sum total of the conditions of wealth production constitutes the economic structure of society, the real basis on which is raised an ethical and political superstructure to which correspond certain forms of social consciousness ... It is not the mind of man which determines his life in society, but it is this material economic life that determines his mind.' The world has beheld one fact which gives the lie to all that flimsy theory. Christ brought into the world so deep and wide and lasting a change that there has been no other ever like it. That change was hostile to economic causes; it came from outside the business world. But it determined a new world of thought and conduct, and through these moral causes it changed the social and economic lives of men. It brought into the civilised world the duty and honour of labour, the breaking of the fetters of the slave, the lifting up of woman to be man's helpmate and equal, not his mere plaything or his property, the recognition of the rights of the poor to the ownership of the superabundance of the wealthy.

Such a statement as that Christ brought into the world a change hostile to economic causes could only be made by a lecturer who presumed either upon lack of historical knowledge on the part of his audience, or upon the fact that as he spoke from a pulpit none of his immediate listeners would dare to point out his errors upon the spot. All but the merest dabblers in Scriptural history know that the economic oppression of the Jewish people was so great immediately before the coming of Christ that the whole nation had been praying and hoping for the promised Redeemer, and it was just at the psychological moment of their bondage as a nation and their slavery as a race that Christ appeared. And it is equally well known that the priests and comfortable classes—the 'canting, fed classes'—refused to acknowledge His message and intrigued to bring about His crucifixion, whereas it was the 'common people' who 'heard Him gladly' in Judea, as it was the slaves and labourers who formed the bulk of His believers throughout the Gentile world until the fury of the persecutions had passed. Roman and Jewish historians alike speak contemptuously of early Christianity as a religion of slaves and labourers. These early Christians had been socially enslaved. Christ and His Disciples spoke to them of redemption, of freedom. They interpreted, rightly or wrongly, the words to mean an earthly redemption, a freedom here and now as a prelude possibly to the freedom hereafter; and hence they joined with enthusiasm the sect hated by their oppressors. We have had a similar experience in Ireland. The passionate adherence of the Irish to Catholicity in Reformation times was no doubt largely due to the fact that the English Government had embraced Protestantism.

For the last portion of the part quoted it should not be necessary to point out to anyone other than Father Kane that of all those things which he asserts Christianity has 'brought into the world' most are not here yet. The 'duty and honour of labour.' The greatest honours of Church and State are reserved for those classes whose members do not labour, and highest honours of all for those who claim that their ancestors have not laboured for a hundred generations. 'The lifting up of woman to be man's helpmate and equal, not his plaything or his property.' She has not yet attained to that elevation in fact, and the Socialists are the only ones who claim it for her in their programmes, whereas his Holiness the Pope has recently denounced her for seeking the right to vote. 'The rights of the poor to the superabundance of the wealthy' is so far from being recognised that a starving man would be sent for seven years to prison for stealing a loaf of bread, and a rich man sent to the House of Lords for stealing a nation's liberty.

Universal ownership by the State of all means of wealth production is one cardinal doctrine of Socialism. The Erfurt platform lays down: 'Private property in the means of production has become incompatible with their proper utilisation and full development.' The platform of the Socialists of the United States lays down: 'The aim of Socialism is the organisation of the working classes for the purpose of transforming the present system of private ownership of the means of production into collective ownership by the entire people.' The International Social Convention at Paris, 1900, lays down as an essential condition of membership the admission of the essential principles of Socialism; amongst them, 'the socialisation of the means of production and distribution.'

Now consider the colossal magnitude of such a scheme. The taking of a census entails a strange amount of time and trouble. Try to imagine what it would mean to ascertain the wants, needs, desires, helps or difficulties of every man, woman and child in a nation, not merely in one branch, but in every possible branch of human life; all possible food stuffs, all possible dress stuffs, all possible lodging accommodation, all possible means of transit, travel or communication. Then imagine what it would mean that all this should be catered for; that all the possible labour should be applied in the right time, place and manner; that all the possible materials and tools for work should be made ready beforehand; that all possible difficulties or accidents should be anticipated. Surely so vast, so unending, so complex, so intricate a task would require many men of most surpassing genius. Further, consider the enormous multitude of officials which all this would require. The percentage of officials amongst the people would be really alarming, and these flunkeys would grow fat on the labour of the common fellows. It is absurd to suggest that every man would get his turn at being a full-blown flunkey with a pet position, or a full private with hard and nasty work to do.

With a childishness born of a training in a profession 'not

concerned with this world,' the reverend gentleman does not realise that the task of ascertaining and catering for the 'wants, needs, desires,' etc., of the nation is done every day by the common everyday men and women he sees around him—done in a blundering, imperfect manner it is true, but still it is done. And what is done imperfectly by the competing forces of capitalism today, can be done more perfectly by the organised forces of industry under Socialism. Government under Socialism will be largely a matter of statistics. The chief administrative body of the nation will be a collection of representatives from the various industries and professions. From the industries they represent these administrators will learn of the demand for the articles they manufacture; the industries will learn from the storekeepers of the national stores and warehouses what articles are demanded by the general public who purchase at these stores, and the cumulative total of the reports given by storekeepers and industries will tell the chief administrative body (Congress, if you will) how much to produce, and where to place it to meet the demand. Likewise the reports brought to the representatives from their Industrial Union as to the relative equipment and power of their factories in each district will enable them to place their orders in the places most suited to fill them, and to supervise and push forward the building and developing of new factories and machinery. All this is so obvious to a mind acquainted with the processes of modern industry that it gives the Socialist a feeling of talking to the baby class when he has to step aside in order to explain it. All the talk of Socialist flunkies, bosses, corruption, favouritism, etc., is the product of minds who are imagining the mechanism of capitalist business at work in a Socialist commonwealth, which is as absurd as to suppose that an Atlantic liner of the present day could be handled on the methods of a fishing boat on the sea of Galilee in the days of St. Peter. When the workers elect their foremen and superintendents, and retain them only during effective supervision and handling of their allotted duties, when industries elect their representatives in the National Congress and the Congress obeys the demand emanating from the public for whom it exists, corruption and favouritism will be organically impossible. Being a merely human society there will be faults and imperfections of course, but it has also been whispered that faults and imperfections exist even in the Society of Jesus. And yet that institution does its work.

Father Kane says:

> They suppose that they could avoid class distinctions, but unless the State should lapse into barbarism it must have its specialists, its great engineers, its great doctors, its great scientists, its great writers, its great statisticians, its great inventors, its great administrators, and, above all, its great officials. All these men should have their lives devoted to their profession with material comfort and studious ease, with high incentive to their talents' use, and with right reward for their labour done.

Observe the phrase, 'with high incentive to their talents' use,' and its implied meaning, with great *monetary* reward. It is a strange fact that when Socialists preach the necessity and duty of the men and women of genius *serving* their fellows, instead of using their God-given genius to *rob* their 'fellow brothers and sisters of Christ,' it is always a paid servant of Christ who gets up to denounce the idea, and to insist that progress will cease unless men gifted by God get the right to plunder their fellow-men. And yet Christ said, 'Give, hoping for nothing in return.' Fortunately, history knows and teaches us better than the Church-men. It teaches us that the greatest 'engineers, doctors, scientists, writers, statisticians and inventors' reaped nothing but their labour for their pains, that for the most part they died in poverty, and that the highest incentive they ever possessed was the inward desire to give outward expression to the divine passion to create planted in their bosoms by Him who knew better than Father Kane. Under Socialism all will enjoy a full, free and abundant life, with every possibility and appliance provided them to serve well their fellows. And what more could the 'specialists' desire?

> At present the two great Socialist organisations in the United States are at war. Amongst other choice epithets bandied between them one stigmatised the other as a

> party of 'scabs.' Amongst German Socialists there are signs of a cleavage, which must inevitably split in twain any Socialist State. A fierce jealousy between the educated and the proletarians; between, on the one hand, writers or speakers of good family, mostly the madcaps of atheistic universities and, on the other hand, the mere workmen, who are suspicious of any leaders who do not belong to the labour class. This is easily understood, for Socialism must logically work out into a solid class organisms to steady it, must oscillate wildly between a despotism, an oligarchy, and universal muddle; for a pure democracy has no other standard of right than the will of the masses, and the will of the masses is at the mercy of wire-pullers and demagogues. Thus a Socialist State would in theory be under the sovereignty of the mob in the street, but in reality it would be under the slavery of the conspirators in their den.

In previous portions of his tirade the reverend lecturer has been insisting vehemently that Socialism will inevitably mean a despotism in which political freedom will be impossible, and all must conform to the common mould. In this portion he finds fault with the Socialists because while in perfect agreement as to their object they quarrel over other matters. He says this 'must inevitably split in twain the Socialist State,' but he carefully avoids explaining how the existence of two or more parties will destroy Socialism any more than it destroys capitalism. There are two, and more than two, purely capitalist parties in every nation in the civilised world. The fact that Socialists are as a rule men and women of strong individuality who fiercely contest for their rights, while it makes occasional unseemly squabbles in the Socialist ranks to-day, is the best guarantee that they are not likely to be working for a system which will crush their individuality or destroy their personal or political liberty. Also if splits in the party, harsh words among the members, and even hatreds could destroy the movement it would have died long ago, instead of growing stronger and more rapidly every day. And surely when we remember how fiercely hatreds have developed within the Christian fold—how the Dominicans have fought the Jesuits, and the Jesuits have denounced the Dominicans, how the Lutherans have burned the Calvinists and the Calvinists have burned the Lutherans—we have no right to demand from an organisation of mere earthly origin more than was shown by organisations claiming Divine inspiration. Quarrels among Socialists, forsooth! Have we not had quarrels among Catholics? For 68 years the Christian world saw two Popes directing and claiming its allegiance. The Pope at Avignon, supported by half of the bishops and clergy of the world, excommunicated the Pope at Rome and all his supporters; and his Holiness at Rome hurled back his curse in return. In 1064 Henry III of Germany entered Italy and found three Popes in Rome—all claiming the allegiance of the Catholic world, and denouncing each other worse than Socialists are denounced today. In 1527 an army of 30,000 troops under the Catholic Constable of Bourbon attacked and captured Rome, killed the Pope's soldiers, imprisoned his Holiness Clement VII in the Castle of St. Angelo, and put the sacred city to the sack. They were all Catholic soldiers under Catholic officers, and they plundered and ravished the centre of Catholicity. But, it will be said, these were only quarrels; they were not disputes over doctrine. Father Kane is a Jesuit; the majority of priests who at present are in the forefront of the attack upon Socialism are also Jesuits. Let us remind our reverend critics of a few incidents in the history of their own order—instances of the fierce disputes between the Jesuits and other Catholics on points of important Catholic doctrine.

In India Jesuit missionaries adopted the life and practices of the Brahmins in 1609 in order to make converts, and in their desire to conciliate that caste *they even refused the Holy Sacrament to no-caste pariah converts*. This outrage upon Catholic teaching and practice was reported to the Pope by a Capuchin Friar, Norbert, and by the Bishop of Rosalia, and condemned in the strongest terms by Pope Innocent X in 1645, by Clement IX in 1669, by Clement XII in 1734 and 1739, and by Benedict XIV in 1745. Pope Benedict XIV in 1741 denounced the Jesuits as 'disobedient, contumacious, captious and reprobate persons.' Melchior Cano, Bishop of the Canary Islands, banished the Jesuits from his diocese for teaching false doctrines, and for the same reason St. Charles Borromeo expelled them from the diocese of Milan, as did also his successor, Cardinal Frederick Borromeo. We do not presume to say which side was right in these controversies, but we submit that if Popes and Jesuits could be wrong then on a point of doctrine they can be wrong now on Socialism—a point of economics and politics.

At the beginning of the seventeenth century a Jesuit missionary, Father Ricci, gained the favour of the Chinese Emperor, and he appointed Catholics to all high positions. The Catholic religion gained a strong foothold in China, established scientific observatories, and founded schools and universities. But the Dominican Fathers accused the Jesuits of allowing their converts to practise their old idolatry, and a fight started between the Jesuits and Dominicans over this question of what were called the 'Chinese Rites.' Nine different Popes condemned these 'Chinese Rites,' but the *Jesuits refused to obey the Popes*, and in 1710 imprisoned the Papal Legate of Clement XI in the prison of the Inquisition at Macao, where he died. Sixtus V, Urban VIII and Clement VIII all died so soon after opposing the Jesuits that popular prejudice accused the Society of having had them assassinated. The Bishop of Pastoia, Scipio de Ricci, accused the Jesuits of having poisoned Pope Clement XIV, as did also Cardinal de Bernis, and the Spanish ambassador to the Court of Madrid declared that several Jesuits had told the Vicar-General of Padua the approximate date on which the Pope would die. In China the Jesuits in 1700 got an edict from the Pagan Emperor defending them against the charges of heresy brought by the Pope, but eventually the fight between the Catholics became so scandalous that the heathens withdrew their toleration and suppressed the Christian religion in the empire. In 1661 the Jesuits alone had possessed 151 churches and 28 residences in China, had written 131 works upon religion, 103 on mathematics, and 53 on physical and moral science. All this was lost to Catholicity because of Jesuit perversion of Catholic doctrine, and consequent disgraceful feuds between Catholics. As the Jesuits perverted Catholic doctrine in India and China to gain the support of the great and powerful, is it wonderful if some think that they and other ecclesiastics are now again perverting Catholic doctrine for a like purpose?

The reader who has studied the facts set forth in our little excursion into Irish history in the introduction will appraise at its full value our reverent opponent's disquisition upon patriotism in the next passage:

> There is a patriotism that is false. It is a mere morbid, hysterical idolatry of a fetish, with an unreasoning rancorous hatred of those people who are not of its own ilk. But there is a patriotism that is true. It is a thoughtful, manly worship for the nation of which one is the son; it is a chivalrous allegiance to her honour, a disinterested service of her fortune, a prayerful veneration for her name, a devotedness unto death to her life. The Socialist will say that that is sentiment. No wonder, then, that the Socialist is the enemy of his country. The French Socialists are the worst enemies of France. The German Socialists are the worst enemies of Germany. The English Socialists are the worst enemies of the power, the greatness and the empire of England. But our sentiment is the heartbeat of men true to their country; their Socialism is the heartburn of traitors to their Fatherland. If it be sentiment that a child should love its mother, that a man should love his home? Then it is sentiment that a citizen should love his country, that a patriot should love his nature. But if this be sentiment, then I say that is the power which makes a nation. Ah! there is something in your inmost nature that affirms the truth and re-echoes the enthusiasm of what the poet sang:
>
> Breathes there the man with soul so dead,
> Who never to himself hath said,
> This is my own, my native land.

The Socialist doctrine teaches that all men are brothers, that the same red blood of a common humanity flows in the veins of all races, creeds, colours and nations, that the interests of Labour are everywhere identical, and that wars are an abomination. Is not this also good Catholic doctrine—the doctrine of a Church which prides itself upon being universal or Catholic? How, then, can that doctrine which is high and holy in theory on the lips of a Catholic become a hissing and a blasphemy when practised by the Socialist? The Socialist does not cease to love his country when he tries to make that country the common property of its people; he rather shows a greater love of country than is shown by those who wish to perpetuate a system which makes the great majority of the people of a country exiles and outcasts, living by sufferance of capitalists and landlords in their native land. Under Socialism we can all voice the saying of the poet, at present 'our' native land is in pawn to landlords and capitalists.

When the reverend lecturer hurls at the Socialists the taunt that they are the worst enemies of their own country, whatever that country be, he is only repeating against us the accusation made more truly in times past against the order of which he is such an ornament. The Jesuits have been expelled from every Catholic Country in Europe, and the grounds on which they have been expelled were everywhere the same, viz., that they were the worst enemies of their country, and were constantly intriguing against the Government and national welfare, that their teaching made bad subjects, and all their influence was against the welfare of the State—just what they allege against Socialists today. They were expelled from Venice during the first half of the seventeenth century, from Portugal in 1759, from the French dominions in 1764 and 1767, from Spain in 1767, from Naples, Parma and Modena about the same time. Maria Theresa of Austria and Emperor Joseph, her son, also expelled them. The kings of Spain, Portugal and France united in an ultimatum to the Pope threatening to withdraw their countries from fealty to Rome and to create a schism unless the Pope suppressed them, and finally in a Brief issued July 21st, 1773, his Holiness, Pope Clement XIV, suppressed the Jesuits 'in all the States of Christendom.' As the Catholic author of the article on the Jesuits in the Encyclopædia Americana truly says, 'They have been expelled over and over again from almost every Catholic country in Europe.' In 1601 the secular priests of England issued a pamphlet entitled,

'Important Considerations,' in which they laid the blame of the Penal Laws against Catholics upon the Jesuits. The author of this work, William Watson, afterwards died a martyr for the Catholic faith. The Papal Brief, Dominus ac Redemptor, speaks of their defiance of their own constitution, expressly revised by Pope Paul V, *forbidding them to interfere in politics*, of the great ruin to souls caused by their quarrels with local ordinaries and other religious orders, *their conformity to heathen usages in the East*, and the disturbances resulting in persecution of the Church which they have stirred up even in Catholic countries, so that several Popes have been obliged to punish them. It is instructive to recall that upon their suppression the Jesuits took refuge in Russia under Catherine, and in Prussia under Frederick, both sovereigns being Freethinkers. Not until the French Revolution had frightened all liberal ideas out of the crowned heads of Europe, and the fall of Napoleon enabled the sceptred tyrants of England and the Continent to place their iron heels upon the necks of the peoples did the Jesuits once more receive an invitation to resume their activity and their existence as an order. That invitation was coincident with the suppression of all popular liberties, and the enthronement of absolute power.

Is it not, then, a joke to see Socialists accused of being unpatriotic, and accused by a Jesuit?

CHAPTER V

God or Mammon

In his fifth lecture our reverend critic simply refurbishes up and places upon exhibition all the individual opinions of individual Socialists he can find antagonistic to religion, and tells us that their individual opinions are orthodox Socialist doctrines. After having for four weeks beaten the air in a wild endeavour to convince us that the Church is and always was against Socialism, that Socialists were and are beasts of immorality, uncleanness and treason, he affects to be horrified at the idea of those Socialists thinking and saying harsh things about the religion whose priests have been so busy slandering and vilifying them. We would say to him, and all others, that if the pioneers of the Socialist movement were indeed Freethinkers, so much the more shame to the Church that by neglecting its obvious duty left Freethinkers to do the work in which Churchmen ought to have been their leaders.

Sufficient to remind our readers that, even according to the oft-repeated assertion of Father Kane, Socialism means a State of society in which the will of the people should be supreme, that therefore Marx and Bebel and Liebknecht and Vandervelde and Blatchford were not and are not working for the establishment of a system in which they would be able to force their theories about religion upon the people, but for a system in which the people would be free to accept only that of which their conscience approved. In the light of that central truth how absurd seems the following passage:

> Now, in Socialism there are principles which no real Catholic can hold. First, Socialists hold that private ownership is in itself wrong; that, no Catholic can admit. Secondly, Socialists maintain that the child is the property of the State as against the father's right; that, no Catholic can admit. Thirdly, Socialists recognise divorce as a breaking of the marriage bond; that, no Catholic can admit. Fourth, Socialists limit and confine religion to mere personal private worship; that, no Catholic can admit.

We have seen that saints and Popes denounced private ownership of the means of life. We challenge the reverend Father to produce from any Socialist Congress or Party a declaration that Socialists desire to take the child from the father or mother, but we will produce many declarations that it is the right of the State to help fathers and mothers to support their children, and finally we flatly deny, and brand as an unqualified falsehood, the statement that the Socialist programme declares for the breaking of the marriage bond. Our reverend and holy critics make it appear that the Socialist idea of society must be responsible for the other ideas held by some of its sponsors. Why not apply this to the Catholic Church then? When King Edward VII of England ascended the throne he swore that the Mass was blasphemous and idolatrous; and when he died the Vatican went into mourning. Did the

Vatican believe that the institution of monarchy was not to be blamed for the official declarations of its supporters? And if so, why blame Socialism for the private, non-official, declaration of a few of its supporters.

Recently there died in Europe a king—King Leopold of Belgium—whose private life was so disgracefully immoral that it was the scandal of Europe. A married man with a grown-up family, he kept a Parisian actress as his mistress, and led so scandalous a life that the females of his family refused to follow his body to the grave. Yet when he died the whole official Catholic world went into mourning for him. He was more of a representative of the institution of monarchy than any private individual can ever be of Socialism; but the Rev. Father Kane or his Holiness the Pope did not therefore deliver sermons against the wickedness of supporting kings. And what is true in these two striking examples is also true of kings, nobles and capitalists all the world over. In the United States the divorce rate for 100,000 of the population rose from 23 in 1880 to 73 in 1900. Between 1887 and 1906 the total number of divorces was 945,625. *This enormous increase of divorces was almost entirely among the classes least affected by Socialist teaching*—the middle and upper capitalist class. That is to say, among the class our reverend opponent is defending. Why all this howl about supposed Socialist theories of divorce, and all this silence about the capitalist practice thereof?

> Is there any logical connection between Socialism and Atheism? This question has two aspects; first, does Atheism logically lead to Socialism? and secondly, does Socialism logically lead to Atheism? As regards the first question it is very evident that a wealthy Atheist is little likely to be a genuine Socialist. For him his wealth and pleasure will be the only objects of his worship, and he will not sacrifice them in order to secure the honour of being a Socialist labourer. But with the Atheist who is penniless it is quite another matter. For him there is no moral law, because there is no law without a lawgiver, and there is no lawgiver but God; hence, there is no right that can restrain him from taking all the wealth on which he can lay

> his hands, and Socialism supplies him with the means of doing this. A beggar Atheist is a Socialist, unless he be a fool. The answer to the second question is not so clear. Does Socialism logically lead to Atheism? *If we understand Socialism exclusively in its real and essential sense as a social system, which would give exclusively to the State all ownership of capital, of means of wealth production, and kindred powers, with also the exclusive right of distribution and administration of such goods, then we admit that Socialism is not logically the same thing as Atheism.* However wrong a man may be in ethical or economic matters, he may yet be right in recognising God. This, however, is vague and abstract. Is Socialism logically incompatible with Catholicity? To this we must fearlessly answer this; a true Catholic cannot be a real Socialist. Understand what this does not mean and what it does mean. It does not mean that the Catholic who calls himself a Socialist is thereby a heretic. It does not even follow that a Catholic who is a real Socialist is thereby a heretic; but it does logically follow that a real Catholic cannot be a real Socialist. Do not push this statement unfairly towards one side or towards the other.

When he makes the damaging admission he does in the point we have put in [italics][1], our reverend friend knocks the feet from under his own case; and when he goes on to wriggle still further in an attempt to cloud the issue he reveals that his purpose is not to discuss Socialism so much as to traduce it. He admits that logically there is no connection between Socialism and Atheism, and yet his whole discourse was a long-drawn-out attempt to prove such a connection. In what other walk of life would a man be tolerated who indulged in such senseless hairsplitting as the foregoing, or in such vilification as the following?

> What will you then have in your Socialist paradise? A herd of human cattle, some of them intelligent, educated, cultured, a very suspected lot in the Socialistic State, most of them, practically all of them, a Godless, unprincipled, immoral crowd. In our Christian commonwealths there

[1] 'heavy type' in the original.

> are many criminals, but they are the exception. They are an offence against our principles and rebels against our right. Under Socialis mcriminals would be the authorised spokesmen of your principles and the ruthless henchmen of your lawlessness. Again and again, without God there is no morality, and without morality there is only left the God of the Socialist—irreligion, immorality, degradation of the man and suicide of the nation.

Note the words, 'Under Socialism criminals would be the authorised spokesmen of your principles.' He has repeatedly asserted that under Socialism the will of the people would rule, and now he asserts that the people would choose criminals as their spokesmen. Yet such a thing as a Socialist criminal is practically unknown in the records of the police courts of the world. Can any sane man believe that if the 'means of wealth production and kindred powers' were common property that the people would be so debased by the enjoyment of the full fruits of their labour that they would elect criminals to be their spokesmen and rulers? Or that a man cannot worship God unless he concedes the right of a capitalist to three-fourths or more of the fruits of his labour? Or that a people cannot love their country if they own it as their common property? Or that a nation would commit suicide if it refused to allow a small class to monopolise all its natural resources and means of life? Or that the nation which refused to allow a class to use the governmental machinery for personal aggrandisement, to stir up wars and slaughter thousands of men 'made in the image of God' for the sake of more profits for a few, that the nation which should refuse to allow this would be 'powerless in the moral order,' and hastening on to decay? Yet it is this monstrous farrago of nonsense Rev. Father Kane attempts to establish in his fifth lecture.

CHAPTER VI

The Firebrand or the Olive Leaf

> Socialists will not shrink from resorting to brute force. A Socialist ring will not scruple when there is a question of

> finally superseding the old order of society to snatch up Anarchist weapons—the dagger, the torch, the bomb. Listen to the candid utterances of the great founder of Socialism, Karl Marx, with his henchman, Engels, [who] declared in their manifesto 'that their purpose can be obtained only by a violent subversion of the existing order. Let the ruling classes tremble at the Communist revolution.' Again, at the Congress of The Hague, Karl Marx, as the mouthpiece of Socialists, officially declared: 'In most countries of Europe violence must be the lever of our social reform. This violent upheaval must be universal. A proof of this was witnessed in the Commune of Paris, which only failed because in other capitals—Berlin and Madrid—a simultaneous revolutionary movement did not break out in connection with the mighty upheaval of the proletariat in Paris.' Again, Bebel, one of the greatest leaders of Socialist thought, dared to say in the German Reichstag: 'The Commune in Paris was only a slight skirmish in the war which the proletariat is prepared to wage against all palaces.' Again, Bebel said elsewhere this Socialistic change cannot be brought about by 'sprinkling rose-water.' At the Socialist Convention at Ghent in 1877 one of their leaders said: 'When our day comes, rifle and cannon will face about to mow down the foes of the Socialist people.' At a public meeting during the recent elections in England an M.P. supporter of the Liberal Government is reported to have said: 'I honour the man or woman who throws a bomb.'

That some Socialists believe that force may be used to inaugurate the new social order only indicates their conviction that the criminal capitalist and ruling classes will not peacefully abide by the verdict of the ballot, but will strive by violence to perpetuate their robber rule in spite of the declared will of the majority of the people. In this conviction such Socialists are strengthened by the record of all the revolutions of the world's history. It is a well-established fact that from the earliest revolutionary outbreak known down to the Commune of Paris, or Red Sunday in Russia, the first blood has been shed, the first blow struck, by the possessing conservative classes. And we are not so childish as to imagine that the capitalist class of the future will shrink from the shedding of the blood of the workers in order to retain their ill-gotten gains. They shed more blood, destroy more working-class lives every year, by the criminal carelessness with which they conduct industry and drive us to nerve-racking speed, than is lost in the average international war. In the United States there are killed on the railroads in one year more men than died in the Boer War on both sides. When the capitalists kill us so rapidly for the sake of a few pence extra profit it would be suicidal to expect that they would hesitate to slaughter us wholesale when their very existence as parasites was at stake. Therefore the Socialists anticipate violence only because they know the evil nature of the beast they contend with. But with a working class thoroughly organised and already as workers in possession of the railroads, shops, factories and ships we do not need to fear their violence. The hired assassin armies of the capitalist class will be impotent for evil when the railroad men refuse to transport them, the miners to furnish coal for their ships of war, the dock labourers to load or coal these ships, the clothing workers to make uniforms, the sailors to provision them, the telegraphists to serve them, or the farmers to feed them. In the vote, the strike, the boycott and the *lock-out exercised against the master class* the Socialists have weapons that will make this social revolution comparatively bloodless and peaceable despite the tigerish instincts or desires of the capitalist enemy, and the doleful Cassandra-like prophecies of our critic.

And if the capitalists do abide the issue of the ballot and allow this battle to be fought out on lines of peaceful political and economic action, gladly we will do likewise. But if not——

> But the real point is this: it is not merely the Rothschilds or other millionaires who are to be robbed; it is not merely the fashionable people who live in palaces and drive in motor-cars who are to be robbed, but the shopkeepers are also to be robbed; it is not merely the great big shopkeepers who are to be robbed, but every small

> business house will be robbed. The professional classes, the barristers and the doctors will be robbed. The small farmer, the small cottager will be evicted. The cabman's horse and cab will be taken from him. The poor woman who sells apples in the street will have her basket seized upon. These are all ways of making money, and the Socialist says that nobody has any right to make money except the Socialist State. Do you think that men would stand this? Do you think that a tenant who has bought out his land will willingly give it up to the Socialist who promises to spoon-feed him? Do you think that any respectable shopkeeper would give up his shop for the honour of being the shop-boy of a Socialist flunkey? Do you think that any manly man would give up the few shillings that are his own in order to become an irresponsible easy-going loafer in an idealised work-house? No.

This argument is brought in after telling a silly story about a Socialist who wanted Rothschild to divide up, and the story is told despite the fact that the reverend and pious lecturer has frequently explained that Socialism has nothing to do with dividing up. In fact Socialists want to stop dividing up with the 'irresponsible easy-going loafers' called aristocrats and capitalists, in the 'idealised work-houses' known as palaces and mansions. All those poor workers whom he mentions—the small farmer, the cottager, the cabman, the apple-woman, the doctor—all are compelled to divide up with the capitalist, speculator and landlord, and Socialism proposes to them that instead of wearing life out working night and day as in the case of the doctor, or shivering and suffering as in the case of the farmer, the cottager, the cabman and the apple-woman, they shall help to establish a system of society where the functions they now perform shall be performed better through more perfect organisation, with equipment supplied by the community, and where they shall be honoured co-workers with all their fellow-workers with an old age guaranteed against the want and privation they know awaits them under the present order. And they are hearkening to this Socialist promise of relief from their present social purgatory.

Father Kane next proceeds to quote Socialists to prove the beneficence of medieval Catholicism. He says:

> The contrast is reproduced under a different aspect when we compare the Church of Christ with the Church of Luther, King Harry and Queen Bess. Whoever studies Socialism will find that there is much to learn from this contrast. We read in Professor Nitti, of Naples: 'An English Socialist, Hyndman, whose profound historical and economic learning cannot be questioned even by his adversaries, has understood and admirably expressed the many benefits society has derived from the Church of the Middle Ages.' Hyndman wrote: 'It is high time that the nonsense that has been foisted on to the public by men interested in suppressing the facts should be exposed. It is not true that the Church of our ancestors was the organised fraud which it suits fanatics to represent it. The monasteries and priests did far more for elementary education than is at all known ... As to University education, where would Oxford be today but for the munificence of bishops, monks, and nuns? Fourteen of her finest colleges were founded by Churchmen or abbots for the benefit of the children of the people. The Reformation converted these colleges into luxurious preserves for the sons of the aristocracy.' He tells us how the Reformation converted the lands of the monasteries into the properties of rack-renting landlords. Abbots and priors were the best landlords in England. While the Church had power permanent or general pauperism was unknown. One-third of all tithes, one-third of all ecclesiastical revenue was first set aside to be given to the poor. The monks were the road-makers, alms-givers, teachers, doctors, nurses of the country. They built, furnished and attended the hospitals, and gave the poor relief out of their own funds. While the monasteries stood the poor or unemployed were always sure of food and shelter. Look at the other side of the contrast. When Harry VIII was king in Merrie England he wanted to get rid of his wife and he wanted to get money. Both motives moved him to break away from the

Church of Christ, and to confiscate the monasteries. One sad and most pitiful result was that thousands and thousands were driven out on the roads to beg. They were all able men and willing to work, but the monasteries had disappeared, and with them work and shelter and food. These 'sturdy beggars,' or 'stalwart vagabonds,' as they were called, thronged the road. They had been able to earn their bread under the old Church of Christ, but under the new church of King Hal and his merry men these 'sturdy beggars' were a nuisance. In 1547 a law was passed that these 'sturdy beggars' should be branded with hot irons and handed over as slaves to the person who denounced them, or if again caught they were to be hanged. Under good Queen Bess unlicensed beggars over 14 were flogged and branded on the left ear unless someone would take them into service for two years. If they begged again, all over 18 were executed unless someone was willing to take them into service for two years; caught a third time, death was the penalty, without reprieve. Hollingshead asserts that in the reign of the good King Henry VIII 72,000 sturdy beggars were hanged for begging. That was the contrast between the Reformation and the love of Christ's Church for Christ's poor. It was the way in which the Reformation solved the difficulty of the unemployed. Queen Bess, the 'virgin queen,' the good, sweet Queen Bess, found a woman's way of following her father's mood. She had her 'stalwart vagabonds' strung up in batches, like flitches of bacon along the rafters, in order to teach the people the godly way in which they should walk —the way of her Reformation of the Church of Christ. The Church of Christ has always protected the poor.

This long extract should be enlightening and illuminating to our readers. It shows that the Socialists have been uniformly fair in their treatment of the attitude of the Catholic Church of the past towards the poor, that they have defended that Church from the attacks of unscrupulous Protestant historians, upon that point, so that our reverend friend has to admit that a correct knowledge of the contrast between the attitude of the Church and that of the Protestant Reformers can be best attained by whoever studies Socialist literature. But, as we pointed out in a previous chapter, when Father Kane is recounting the numberless murders, outrages and barbarities practised upon the poor by the aristocracy of the Reformation he is telling also where we are to find the title deeds of the landed estates of England and Ireland. And it is just those landed estates, gained by such means, that Father Kane and his like are fighting to perpetuate in the ownership of the English and Irish aristocracy today. How do the Catholic clergy dare to defend the possessors in the present possession of their stolen property, when they publicly proclaim from the altar their knowledge of the inhuman crimes against God and man by which that property passed out of the hands of Church and people? The Reformation was the capitalist idea appearing in the religious field; as capitalism teaches that the social salvation of man depends solely upon his own individual effort, so Protestantism, echoing it, taught that the spiritual salvation of man depends solely upon his own individual appeal to God; as capitalism abolished the idea of social interdependence which prevailed under feudalism, and made men isolated units in a warring economic world, so Protestantism abolished the independent links of priests, hierarchy and pontiffs which in the Catholic system unites man with his Creator, and left man at the mercy of his own interpretations of warring texts and theories. In fine, as capitalism taught the doctrine of every man for himself, and by its growing power forced such doctrines upon the ruling class it created its reflex in the religious world, and that reflex, proclaiming that individual belief was the sole necessity of salvation, appears in history as the Protestant Reformation. Now, the Church curses the Protestant Reformation—the child; and blesses capitalism—its parent.

Now listen to the peroration of our critic:

> Nothing will do but Socialism.
>
> Not so! not so! The Church of Christ teaches both men and masters that for their own sake they should be friends not foes, that their mutual interests are inseparably inter-

> woven, and that they are bound together not merely by the duties or rights of justice, but by a sacred bond of kindliness, which is the same virtue that moves a man to fondly love his home and nobly love his Fatherland. Still, still!—that misery! that most sad poverty, that despairing wretchedness of utter want! Surely! surely! were the kind Christ here, Whose heart was moved to tender pity for the hungering crowd; surely He would give them food. He is not here, but in His stead He has placed you, Christian men and women, that you may do His blessed work. Have pity! have pity on the poor. We cannot stand idly by with folded arms while so many starve, nor can we suffer, while we have wealth to spare, that such multitudes who are brothers and sisters of our human blood should eke out in lingering death a life that is not worth the living. There is no need, no excuse for Socialism. But there is sore need of social reform. The State is indeed bound to enforce such remedial measures as are needed, and of these, whatever be our politics or party, we must all approve. But in our own way and in our own measure we should recognise in actual practice that Christians should be like the great Christ Who had pity on the poor.

And so he concludes—with an appeal for pity for the poor. After all his long discourse, after again and again admitting the tyranny, the extortions, the frauds, the injustices perpetrated in our midst every day by those who control and own our means of existence he has no remedy to offer but pity! After all his brave appeal to individuality, to national honour, to the heroic spirit in poor men and women, he shrinks from appealing to that individuality, to that national honour, to that heroic spirit in the poor and asking them to so manifest themselves as to rescue their lives from the control of the forces of Mammon. Professing to denounce Mammon, he yet shrinks from leading the forces of righteousness against it, and by so shrinking shows that all his professed solicitude for justice, all his vaunted hatred of tyranny, were 'mere sound and fury, signifying nothing.'

Is not this attitude symbolic of the attitude of the Church for hundreds of years? Ever counselling humility, but sitting in the seats of the mighty; ever patching up the diseased and broken wrecks of an unjust social system, but blessing the system which made the wrecks and spread the disease; ever running Divine Discontent and pity into the ground as the lightning rod runs and dissipates lightning, instead of gathering it and directing it for social righteousness as the electric battery generates and directs electricity for social use.

The day has passed for patching up the capitalist system; it must go. And in the work of abolishing it the Catholic and the Protestant, the Catholic and the Jew, the Catholic and the Freethinker, the Catholic and the Buddhist, the Catholic and the Mahometan will co-operate together, knowing no rivalry but the rivalry of endeavour toward an end beneficial to all. For, as we have said elsewhere, Socialism is neither Protestant nor Catholic, Christian nor Freethinker, Buddhist, Mahometan, nor Jew; it is only HUMAN. *We of the Socialist Working Class realise that as we suffer together we must work together that we may enjoy together*. We reject the Firebrand of Capitalist Warfare and offer you the Olive Leaf of Brotherhood and Justice to and for All.

3. ROME AND IRISH CATHOLICS

It was not to be expected that the influential and somewhat haughty Fathers of the Society of Jesus would rest content with having their chosen spokesman worsted in polemic by a mere labourer, to say nothing of the need for controverting socialism which most of them would have regarded as a matter of extreme urgency. An occasion offered itself when on September 25th, 1912, 'Democrat', a columnist in the Labour journal, the London Daily Herald, *devoted much praise to* Labour, Nationality, and Religion, *viewing Connolly as voicing the opinions of 'candid and thoughtful Irish Catholic laymen'. It may well have been that the Jesuits were anxious to restrict their literary, as opposed to their sacerdotal, refutations of the pamphlet to arenas which would obviate the need for specific defence of their own man; certainly Father MacErlean, S.J., who was undoubtedly acting with the approval, and possibly under the orders, of his Jesuit superiors, rather disingenuously avoided any mention of Father Kane, S.J., confining his attack on Connolly, which appeared as an article in the* Catholic Times *on October 18th, 1912, to the foreword of* Labour, Nationality and Religion. *After baldly denying Connolly's Catholicism in view of his socialism, Father MacErlean continued: 'No matter how ignorant a writer may be, if he but rehash for unthinking Protestant prejudice some old libels on the Catholic Church, he at once becomes a candid, thoughtful, intelligent Catholic layman. We do not know of Mr Connolly as distinguished for historical research, but "Democrat" informs us he may be found in Corporation Street, Belfast, where as everybody knows, the inhabitants are so anxious for the welfare of Irish Catholics and so celebrated for the accuracy of the views they entertain upon all questions of the past and present policy of the Catholic church.' He took particular exception to the quotation from Judge Maguire, and made elaborate efforts to defend the Papacy from his and Connolly's criticisms. 'Democrat' may well have been Connolly's friend the Irish labour historian W. P. Ryan, father of Desmond Ryan and a victim of Catholic clerical hostility to liberalism; as a* Daily Herald *staff writer he would both have been likely to see the attack, to get Connolly—hardly a reader of the London* Catholic Times*—to reply,* *and to have that paper arrange for an article by him to appear. The* Catholic Times *printed it on November 8th, 1912.*

FATHER MacERLEAN, S.J., AND A LABOUR PUBLICATION

In the issue of the *Catholic Times* of October 18 there appeared a long article upon the above subject by Father MacErlean, S.J., upon which I crave the permission of the Editor to make a few comments. In craving this permission I, of course, assume that the Editor is not at all responsible for the totally disingenuous insinuation of the article in question that my little book was, or is, a 'rehash for unthinking Protestant prejudice,' or that because my address is in Belfast I must therefore be under suspicion by all true Catholics. The book was primarily written for and first published in Dublin amongst people of our own Catholic Faith; and we can afford to treat with contempt the suggestion that the Catholics living in Belfast and bearing the brunt of the struggle against Orangeism must also bear the odium of suspicion amongst Catholics elsewhere because of that very Orange bigotry from which they are the sufferers.

Father MacErlean's Indictment

Father MacErlean says: 'Mr. Connolly's Catholicity may be gauged by his profession of Socialism; his thoughtfulness is disposed of by the exhibition he has given of his ignorance of history; and his candour may be judged from his falsification and misrepresentation of facts.' After this indictment one would expect to read at least some little proof of the 'ignorance,' 'falsification,' and 'misrepresentation' so blatantly alleged, for in public controversy we do not expect a clergyman to be less honourable than a layman, and to frame such an indictment and then to calmly walk away and leave it totally unsupported would not be considered honourable nowadays by any reputable lay writer. Yet this is what Father MacErlean has done. The sneer at my Socialism we can leave unheeded save for the passing remark that as no Catholic doctrine forbids the State to hold a thousand acres of land it cannot therefore be immoral for it to hold a million acres; if it, the State, has the moral right to own a square mile of land, it cannot be denied the moral right to own 32,524 square miles—the total area of Ireland. Or, if it can be denied such right, at what point of magnitude does the extent of its possessions become immoral? And if the State can,

According to Catholic Doctrine,

morally own and conduct factories for the production of death-dealing instruments of war, as at Woolwich, why may it not own and conduct factories for the production of life-supporting articles, such as food, clothing, and other necessaries? And if it is permissible according to Catholic doctrine that Democracy should be applied to the government of countries, it cannot be immoral for Catholics to advocate the democratic ownership and control of workshops, fields, mills, and factories. If this is conceded—and it cannot logically be refused—then my Socialism is consistent with Catholicism, and we can leave my critic to waste his sneers upon some crude and fantastic Socialism of his own imaginings, but unrecognised in the authorised Socialist programmes of the world.

In a column and a half of an article ostensibly an onslaught upon my poor self the critic does not once quote any words of my own, but spreads himself upon a

Quotation from a Book by Judge Maguire

of the Supreme Court of California, and upon an opinion expressed in a review of my book by a writer in the *Daily Herald.* The opinion expressed by the latter writer upon the real attitude of the Pope and the higher clergy of Ireland towards Home Rule are his own opinions presumably, but I have never expressed myself upon the matter (having no means of informing myself reliably upon the question), despite the unwarranted assertion of my reverend critic. But of the substantial accuracy of the statement of Judge Maguire whatever Father MacErlean may say, there is ample historical confirmation. Let me quote it again: 'Under all their Catholic Majesties from Henry II to Henry VIII (nearly four hundred years), the Irish people, with the exception of five families, were outlaws. They were murdered at will, like dogs, by their English Catholic neighbours in Ireland, and there was no law to punish the murderers. Yet during all of this unparalleled reign of terror history fails to record a single instance in which the power of the Catholic Church was ever exerted or suggested by the Pope for the protection of her faithful Irish children.' To refute this Father MacErlean cites

A Letter from Pope John XXII

to the Papal Nuncio in 1317 urging King Edward II to take steps for the 'immediate correction and reformation of the aforesaid grievances,' and carefully avoiding any explanation of the accompanying circumstances, he seeks to create the impression that this is a crushing refutation of the statement of Judge Maguire. What were the circumstances attendant upon that letter? Donald O'Neill, King of Ulster, and a number of other Irish princes had united in sending to his Holiness a Remonstrance setting forth the sufferings of Ireland under the English, and the determination of the Irish to end those sufferings. They informed his Holiness that they had no hope of getting justice from the English King, and had invited the brother of Robert the Bruce of Scotland to aid them in throwing off the English yoke. Pope John XXII responded by sending a letter to King Edward counselling him to take steps for the 'immediate correction and reformation of the aforesaid grievances,' 'lest,' the letter goes on to say, 'it might be too late hereafter to apply a remedy when the spirit of revolt has grown stronger.' It might be difficult to say whether this was intervention on behalf of the Irish, or rather intervention on behalf of English dominion over the Irish, but that there might be no doubt about his meaning the Pope also *threatened with excommunication all those Irish who refused to trust to the clemency of an English King*, but preferred to take up arms for the holy cause of their national independence. Father MacErlean says: 'We do not know of Mr. Connolly as distinguished for historical research.' Alas, we are utterly crushed by thinking of the things Father MacErlean does not know of, but surely even Father MacErlean must know of

Father D'Alton,

a brother clergyman and author of a History of Ireland which, although but recently published, has already become a standard work of reference. Here is how Father D'Alton tells of the incident we are discussing. Will the reader please compare his account with the garbled and utterly misleading version given by our reverend critic? Father D'Alton says: 'Donald O'Neill reminded the Pope that one of his predecessors, Adrian IV, led by false representations and by his partiality for England, had granted Henry II dominion over Ireland, but that he had done so for the good of Ireland itself, and in the hope that it would prosper under English rule. He now instanced the evils his country had suffered and was suffering still; his countrymen and himself had no hope of getting justice from England, and had in consequence invited Edward Bruce, brother of King Robert of Scotland, to come and reign over them, and they hoped he would receive the Pope's blessing and support. John XXII did not grant the prayer of the Remonstrance; he had no love for the Bruces, King Robert was already excommunicated, and far from approving Edward Bruce's invasion *he even warned the Irish against supporting it, and threatened with excommunication those who did.*'

Thus Father D'Alton on pages 282–283 of Volume I, and in confirmation of his account he quotes in a note from Volume I, page 275, of Leland, and from Volume III, pages 19 and 20, of Lingard. In fact, no reputable historian tells the story otherwise. Although some slur over the account of the threatened excommunication of the patriotic Irish, it was left for my critic to attempt to give a totally wrong impression of the matter by telling one part of the story and suppressing the other and the most vital part.

For the other incidents mentioned in refutation of Judge Maguire's statement suffice it to say that they all appear to have been interventions on behalf of the right of the Holy See to control all ecclesiastical appointments in Ireland (as elsewhere), and against the continual encroachments of the English monarchy in

Matters of Church Government.

In short, they were not interventions on behalf of the Irish people, but were interventions in assertion of the immunity of ecclesiastical powers from civil control. On some occasions they worked out in favour of the Irish, on more occasions they operated in favour of English rule in Ireland, but on all occasions they were inspired primarily by considerations for the welfare of the Church. I find no fault with this, nor yet do I waste time by carping at its effects. First as an Irish Nationalist and latterly as a Socialist I have always accepted and understood the doctrine so well expressed by Father MacErlean that the Holy See must always 'acknowledge the *de facto* government in any country without examining or deciding the question of its rightful title.' But the considerations which compel the Holy See as such to recognise the *de facto* government, and the *de facto* social order, are not binding upon individual Catholics, and we therefore retain to the full all our rights and prerogatives as citizens and workers for social betterment, without abating necessarily one jot of our Catholicity. As individual Catholics we claim it as our right, nay, as our duty, to refuse allegiance to any power or social system whose authority to rule over us we believe to be grounded upon injustice.

4. ROME AND IRELAND'S STRUGGLES

The Rev. John MacErlean, S.J., returned to the charge on November 18th, 1912, with another article. Its medieval scholarship, to which its author brought considerable powers of research, was more soundly based than its modern: he concluded with the somewhat dubious argument that Pope Innocent XI was not in support of William III's Irish campaign in that the Pope was not a signatory to the League of Augsburg. The weight of reputable historical opinion then and now would have had little respect for this proposition, but Connolly deferred—permanently, as it happened—his reply to that point in the Catholic Times. *He did reply to the general argument in a later essay, printed below, and another critic of Father MacErlean took up the matter in the* Catholic Times *itself. Father MacErlean was inhibited by his priestly calling in refuting Connolly's citation of Father (later Canon) D'Alton: he could hardly assert the truth, which was that D'Alton's scholarship was much inferior to his own. Dictates of modesty apart, to have done so would have been to have conceded Connolly's insistence that churchmen could err, which Father MacErlean was at least implicitly denying. The high point in his rejoinder to Connolly was as follows:*

Mr. Connolly now admits that Judge Maguire's statement is not strictly true; that the Popes were justified in recognising the rights of the *de facto* government, that is, in the present case, the rights of the King of England over those parts of Ireland that had acknowledged his lordship; that the interventions of the Popes worked out on some occasions in favour of the Irish; and that he has no fault to find with the Popes for their being on all occasions inspired primarily by considerations for the welfare of the Church. Let us see also

What Mr. Connolly does Not now Deny.

He does not deny that Pope John XXII sternly commanded King Edward II to remedy the grievances of which the Irish complained; that the Popes refused to recognise any claim of the Kings of England to interfere in the affairs of independent Irish dioceses; that the Popes frequently resisted the pressure brought to bear on him [*sic*] by the King of England and the Anglo-Norman nobles; that there was no systematic favouring of the Norman as against the Irish clergy by the Pope; that a Pope refused to recognise ignorance of English as a bar to an Irishman's being appointed to a bishopric in the English domain; or that the Pope favoured the establishment of an Irish University for the education of Irish students at home. All that is as satisfactory as it is undeniable; but what then becomes of Mr. Connolly's quotation from Judge Maguire that history fails to show a single instance of the Church's intervening for the protection of her faithful Irish children?

What Mr. Connolly Complains of.

Mr. Connolly complains that I have tried to create suspicions against the Catholics of Belfast in the minds of Catholics elsewhere; that I attacked him without quoting any words of his; and that I suppressed the fact that the Pope ordered the adherents of Bruce to be excommunicated. A few words will suffice to dissipate these suggestions. Far from trying to create suspicion against the Catholics of Belfast I wrote that article to counteract the statements of Mr. Connolly and others which would tend just to create such suspicions. The Catholics of Belfast have never had any sympathy with such sentiments as those of Mr. Connolly. Their faith and their nationality are spoken of throughout the world. They have ever been loyal to Ireland and loyal to the Church, and have always shown themselves ready to shed their blood, if necessary, in defence of either. If Mr. Connolly wishes to share in the glory of the Catholics of Belfast, let him learn their spirit and do their works. To attempt to divorce the national spirit of the Catholics of Belfast from their spirit of

Traditional Loyalty to the Church

by publishing a pamphlet in which the Church is falsely abused and openly maligned is the work of an enemy, even though he should masquerade as a friend. Cockle is cockle, even though it grow in a cornfield.

Connolly's understandably testy reply appeared in the Catholic Times *on November 22nd, 1912.*

THE CONTROVERSY WITH FATHER MACERLEAN, S.J.

He would indeed be a hardened controversialist who could repress a feeling of sympathy for Father MacErlean in his latest pitiful attempt to wriggle out of the absurd position created by his first article on the above subject. By no other name can his article be described. A pitiful wriggle exciting a feeling of sympathetic wonderment that he should rush in so lightly to essay a task for which he was so poorly equipped. An attempt to suppress a material incident in a certain period of Irish history when exposed is airily followed by a declaration that he was not discussing that material incident. Such antics may serve to obscure the issue—and perhaps that is why they are introduced—but that they can deceive the discriminating reader I refuse to believe.

I have proven that the so-called intervention of Pope John XXII in favour of the Irish was in reality an intervention in favour of the English power over the Irish, and a threat to excommunicate all those who preferred the chance of national independence to the hopes or promises of English justice.

The Fact of the Excommunication

was the dominating factor in the national war for national liberty, and an attempt to explain the letter of his Holiness without mentioning that threat of excommunication would be more ridiculous than the proverbial play of Hamlet with Hamlet left out. Yet it is this ridiculous travesty which Father MacErlean attempts to foist upon us as history. Save us from such history! In a similar manner he most disingenuously attempts to misinterpret my statement that I found no fault with, nor spent any time in carping over the obligations resting upon the Holy See to recognise the *de facto* government in any given country. He says that I admit that 'the Popes were justified in recognising the rights of the King of England over those parts of Ireland which had acknowledged his lordship,' but he adds quite gratuitously and unjustifiably that this is an admission of the justice of the act of the Pope in excommunicating all those who refused to acknowledge such lordship, as in the case under discussion. As this point is as vital today as it was then, and is of the last importance to the understanding of

My True Position,

which he is so studiously striving to distort, permit me to again re-state the position as indicated in the conclusion of my last letter.

I admit unquestioningly the obligation resting upon the Holy See to recognize the *de facto* government and *de facto* social order in any given country or age. But side by side with, part and parcel of that admission, and not to be divorced from it, I insist upon the right of the individual Catholic to disregard that obligation, and to be a reformer of, or rebel and revolutionist against the government which the Holy See is compelled by its international relations to recognise. Without this right Catholicity would be synonymous with the blackest reaction and opposition to all reform. As an example Ireland is illuminating. For the greater part of seven centuries

The 'de facto *Government' of Ireland*

has been a foreign government imposed upon the country by force, and maintained by the same means. The Holy See was compelled by its position to recognise that government, but the holiest and deepest feelings of the Catholics of Ireland were in rebellion against that government, and in every generation the scaffold and the prison, and the martyr's grave have been filled in Ireland with devout subjects of the Holy See, but unrelenting enemies of the *de facto* government of Ireland.

The firm distinction in the minds of Irish Catholics between the *duties* of the Holy See and the *rights* of the individual Catholics has been a necessary and saving element in keeping Ireland Catholic, and he, by whatever name he calls himself or to whatever order he belongs, who would seek to destroy that distinction or make acquiescence in the political obligations of the Papacy a cardinal article of Catholic faith is an enemy of the faith and liberties of our people.

My Pamphlet

was and is no more than a setting forth of the above position—illustrated by such references to recorded facts as serve to prove the point that disregard of the political instructions or commands of the Vatican has in the past been practised upon occasions by devout Catholics, and such disregard has been justified by the event. My pamphlet was published for Catholics. I know of no way by which Protestants could be prevented from reading it, were I ever so desirous, but I do not believe that the Catholic Church need fear the result of a difference of opinion, or even a sharp discussion amongst Catholics upon matters of historical interest to all.

We have long since learned that some clergymen are more Catholic than the Pope, and that some others seem to see an enemy in everyone who refuses to see eye to eye with them upon all points as well as upon Church doctrine, but we believe that the hope of the Church is in those who refuse to accept such bull-dozing and who stand by their rights as citizens, whilst observing their duties as Catholics.

Upon the historical points raised—the questions of fact, as, for instance, that of

The Battle of the Boyne

I shall, with the Editor's permission, write hereafter. But upon the interpretation of such points as, for instance, whether the letter already discussed of Pope John XXII was an 'intervention in favour' or a condemnation, I shall not endeavour to further follow Father MacErlean in his casuistry or verbal gymnastics.

5. LEARNING THEIR LESSON

In a rather different sense to that implied by the Rev. John MacErlean, S.J., Ulster was integral to Connolly's ideas on the relationship of religion to socialism. The problem he faced was that Irish socialists in Ulster seemed likely to divide on religious sectarian lines, as indeed they very largely came to do. Fundamental to the division was the debate as to whether socialism in Ireland was to assume a primarily Irish or British identity. In 1906 William Walker (1870–1918) and other working-class leaders in Belfast had built up a strong electoral challenge to the Unionist ruling class, drawing support from both Catholics and Protestants. But in the next years, setbacks and the imminent possibility of Home Rule once more led to division. In 1907 the thrust of working-class radicalism in Belfast moved under the direction of Jim Larkin, who was organizing the dockers with emphasis on the power of the sympathetic strike rather than Walker's more elitist emphasis on the ballot. By 1909 Walker was becoming defensively hostile to Home Rule. Connolly, in the U.S.A., saw possibilities in his attitude and wrote accordingly as an editorial in The Harp *for September 1909.*

Our Socialist friends in the North of Ireland are learning their lesson. As readers of *The Harp* are aware, there is in Belfast and its neighborhood a strong Socialist movement, born out of the advanced industrial conditions which prevail in that district. But, as was perhaps natural under the historical circumstances, that Socialist movement keeps itself apart from the life of the rest of Ireland. Its associations are with England, its chief speakers are imported from England, and its methods are distinctly those of the English Labor Party. Indeed, it is a part of the English movement known as the Independent Labor Party. As a result, it has never yet run a candidate as a Socialist Party distinctly and avowedly with a revolutionary purpose and aim, differing in this from the Socialist movement in Dublin, which has on four or five different occasions contested municipal elections as an avowedly Socialist Party separate and distinct from all others. The different tactics employed were characteristic of the religious thought dominant at either part of the country. Protestantism is essentially of the nature of a compromise between the spirit of authority and the spirit of free inquiry, and when a Protestant breaks with any tradition he does so in a halting and tentative manner, perpetually retreating to his starting-point, and as he disavows allegiance to one idol, hastens to create another. On the other hand, the Catholic is positive and dogmatic, and ever inclined, when he swings from his moorings at one point of the compass, to scorn all intermediate stages between that point and its opposite pole. Out of this curious anomaly arose the fact that even while the Belfast Socialists were proclaiming that the Irish Catholics were too much under the heel of priests to be Socialists, these same Irish Catholics in Dublin were proudly nailing to the mast those Socialist colors which their Northern brethren were furtively seeking to hide at every election. This was not the least puzzling and disconcerting feature of the situation. The Belfast Socialists are, as we have said, affiliated to the Independent Labor Party in Great Britain, and while they have had their faces set towards that country have at all times kept out of touch with the toilers of the rest of Ireland, never at any time making any effort to understand their point of view. This attitude of theirs has ever been destructive to the hopes of a real revolutionary labor movement in Ireland; indeed, the Northern men have never, apparently, understood that the Socialist movement is a revolutionary labor movement. Their standpoint and intellectual bias has ever been towards the Fabian opportunism of England, while the Irish Socialists of Catholic training have been most attracted by the Revolutionary Social-Democracy of the Continent of Europe. This problem does not arise out of any distinction of race; indeed, despite the prevalent opinion to the contrary, the Irish Protestants of the North are as purely Celtic as the Catholics of any part of Ireland. The parts of Scotland from whence their forefathers re-emigrated into Ireland were and are as Celtic in the make-up of their population as any part of

Munster, and a deal more so than many parts of Leinster. But from whatever source it arises, this attitude of the Northerners has frustrated the hopes of those who longed for a Socialist Party in Ireland of national scope and reach. In a Socialist Party embracing all the toilers of Ireland, resting upon Irish conditions, and shaping itself to reflect Irish needs, the sturdy men of the Northern capital would be a force of incalculable value, but they have up to the present been singularly blind to realise their opportunity. They failed to see, what a moment's reflection should have shown them, that they would be the backbone and dominating element in an Irish Socialist Party, whereas they can never be anything but the insignificant tail of a Socialist Party in England. And we say this without any feeling of hostility towards the Socialists of England. We are sure that the latter would have no objection to the Belfast branches throwing in their lot with the rest of Ireland in a distinct party, if the result of such action was to build up a Socialist Party in Ireland strong enough to contest the field with the Home Rulers. For the Labor Party of England is, after all, primarily a vote-gathering party. It recognizes that the Irish vote is a strong factor in English cities, and it seeks to conciliate the Home Rule Party as an essential towards having an Irish representative on its side when it appeals to that Irish vote during an election. It would just as soon, indeed much rather, have a representative of a strong Irish Socialist and Labor movement on its platform at such a time to appeal to the Irish workers in English cities. But such an Irish Labor representative is of no value to them if he comes as the Irish member of an English party. Hence they court the assistance of the Home Rulers, despite the protests of Irish Socialists. Were the Belfast Socialists to withdraw in a body from the Independent Labor Party and throw in their lot with the organization of Irish Socialists recently formed in Dublin, their action would be of incalculable service not only to the cause of Socialism in Ireland, but also to the Socialists and Labor Party in England. It would help to save the latter from all the dangers of a Home Rule alliance by bringing into relief the reactionary attitude and policies of the Home Rulers as opposed to the Socialist movement of the Irish working class. We believe such a move would be welcomed by the most astute and farseeing of the Labor Party, since it would enable them to appeal to the Irish voters of Great Britain on their class interests as well as through their national bias. But even if it failed to arouse the sympathetic appreciation of English Labor leaders, the move ought to be taken. We have long ago given up all hopes of making Englishmen understand the Irish character. The English Socialists have failed utterly to fathom the character of the capitalist Home Rulers of Ireland. Their failure arises from their inability to understand the difference between 'rebelly' talk and serious revolutionary purpose. The Home Rulers are adepts at 'rebelly' talk, but of serious revolutionary purpose, even in a Nationalist sense, they are absolutely lacking. They easily succeed in fooling the so-called 'hard-headed' English working man, but they never succeed in fooling the Socialists of Ireland. The latter know their men too well; they know in what an inferno of reaction they have succeeded in keeping the domestic affairs of Ireland, such as education and municipal housing and sanitation, and they see them ever in league with the most merciless exploiters of labor on the island.

Hence the Catholic masses regard the Catholic (?) Home Rule leaders with ill-concealed distrust, and if the Protestant working men would only throw off their senseless distrust of their Catholic fellows, realize that class interests are stronger in political warfare than religious bias, and so realizing, unite with their Catholic fellow-workers of the rest of Ireland on the basis of those class interests, they would find the latter not only willing, but madly anxious to receive them.

We have been moved to make these comments by reading in the *Labor Leader*, of London, England, two articles, or rather letters, upon the subject of the attitude of the Labor Party of England towards the Land Question in Ireland. The first was written by Mr. Walker, of Belfast, a Socialist member of the Belfast branch of the Independent Labor Party, and twice Labor candidate for a parliamentary seat in Belfast. Mr. Walker complains that the Labor Party is apparently influenced by the Home Rulers, and voted along with them on the recent Land Bill, which, he says, and truly, tends to make the farming class more conservative and anti-Socialistic. He cites the case of one constituency, in which the Protestant farmers who have hitherto been Liberal, for the first time voted Conservative at a recent election. He then goes on to say some very severe things about the Home Rule crowd in Parliament. The second letter was from an English labor leader, a Mr. Clynes, and he, of course, tells Mr. Walker that there was no use to talk in Parliament about Land Nationalisation, because a bill on such lines would not pass at present. He thus lays down the axiom that a parliamentary minority must not talk about a measure in Parliament unless it has an immediate chance to pass; quite a new conception of Parliamentary activity! He then goes on to chide Mr. Walker for saying hard things about the Home Rulers—those dear friends of Labor—and in general is serenely indifferent to the Belfast man's protest. It is an old story. Some years ago, when editing the *Workers' Republic* in Dublin, we also protested against the fulsome praise of Home Rule leaders by English Socialists at a time when these same capitalist gentry were bitterly antagonizing the Labor candidates of the Irish trade unions in the Local Government elections of 1899. We, under direction of the Irish Socialist Republican Party, drew up a statement of the case, containing specific citations of the anti-Labor record in Ireland of the Irish capitalist politicians, and we informed our English comrades that their senseless praise of the Home Rule Party in England was being used in Ireland against the Labor candidates who were opposing capitalist Home Rulers. But the leaders of the Independent Labor Party in England paid no attention to our protests, and went joyously on supplying ammunition to our enemies, although a paper so far away as *Vorwaerts*, of Berlin, Germany, the organ of the German Social Democratic Party, quoted our manifesto and expressly approved of our position.

Now it is the turn of the Belfast men! We hope that our Dublin comrades will send them a copy of that earlier manifesto, and that they will learn the lesson of both incidents and join where they belong—in a militant Irish movement of Labor.

6. JULY THE 12TH

By the time Connolly had returned to Ireland and established himself in Belfast, religious sectarian ill-feeling was biting deep within the Belfast working class. He himself was drawn into bitter controversy with Walker in Forward *on May 27th, 1911, and in several subsequent issues. It was sparked off by Walker's having committed the Irish Trade Union Congress to support for the British Labour Party as against Connolly's demand for an Irish Labour Party, on an all-Ireland basis. For details see William McMullen's introduction to the selection of Connolly's writings* The Workers' Republic, *edited by Desmond Ryan,*[1] *and J. W. Boyle's essay 'William Walker' in* Leaders and Workers *edited by him.*[2] *The Walker–Connolly exchanges exacerbated the polarization of the Belfast Socialists on religious lines, as well as on syndicalist versus craft-unionist stances. The beneficiary was Sir Edward Carson's militant Unionism, which won very heavy Protestant labour support in 1912 and 1913. Connolly offered his analysis of the Orange politico-religious festival to his Scots audience in* Forward, *where it was appropriately printed on July 12th, 1913.*

As this Saturday is the 12th of July, and as I am supposed to be writing about the North of Ireland in particular, it becomes imperative that I say something about this great and glorious festival.

The Anniversary of the Battle of the Boyne is celebrated in Belfast by what is locally known as an Orange Walk. The brethren turn out and take possession of the principal streets of the city, and for the space of some hours they pass in processional order before the eyes of the citizens, bearing their banners, wearing their regalia, carrying symbols emblematic of the gates of Derry, and to the accompaniment of a great many bands.

[1] See Bibliography.

[2] Mercier Press, Cork, n.d. [1964].

Viewing the procession as a mere 'Teague' (to use the name the brethren bestow on all of Catholic origin), I must confess that some parts of it are beautiful, some of it ludicrous, and some of it exceedingly disheartening.

The regalia is often beautiful; I have seen representations of the Gates of Derry that were really a pleasure to view as pieces of workmanship; and similar representations erected as Orange arches across dingy side streets that, if we could forget their symbolism, we would admire as real works of art.

The music (?) is a fearful and wonderful production, seemingly being based upon a desire to produce the maximum of sound in the minimum of space. Every Orange Lodge in the North of Ireland, and many from the South make it a point to walk, and as each Lodge desires to have a band without any regard to its numbers, the bands are often so near that even the most skilful manipulator cannot prevent a blending of sounds that can scarcely be called harmonious.

I have stood on the sidewalk listening to a band, whose instruments were rendering:

> Jesus, lover of my soul,
> Let me to thy bosom fly.

Whilst another one about twenty yards off was splitting the air with:

> Dolly's Brae, O Dolly's Brae,
> O, Dolly's Brae no more;
> The song we sang was kick the Pope
> Right over Dolly's Brae.

But the discord of sound allied to the discord of sentiment implied in a longing to fly to the bosom of Jesus, and at the same time to kick the Pope, did not appear to strike anyone but myself.

For that matter a sense of humour is not one of the strong points in an Orangeman's nature. The dead walls of Belfast are decorated with a mixture of imprecations upon 'Fenians,' and the Pope, and invocations of the power and goodness of the Most High, interlarded with quotations from the New Testament. This produces some of the most incongruous results. What would the readers of *Forward* say to seeing written up on the side of a wall off one of the main streets, the attractive legend:

God is Love,
Hell Roast the Pope.

Of course, the juxtaposition of such inscriptions on the walls appears absurd, and yet, the juxtaposition of sentiments as dissimilar is common enough in the minds of all of us, I suppose.

To anyone really conversant with the facts bearing upon the relations of the religious in Ireland, and the part played by them in advancing or retarding the principles of civil and religious liberty, the whole celebration appears to be foolish enough.

The belief sedulously cultivated by all the orators, lay and clerical, as well as by all the newspapers is, that the Defence of Derry and the Battle of the Boyne were great vindications of the principles of civil and religious liberty, which were menaced by the Catholics, and defended by the Protestants of all sects.

The belief we acquire from a more clear study of history in Ireland is somewhat different. Let me tell it briefly. In the reign of James I, the English Government essayed to solve the Irish problem, which then, as now, was their chief trouble, by settling Ireland with planters from Scotland and England. To do this, two million acres were confiscated, i.e., stolen from the Irish owners. Froude, the historian, says: 'Of these, a million and a half, bog-forest and mountain were restored to the Irish. The half a million of fertile acres were settled with families of Scottish and English Protestants.'

A friendly speaker, recently describing these planters before a meeting of the Belfast Liberal Association, spoke of them as:

> Hardy pioneers, born of a sturdy race, trained to adversity, when brought face to face with dangers of a new life in a hostile country, soon developed that steady, energetic, and powerful character which has made the name of Ulster respected all over the world.

And a writer in the seventeeth century, the son of one of the ministers who came over with the first plantation, Mr. Stewart, is quoted by Lecky in his *History of England in the Eighteenth Century*,[1] as saying:

> From Scotland came many, and from England not a few, yet all of them generally the scum of both nations, who from debt, or breaking the law or fleeing from justice, or seeking shelter, come hither, hoping to be without fear of man's justice in a land where there was nothing, or but little as yet, of the fear of God ... On all hands Atheism increased, and disregard of God, iniquity abounded, with contentious fighting, murder, adultery.

The reader can take his choice of these descriptions. Probably the truth is that each is a fairly accurate description of a section of the planters, and that neither is accurate as a picture of the whole.

But while the Plantation succeeded from the point of view of the Government in placing in the heart of Ulster a body of people who, whatever their disaffection to that Government, were still bound by fears of their own safety to defend it against the natives, it did not bring either civil or religious liberty to the Presbyterian planters.

The Episcopalians were in power, and all the forces of government were used by them against their fellow-Protestants. The planters were continually harassed to make them abjure their religion, fines were mutiplied upon fines, and imprisonment upon imprisonment. In 1640, the Presbyterians of Antrim, Down, and Tyrone, in a petition to the English House of Commons, declared that:

> Principally through the sway of the prelacy with their factions our souls are starved, our estates are undone, our families impoverished, and many lives among us cut off and destroyed ... Our cruel taskmasters have made us who were once a people to become as it were no people, an astonishment to ourselves, the object of pittie and amazement to others.

What might have been the result of this cruel, systematic persecution of Protestants by Protestants we can only

[1] Longmans, London, 1892.

conjecture, since, in the following year, 1641, the great Irish rebellion compelled the persecuting and persecuted Protestants to join hands in defence of their common plunder against the common enemy—the original Irish owners.

In all the demonstrations and meetings which take place in Ulster under Unionist Party auspices, all these persecutions are alluded to as if they had been the work of 'Papists,' and even in the Presbyterian churches and conventions, the same distortion of the truth is continually practised.

But they are told 'all this persecution was ended when William of Orange, and our immortal forefathers overthrew the Pope and Popery at the Boyne. Then began the era of civil and religious liberty.'

So runs the legend implicitly believed in in Ulster. Yet it is far, very far, from the truth. In 1686 certain continental powers joined together in a league, known in history as the league of Augsburg, for the purpose of curbing the arrogant power of France. These powers were impartially Protestant and Catholic, including the Emperor of Germany, the King of Spain, William, Prince of Orange, and the Pope. The latter had but a small army, but possessed a good treasury and great influence. A few years before a French army had marched upon Rome to avenge a slight insult offered to France, and His Holiness was more than anxious to curb the Catholic power that had dared to violate the centre of Catholicity. Hence his alliance with William, Prince of Orange.

King James II, of England, being insecure upon his throne, sought alliance with the French monarch.

When, therefore, the war took place in Ireland, King William fought, aided by the arms, men, and treasures of his allies in the League of Augsburg, and part of his expenses at the Battle of the Boyne was paid for by His Holiness, the Pope. Moreover, when news of King William's victory reached Rome, a *Te Deum* was sung in celebration of his victory over the Irish adherents of King James and King Louis.

Therefore, on Saturday the Orangemen of Ulster, led by King Carson, will be celebrating the same victory as the Pope celebrated 223 years ago.

Nor did victory at the Boyne mean Civil and Religious

Liberty. The Catholic Parliament of King James, meeting in Dublin in 1689, had passed a law that all religions were equal, and that each clergyman should be supported by his own congregation only, and that no tithes should be levied upon any man for the support of a church to which he did not belong. But this sublime conception was far from being entertained by the Williamites who overthrew King James and superseded his Parliament. The Episcopalian Church was immediately re-established, and all other religions put under the ban of the law. I need not refer to the Penal Laws against Catholics, they are well enough known. But sufficient to point out that England and Wales have not yet attained to that degree of religious equality established by Acts XIII and XV of the Catholic Parliament of 1689, and that that date was the last in which Catholics and Protestants sat together in Parliament until the former compelled an Emancipation Act in 1829.

For the Presbyterians the victory at the Boyne simply gave a freer hand to their Episcopalian persecuters. In 1704 Derry was rewarded for its heroic defence by being compelled to submit to a Test Act, which shut out of all offices in the Law, the Army, the Navy, the Customs and Excise, and Municipal employment, all who would not conform to the Episcopalian Church. The alderman and fourteen burgesses are said to have been disfranchised in the Maiden City by this iniquitous Act, which was also enforced all over Ireland. Thus, at one stroke, Presbyterians, Quakers, and all other dissenters were deprived of that which they had imagined they were fighting for at 'Derry, Aughrim, and the Boyne.' Presbyterians were forbidden to be married by their own clergymen, the Ecclesiastical Courts had power to fine and imprison offenders, and to compel them to appear in the Parish Church, and make public confession of fornication, if so married. At Lisburn and Tullylish, Presbyterians were actually punished for being married by their own ministers. Some years later, in 1712, a number of Presbyterians were arrested for attempting to establish a Presbyterian meeting house in Belturbet.

The marriage of a Presbyterian and an Episcopalian was declared illegal, and in fact, the ministers and congregations of the former church were treated as outlaws and rebels, to be fined, imprisoned, and harassed in every possible way. They had to pay tithes for the upkeep of the Episcopalian ministers, were fined for not going to the Episcopalian Church, and had to pay Church cess for buying sacramental bread, ringing the bell, and washing the surplices of the Episcopalian clergymen. All this, remember, in the generation immediately following the Battle of the Boyne.

The reader should remember what is generally slurred over in narrating this part of Irish history, that when we are told that Ulster was planted by Scottish Presbyterians, it does not mean that the land was given to them. On the contrary, the vital fact was, and is, that the land was given to the English noblemen and to certain London companies of merchants who had lent money to the Crown, and that the Scottish planters were only introduced as tenants of these landlords. The condition of their tenancy virtually was that they should keep Ireland for the English Crown, and till the land of Ireland for the benefit of the English landlord.

That is in essence the demand of the Unionist Party leaders upon their followers today. In the past, as the landlords were generally English and Episcopalian, they all, during the eighteenth century, continually inserted clauses in all their leases, forbidding the erection of Presbyterian meeting houses. As the uprise of democracy has contributed to make this impossible today in Ireland, the landlord and capitalist class now seek an alliance with these Protestants they persecuted for so long in order to prevent a union of the democracy of all religious faiths against their lords and masters.

To accomplish this they seek insidiously to pervert history, and to inflame the spirit of religious fanaticism. The best cure I know of for that evil is a correct understanding of the events they so distort in their speeches and sermons. To this end I have ever striven to contribute my mite, and while I know that the sight of the thousands who, on July 12, will march to proclaim their allegiance to principles of which their order is a negation, will be somewhat disheartening. I also know that even amongst the Orange hosts, the light of truth is penetrating.

In conclusion, the fundamental, historical facts to remember are that:

> The Irish Catholic was despoiled by force,
> The Irish Protestant toiler was dispoiled by fraud,
> The spoliation of both continues today under more insidious but more effective forms,

and the only hope lies in the latter combining with the former in overthrowing their common spoilers, and consenting to live in amity together in the common ownership of their common country—the country which the spirit of their ancestors or the devices of their rulers have made—the place of their origin, or the scene of their travail.

I have always held, despite the fanatics on both sides, that the movements of Ireland for freedom could not and cannot be divorced from the world-wide upward movements of the world's democracy. The Irish question is a part of the social question, the desire of the Irish people to control their own destinies is a part of the desire of the workers to forge political weapons for their own enfranchisement as a class.

The Orange fanatic and the Capitalist-minded Home Ruler are alike in denying this truth; ere long, both of them will be but memories, while the army of those who believe in that truth will be marching and battling on its conquering way.

7. A FORGOTTEN CHAPTER OF IRISH HISTORY

Connolly returned to the evangelization of Ulster Protestants for Irish Socialism, employing a characteristic deduction from Ulster Protestant history. No doubt he hoped that Scottish Protestant readers of Forward *would draw the argument to the attention of their Ulster co-religionists, with whom close links existed. He could certainly have counted on some Ulster Protestant readership for the article, which* Forward *printed in its issue of September 9th, 1913.*

A writer in *Forward* recently expressed the desire that someone would prepare literature that would be suitable for the conversion to Socialism of Orangemen. It is a desire with which I most heartily sympathise. I cannot resist the feeling that the Socialist movement of these countries has a legitimate grievance against the Socialists in the North of Ireland for never having seriously essayed this task before. Unfortunately the Socialists of this district seem to have been possessed with the idea that it was good tactics to talk about every place under the sun except about the North of Ireland, to read every history except Irish history, and to profess unlimited faith in the democracy of every country except Ireland.

This it was, and is, argued, showed a good broad-minded attitude, proved that they were true internationalists, whereas to talk about Ireland, to dissect and analyse the claims made by Irish politicians, to expose the hollowness of their shibboleths, to direct attention to the merciless expropriation that underlay the so-called religious issues of past wars in Ireland, and the equally callous desire to hide present exploitations on the part of those who seek to keep alive animosities supposedly arising out of these wars—all this is supposed to betray a parochial, Chauvinistic, narrow spirit alien to the true Internationalist.

I have always argued that although the Socialist movement requires a world-literature, a stock of books dealing with capitalism as a world force, constituting as it were the classical literature of the movement, yet that each country requires also a local or native literature and spoken propaganda translating and explaining its past history and present political developments in the light of the knowledge derived from a study of Socialist classics.

Any country which is content to depend solely upon these great Socialist classics will never have a Socialist movement of the working class; it may have a Socialist sect of a few true believers, but it cannot hope for the adhesion of the great mass of the toilers.

It is only when Socialism is brought down from the clouds and is shown to have a direct bearing upon the political life of each country as a reflex of the economic history of that country, and to have a message bearing upon the political problems of the day, it is only then that Socialism has an opportunity of developing from being the cult of the few to become the faith of the many.

In every country this has been learned, and in proportion as the local literature grew, the Socialist movement of which it was the expression grew also. The stronger and the more widespread is that local translation of Socialist generalisations the more deeply rooted, not the less, became the faith in the world-wide nature of the movement.

As long as the movement in this district is content to draw its literature from England and its illustrations from British conditions, so long will it be but an echo of the fight of our British brothers and sisters. So soon as we build up a literature and spoken propaganda dealing with conditions in Ireland, as our fathers knew and as we know them, so soon will the movement here draw strength and power to itself.

Like the mythological character who lost his strength when raised from the earth, but renewed his strength and power whenever his feet once more come in contact with the soil—so the Socialist movement drains itself to mere impotence or raises itself to power in proportion as it rests upon the immediate realities of the people to whom it is appealing.

The industrial movement, the rebellion in the shops, ships, docks, and factories needs to care little for the moment about questions arising out of past history, but the Socialist movement seeking to challenge the political powers of the political lords, or the rights of ownership of the machine lords, cannot evade the duty of an investigation of the historical origins of these powers and rights.

And when we find that the landlords and machine, or mill and factory lords of our own country have become the political leaders of our own district, nothing can absolve us from the duty of investigating and exposing the sources of that social power which has also vested them with their evil political dominance.

These things are of course commonplace among the thoughtful Socialists elsewhere, but are, I am sorry to relate, regarded as extraordinary innovations here. The fact is indicative of the unformed state of our Socialist movement, and the immense spade-work that is still to be done.

When that ex-Orange exploiter of Socialism does arrive, he will not lack materials to go upon if he is courageous enough to resolve to give his readers the facts about the past record of the Orange aristocracy they now so slavishly worship.

As a humble contribution to his arsenal, allow me to state briefly the story of the Antrim Leases of 1772.

I have pointed out before that the Ulster plantation of James I was a scheme under which the lands stolen from the natives were given to certain Crown favourites and London companies, and that the rank and file of the Protestant English and Scottish armies were only made tenants of these aristocrats and companies. Tyrone, Derry, Donegal, Fermanagh, Armagh and Cavan were entirely confiscated. The plan was worked out by Sir Arthur Chichester, ancestor of the Marquis of Donegal. For his share in the transaction he received the entire territories of the clansmen of Sir Cahir O'Doherty; the London companies, which had financed the war, received 209,800 acres out of a total of 500,000 acres, and other ancestors of the Orange aristocracy got the rest. In addition to the above-mentioned plunder, when Sir Arthur

Chichester resigned his position as Lord Deputy in 1616, he received certain lands in Antrim and the title of Baron of Belfast.

All the Antrim lands were settled by a Protestant tenantry, the Catholics being driven to the hills and glens. As was natural from the political circumstances of the time, and in order to preserve the appearance of fairness, these Protestant tenants were at first granted very long leases. Under the security of tenure afforded by these leases, they worked hard, reclaimed the land, built houses, drained, fenced and improved the property. Also under the terms of the promise given by William III, when in answer to the petition of the English woollen manufacturers he suppressed that industry in Ireland but promised bounties to the linen industry as a compensation, the cultivation of flax and the manufacture of linen grew up in Antrim as a further contribution to the prosperity of the tenants of Lord Donegal.

But in and about the year 1772 the leases began to expire all over the county. What happened then is best told in the words of the 'Remonstrance of Northern Protestants' sent to the Lord Lieutenant, Lord Townshend, in that year:

> The landlords thirsted to share the people's benefits by raising their rents, which would have been very reasonable to a moderate degree, but of late they had run to great excesses.
>
> When the tenant's lease was ended, they published in the newspapers that such a parcel of land was to be let, and that proposals in writing would be received for it. They invited every covetous, envious, and malicious person to offer for his neighbour's possession and improvements. The tenant, knowing he must be the highest bidder, or turn out he knew not whither, would offer more than their value. If he complained to the landlord that it was too dear, the landlord answered that he knew it was, but that as it was in a trading country, the tenant could make up the deficiency by his industry. Those who possessed the greatest estates were now so rich that they could not find delicacies enough in their own

> country to bestow their wealth on, but carried it abroad to lavish there the entire day's sweat of thousands of poor people.

The two worst extortioners were Lord Donegal and a Mr. Upton. On the estate of Lord Donegal a large number of the leases expired simultaneously. The landlord refused to renew them unless he received the enormous sum of £100,000 in fines, as a free gift for his generosity. As the tenants could not raise this great sum, they offered to pay the interest upon it in addition to their rent, but this was refused, and then some 'hard-headed, shrewd and enterprising' Belfast capitalists offered the money to my lord and secured the farms over the head of the tenants, who were accordingly evicted. According to Froude in his *English in Ireland in the Eighteenth Century*[1] (and Froude was as bitter, malevolent and anti-Irish a historian as ever wrote)—'In the two years that followed the Antrim evictions, thirty thousand Protestants left Ulster for a land where there was no legal robbery, and where those who sowed the seed could reap the harvest.'

Those who remained at home did not accept their fate with complacency, nor show that voluntary abasement before the aristocracy characteristic of their descendants today. They formed a secret society—the 'Hearts of Steel'—which strove by acts of terrorism to redress some of their grievances. In a manifesto issued by this organisation in 1772, the following sentence appears:

> The supreme judge himself had excited them to commotion to cause the landlords on whom no mild means will prevail to observe the pale faces and the thin clothing of their honest Protestant subjects who had enriched the country by their industry.

When in the same year six of their number were arrested and lodged in the town jail of Belfast, the members of this society assembled from all parts of Down and Antrim, marched upon Belfast, stormed the jail, and released their comrades. The thin clothing and pale faces of honest Protestant workers are

[1] Longmans, London, 1872–4.

still in evidence in Belfast, but the only things they are storming nowadays are the homes of their fellow sufferers who profess different political faith.

Here then is the reality as against all the vaunted 'Civil and Religious Liberties' which the Carsons and their breed tell us was established at the Boyne. Some day I will tell the equally shameful story of the suppression of political liberty, of how the Protestant workers were kept outside the franchise whilst the classes manipulated the powers of the State to their own enrichment.

But this story of the Antrim Leases will serve as an illustration of my point that in the treatment of Protestant workers by Protestant exploiters in Ulster, our coming historian will find plenty of material upon which to base his appeal to the Orange masses.

The worker who grasps that point will then be able to fully comprehend the teaching conveyed in the following statement of principle, upon which the Independent Labour Party of Ireland is based, and which it adopted as its own at the joint conference of Socialist bodies in Ireland which saw its formation:

> Whereas the political history of Ireland is a record of the attempts of successive races and classes to obtain possession of the land and other sources of national wealth in order that the yoke of slavery may be laid upon the necks of the non-possessors, and
>
> Whereas in this fight for economic supremacy the marauding races and classes have utilised in the past every possible appeal to racial sentiment, patriotic devotion and religious bigotry, hiding under their various rallying cries the ever-present desire of a dominant section for power and plunder, and
>
> Whereas the working class of Ireland today, like the working class of every other nation, is the heir and representative of all the defrauded and dispossessed generations of the past, embracing in its ranks the descendants of the men and women who, no matter what banner they fought under or what cause they

> envoked were despoiled and subjugated alike in victory and in defeat:
>
> Therefore be it Resolved—'That recognising that, despite their diverse origins, the workers of Ireland are heirs of a common spoliation, and sufferers from a common bondage, that the watchwords and rallying cries of the various parties, led by the various factions of our masters, are but sound and fury, signifying nothing to us in our present needs and struggles; and that it is no longer a question of Celt against Saxon or Catholic against Protestant,
>
> But of All the Workers Against All the Exploiters, we, representing workers from North and South, unite under the following constitution in a common association against the common enemy for the ownership of our common country and the World for the Workers—'

A correspondent, 'A. O.,' writing to *Forward*, suggests that it would be well if I gave my authorities for statements such as that of the alliance of the Pope and King William III at the time of the Battle of the Boyne. I am willing, nay, anxious to give any such when asked, but as a rule I am, I admit, averse to loading my writing with pedantic quotations from other writers, knowing as I do that it might need a page of explanations to introduce and make understood the quotation. For the circumstance of the League of Augsburg the correspondent is referred to Von Ranke's *History of the Popes*,[1] to the recently published work, *Revolutionary Ireland, and its Settlement*,[2] by Murray, a Protestant Unionist writer, and to Guizot's *Civilisation in Europe*.[3] As the latter was a French Protestant, I will here quote from his Thirteenth Lecture:

> The League was so powerful against Louis XIV that openly, or in a hidden but very real manner, sovereigns were seen to enter it who were assuredly very far from being interested in favour of civil and religious liberty.

[1] Translated by E. Foster; Bell & Sons, London, 1846.

[2] Macmillan, London, 1911.

[3] *Lectures on European Civilization.*

> The Emperor of Germany and Pope Innocent XI supported Wiliam III against Louis XIV.

As for the Catholic rejoicings over the victory of William, a Catholic writer in the *Catholic Times* of last year, in answer to another correspondent who questioned my statement, pointed out that these rejoicings took place not only in Rome, but also in Brussels and Madrid.

8. THE WAR IN ULSTER

On March 19th, 1914, a group of British Army officers stationed at the Curragh of Kildare announced their readiness to resign rather than march to reduce Ulster to obedience in response to the Home Rule settlement. The Government proved unable to withstand the moral threat of the mutiny, and from that point all talk of forcing the Ulster Unionists to accept the Home Rule Act ceased to be serious. The partition of Ireland had become a likelihood; moreover, the authority of Parliament had been challenged successfully. Connolly rightly saw bluff and intrigue as the central factors in the situation, though he was somewhat mistaken in his assessment of the intriguers, of whom perhaps the foremost was Major-General (afterwards Field-Marshal) Sir Henry Wilson, Director of Military Operations and the chief link between the mutineers and the Ulster Unionists. Although not directly concerned with religion, the article is of significance as an analysis of the effects of the Ulster sectarianism and its use by the ruling class; it testifies to Connolly's own growing alienation from Ulster social attitudes; and it draws some valuable Marxist lessons from the events, notably from the mutiny itself and its implications. Forward *printed it on March 28th, 1914.*

Now that all the world and its wife has it eyes fixed upon Ulster, and now that I am back at my post in Belfast, it is, I suppose, strictly in order that I shall this week say something about the Ulster crisis.

At the time of writing (Sunday afternoon) all the posters of the Sunday Press are announcing in great letters that 'Ulster is on the brink of war'; that 'The outlook is black'; that '100 officers have resigned'; that 'Regiments throw down their rifles'; that 'Warships are in Belfast Lough'; and that, briefly speaking, hell has been let loose. All of which seems to convince us that we are living in stirring times.

Strangely enough, Belfast itself seems bent upon its usual lines of strict attention to the business of profitmaking, and when I look around for the 'grim, determined faces,' so celebrated in the song and story of the Tory Press, I fail to see them, and see instead in all the shop windows the usual alluring advertisements of next week's sales; in the columns of the Tory Press the usual invitation to buy and sell and leave all sorts of property; and in the faces of the people in the streets the same unimaginative smugness, tempered by the effects of a Calvinistic theology in some cases, and by drink in many more.

Are these, then, the signs of times that try men's souls? Belfast may or may not go to war, but if she does she still wears the outward appearances of respectable mediocrity and slave-driven wagedom. There is none of the enthusiasm of rebellion for a holy cause, nor the excitement of men who do and dare all things for a great principle; here are only the signs and symbols of a people who have pawned their souls for a usurer's promise of prosperity—a people who would breathe the spirit of the Past into all the institutions of the Present, and continually shrinking from a contemplation of the Future, recite as their Litany and Article of Faith a thanksgiving that they are not as other men.

Have the governing forces of these countries shrunk from their people in fear of their powers on the field of battle? Has the Liberal Government really a dread that the motley hosts of Orangemen led by landlord rack-renters, capitalist sweaters, and lawyers on the make, will take the field against the forces of the Crown? If they have, it is at least certain that the Home Rule population of Belfast, indeed of Ulster generally, have no fears whatever upon the score. Nationalists, Socialists, Liberals, to put them in the order of their numerical importance, feel quite confident that were the forces of the Crown withdrawn entirely, the Unionists could or would put no force into the field that the Home Rulers of all sections combined could not protect themselves against with a moderate amount of ease. Why, then, this sudden flurry in Government circles?

The present writer is quite satisfied that the 'war' scare is all part of a great piece of theatricals, carefully arranged between the Liberal Ministry, the official Home Rule party, and the Unionist leaders.

He is quite assured that the exclusion of a part of Ulster from the Home Rule Bill is already agreed upon between those tricky gentry, and that the so-called scene in Parliament between Devlin and Carson, the latter's flight from the House to Ulster, and the rush of troops to this province, are all parts of a carefully arranged programme having for its end the blinding of Nationalist Ireland to the infamous character of the Partition scheme to which Redmond and Devlin had given their consent.

Without some such theatricality the democracy of Nationalist Ireland would have had time to think—to think how any of their leaders in the past would have received such a proposal, and had they so thought those who accepted it now would have been hounded out of Irish public life.

Think, for instance of the position of the Nationalists of Belfast! If they are included in the Home Rule Bill now it will be Sir Edward Carson they will have to thank, as Joe Devlin was willing to leave them out if Sir Edward would agree.

To prevent the people understanding this infamy we are treated to columns of balderdash about civil war. You may think my accusation over-strained. Wait and see. And while you are waiting ponder over the circumstance that Sir Edward Carson has not given a definite refusal, that Bonar Law has given a qualified acceptance, and that all the threats of the Government are accompanied by a renewal of the offer—a renewal made with the tacit consent of the Home Rule leaders.

I wish to state it to be my most solemn conviction that the only real obstacle in the way of the Exclusion policy being accepted by both sides in Parliament is the fear of the business men of Ulster that it would ruin their trade with the other provinces.

That the orders to certain regiments to march upon Ulster has been the cause of a large number of officers resigning is, I am sure, an unwelcome fact to all the official parties. The Carsonite officials are not at all pleased, I suspect, at the readiness with which the poor fools of officers acted. Lawyers and politicians use language inciting to mutiny under certain contingencies, but they always reserve to themselves the right to say whether those contingencies have or have not arrived, and always save their precious skins by deciding that the contingency which justifies mutiny has not arrived, not quite. Thus they save their skins, even although they lose their honour. But they sometimes by their language lead into real mutiny other men who are not quite such discriminating judges, and who are more solicitous of their honour than their skins. I rather think that those officers are in this position, and I suspect that the greatest suffering that will befall them will be the shock to their feelings when they discover that neither Bonar Law nor Carson will stand sponsor for their acts.

But suppose mere privates on being ordered to march against strikers had refused, what would befall them. Imagination fails to picture the columns of the Tory, Liberal, and Home Rule Press during the ensuing week. But of one thing we may be assured, viz., that any one of such privates so refusing who was out of prison inside of twelve months would be a lucky man.

It is to be hoped that the growing number of Socialist privates in the Army and Navy are not forgetting to drive this lesson home to their mess-mates. So Carson will not have lived in vain if he thus helps to popularise amongst these men the idea involved in the historic appeal—don't shoot!

PART III

A SOCIALIST EVANGEL IN NATIONALIST IRELAND

The present writer has spent a great portion of his life alternating between interpreting Socialism to the Irish, and interpreting the Irish to the Socialists. Of the two tasks, I confess, that while I am convinced that the former has been attended with a considerable degree of success, the latter has not. – James Connolly, in *Forward*, May 3rd, 1913

9. ERIN'S HOPE... THE END AND THE MEANS

The following text is taken from the edition of 1909, published in the 'Harp Library' by J. E. C. Donnelly, who was then publisher of The Harp *itself; this edition necessarily commands authority as the last published in Connolly's lifetime and prepared under his direction. Some minor textual changes were made from the first edition, and these have been noted here, apart from the incorporation of a detailed footnote into the main body of the text. Connolly's own introduction to this edition, more detailed than his prefatory note to the first, conveys the circumstances of the work's origins. Printing errors and obvious slips have been corrected; otherwise his text is unchanged from this, his final version. After the 1897 publication,* Erin's Hope *was reissued as a serial in* The Workers' Republic *in May–September 1900, and issued with the paper as an insert in June 1901. At least two editions were published in the U.S.A. before the 1909 one, both of them being under the auspices of Daniel de Leon and his party press, with profuse and reverential advertisements for De Leon's own works appended. The texts of the De Leonite editions are not good and it is doubtful if Connolly saw them before their publication. It may well have been because the 1909 edition made no reference to earlier American publication that on its appearance the London* Industrialist *wrote: 'He only deals with the political organization of the workers and not their economic, this is too bad from an I.W.W. member.' On this Connolly commented: 'Our reviewer forgets that the book was first printed in 1897. We confess to have learnt something since.' The first edition carried the following epigraph: 'It is indeed certain that industrial society will not permanently survive without a systematic organization. The mere conflict of private interests will never produce a well-ordered commonwealth of labour.' The author of the statement was John Kells Ingram, former romantic nationalist, now conservative, don of Trinity College, Dublin; it appeared in his* History of Political Economy.

Our Independence must be had at all hazards. If the men of property will not help us, they must fall; we will free ourselves by the aid of that large and respectable class of the community—the men of no property.

—Theobald Wolfe Tone.

INTRODUCTION

In publishing an American edition of *Erin's Hope* in the interest of the Irish Socialist Federation, the author is of opinion that a few words of explanation of the circumstances attending its first publication in Ireland in 1897 may be both useful and interesting.

The Irish Socialist Republican Party was founded in Dublin in 1896 by a few workingmen whom the author had succeeded in interesting in his proposition that the two currents of revolutionary thought in Ireland—the Socialist and the National—were not antagonistic, but complementary, and that the Irish Socialist was in reality the best Irish patriot, but that in order to convince the Irish people of that fact he must first of all learn to look inward upon Ireland for his justification, rest his arguments upon the facts of Irish history, and be the champion against the subjection of Ireland and all that it implies. That the Irish National question was at bottom an economic question, and that the economic struggle must first be able to function freely nationally before it could function internationally, and as Socialists were opposed to all oppression, so they should ever be foremost in the daily battle against all its manifestations, social and political. As the embodiment of this teaching, the party adopted the watchword, *Irish Socialist Republic*, and by deduction therefrom, the aforementioned name of their organization.

This policy received its formal endorsement by the International Socialist movement when at the International Socialist Congress at Paris in 1900 the delegates of the I. S. R. P. were formally seated as the delegates of a nation separate from England.

It is no exaggeration to say that this organization and its

policy completely revolutionized advanced politics in Ireland. When it was first initiated the word 'republic' was looked upon as a word to be only whispered among intimates; the Socialists boldly advised the driving from public life of all who would not openly accept it. The thought of revolution was the exclusive possession of a few remnants of the secret societies of a past generation, and was never mentioned by them except with heads closely together and eyes fearfully glancing around; the Socialists broke through this ridiculous secrecy, and in hundreds of speeches in the most public places of the metropolis, as well as in scores of thousands of pieces of literature scattered through the country, announced their purpose to muster all the forces of labor for a revolutionary reconstruction of society and the incidental destruction of the British Empire. The Socialists of Dublin conceived of and organized the great Anti-Jubilee Protest of 1897, which startled the world and shattered all the elaborate attempts of the British government to represent Ireland as loyal. They held the first meeting of protest against the Boer war, and at that meeting of over 2,000 persons in College Green, Dublin, passed the first resolution in Ireland calling upon the Irish in the Transvaal to take up arms against the armies of the British capitalist government; they conducted the first campaign against enlistment in the army; they were the first to contest elections upon a platform openly declaring for a revolution, and they were the first to point out all the immense amelioration of the conditions of life in Ireland which could be realized without waiting for Home Rule. In short, the Irish Socialist Republican Party has to itself the credit of having opened up practically all the new fields of thought and action now being exploited by other and less revolutionary organizations.

Needless to say, when this policy was first entered upon it aroused interest alike among Nationalists and Socialists. Thence came requests for enlightenment, each side inquiring upon that part of the policy which seemed to touch most closely their own previous ideas of politics. The advanced nationalists of Ireland had at that time only one monthly literary magazine, the *Shan Van Vocht*, ably edited by Miss Alice Milligan and published at Belfast. In response to a request from that lady, the article, 'Can Irish Republicans be Politicians?' was written and published in that magazine in November, 1896. Mr. J. Keir Hardie, the editor of the *Labor Leader*, Glasgow, and Socialist member of the English Parliament, also wrote asking for a series of articles upon the relation of the Irish Question to Socialism, and in response to the invitation, the other articles were written. The I. S. R. P. afterwards combined the two sets of articles and made of them the pamphlet which we now reproduce.

We now present those articles to the Irish Workers in America in hope that we may induce them to study and accept our position, viz.:

> That the Irish Question is at bottom a Social Question, that Socialism alone can lay the material foundation necessary for the free development of the intellectual and spiritual forces of the scattered children of the Clan-na-Gael, and that the Socialist message to Ireland and to America is identical, and calls for the Industrial and Political Organization of Labor as the Means by which that End may be reached.

ERIN'S HOPE

In the October issue of the *Shan Van Vocht*, the editor, in commenting upon the strictures passed by one contributor on the French Revolution, asks for an expression of opinion on the relative merits of revolutionary uprisings and moral force agitations. As both the article in question and the editorial note suggesting the discussion, apparently take it for granted that the query with which this communication is headed, must be answered in the negative, an assumption which I believe to be entirely erroneous, and the fundamental mistake in the calculation of our modern Irish revolutionists, I would suggest that as the broader and more comprehensive question, this be instead the basis of the proposed controversy. To make my position more plain, I may say, I write as one who believes that the concession to Ireland of such a limited form of local autonomy as that embodied in Mr. Gladstone's Home Rule Bill, would not, in any sense, be a step towards independence, but would more likely create effectual barriers in the way of its realization.

The question thus arises, are those who see in an Irish Republic the only political ideal worth striving for to eschew political action and seek, in secret conspiracy alone, to prepare for revolution? Up to the present every genuine Irish revolutionist has acted on this belief, that political action was impossible for republicans.

Now I assert the contrary. A revolution can only succeed in any country when it has the moral sanction of the people. It is so, even in an independent country; it is doubly so in a country subject like Ireland, to the rule of another. Within this century, no Irish revolutionist had obtained this sanction before he took the field. In 1848 the majority of the Irish people pinned their faith to the Repeal Association, which had disavowed even the right to resist oppression, and the Young Irelanders themselves had made no reasonable effort to prepare the popular mind for revolution, but had rather been precipitated into it against their will. Under such conditions, failure was inevitable. Those who were willing to 'rise' had no means of knowing how far their aspirations were shared by their fellow-countrymen elsewhere, and lacking confidence in themselves, with the recognized leaders of public opinion against them, the effort ended in disaster. The history of the Fenian movement was somewhat similar. The number of actually enrolled members formed but an insignificant minority of the population, the vast majority of our countrymen, though perhaps sympathizing with the Fenian ideal, put their trust in politicians who preached tame submission under the name of 'prudence' and 'caution,' and in the critical period of the movement flung the weight of their influence on the side of 'law and order.'

In both cases the recognized leaders of national thought were on the side of constituted authority, and against every revolutionary effort. The facts are as undeniable as they are lamentable, and they speak in trumpet tones in favor of such a re-modelling of Irish revolutionary tactics as shall prevent a recurrence of similar disasters in the future. This, I hold, can be best accomplished by a political party seeking to give public expression to the republican ideal. One point needs to be emphasized in this connection, viz., it is not republicanism, but the counsel of insurrectionary effort to realize republicanism, which gave to previous Irish movements their odor of illegality. A candidate for political honors(?) is as much at liberty to put the attainment of a republic on his programme as he is to pledge himself to Home Rule, or any other scheme of political reconstruction. Were a political party formed in Ireland to educate the people in sound national ideas by pledging every candidate to openly repudiate the authority of the Crown, and work for the realization of republican principles, it would achieve a much needed transformation in Irish politics.

Hitherto every Irish agitation has sought to make its programme as broad and loosely defined as possible, in order to enrol under its banner every section of Irish national opinion—loyal Home Rulers, Conservative Nationalists, Compromising Whigs, and Nationalist Democrats—all alike were welcome. Such a basis is undoubtedly best for the purposes of an 'agitation,' but it is worse than useless for the purposes of earnest revolutionists seeking a definite end. But such a party as I speak of, with an avowedly republican programme, would, in its very definiteness and coherence, have immense advantage to recommend it to the consideration and support of practical-minded men. It would prevent the emasculation of our young men by the vaporings of 'constitutional' patriots; it would effectually expose the sham Nationalists, and, let us hope, drive them from political life; it would at every election in which it took part, afford a plebiscite of the people for or against the republic; it would enlist the sympathy of many earnest patriots whose open natures shrink from secret conspiracy; it would ascertain with mathematical accuracy the moment when the majority of the Irish people were ripe for revolution, and it could not be suppressed while representative government was left in Ireland.

By adhering steadily to the policy of pledging every candidate to its full programme, whether they stood for Parliament or local governing bodies, it would insure that when a majority of the Irish people had at the ballot boxes declared in favor of the revolutionary party every soldier of the cause would know that in the fight he was waging, he was not merely one of a numerically insignificant band of malcontents, but a citizen soldier fighting under orders publicly expressed in face of all the world by a majority of his fellow-countrymen. This, I hold to be an eminently practical method of obtaining our end. It would exclude the possibility of our national principles being betrayed in the moment of danger, or compromised in the hour of success to suit the convenience of interested party politicians; it would inspire confidence in the most timid by its recognition of the fact that to counsel rebellion without first obtaining the moral sanction of the people would be an act of criminal folly which would only end in disaster. It would make Irish republicanism no longer the 'politics of despair,' but the Science of Revolution.

It may be urged against such a proposal that the first need of Irish politics is unity, and that such a party would only accentuate the division at present existing. This, however, could only be the case if our present representatives refuse to accept the pledge of loyalty to the free Irish Republic, and to it alone. If they do so refuse, then they are unfit to be representatives of the Irish democracy, and cannot be removed too soon. The objection in itself implies a suspicion of the genuine nature of the patriotism so loudly vaunted by our party politicians. Unity is a good thing, no doubt, but honesty is better, and if unity can only be obtained by the suppression of truth and the toleration of falsehood, then it is not worth the price we are asked to pay for it. I would, in conclusion, earnestly recommend my readers to study the suggestions contained in this paper, and to act accordingly. Should this meet with a favorable reception, I may give in a future issue my ideas on the programme of political and social reform, on which such a party might fight in Parliament and the country, while the public opinion of Ireland was ripening behind them, and pending the arrival of the propitious moment for action.

Ireland Before the Conquest

Before the time of the conquest, the Irish people knew nothing of absolute property in land. The land belonged to the entire sept; the chief was little more than managing member of the association. The feudal idea which came in with the conquest was associated with foreign dominion, and has never to this day been recognized by the moral sentiment of the people.

In these few words of Mr. John Stuart Mill the impartial student may find the key for unravelling the whole tangled skein of Irish politics. Latter-day politicians, both on the English and Irish side, have done their utmost to familiarize the public mind with the belief that the Irish question arises solely out of the aspirations of the Irish people to have more complete control over the internal administration of the affairs of their country than it is possible for them to exercise while the seat of goverment is located at Westminster, and that, therefore, some form of local self-government, as, for instance, Mr. Gladstone's Home Rule Bill, is all that is needed to settle this question, and lay forever the troubled spirit of Irish discontent. According to this luminous(?) exposition of Irish history, we are to believe that the two nations have for seven hundred years been engaged in unceasing warfare, that the one country (Ireland) has during all that time been compelled to witness the merciless slaughter of her children by famine, pestilence and the sword; that each succeeding generation has witnessed a renewal of the conflict and a renewal of the martyrdom, until the sensitive mind recoils from a perusal of Irish history as from the records of a shambles, and all, forsooth, because Irishmen and Englishmen could not agree upon the form of political administration best suited for Ireland.

If this new reading of Irish history were true the intelligent foreigner might be forgiven for rating at a very low standard the intelligence of the two nations which during seven hundred years had not evolved a satisfactory solution of such a simple question. At precisely the same low standard may safely be rated the political acumen of the English and Irish party leaders who are today complacently trotting out the discredited abortion of Home Rule as a sovereign remedy for Ireland's misery.

The Irish question has, in fact, a much deeper source than a mere difference of opinion on forms of government. Its real origin and inner meaning lay in the circumstances that the two opposing nations held fundamentally different ideas upon the vital question of property in land. Recent scientific research by such eminent sociologists as Letourneau, Lewis Morgan, Sir Henry Maine, and others has amply demonstrated the fact that common ownership of land formed the basis of primitive society in almost every country. But whereas in the majority of countries now called civilized such primitive communion had almost entirely disappeared before the dawn of history, and had at no time acquired a higher status than that conferred by the social sanction of unlettered and uneducated tribes, in Ireland the system formed part of the well-defined social organization of a nation of scholars and students, recognized by Chief and Tanist, Brehon and Bard, as the inspiring principle of their collective life, and the basis of their national system of jurisprudence. Such a striking fact will, of course, be interpreted in many ways, according to the temperament and political or racial sympathies of the reader. The adherent of the present order of society will regard it as proof of the Irish incapacity for assimilating progressive ideas, and will, no doubt, confidently assert that this incapacity is the real source of Ireland's misery, since it has unfitted her sons for the competitive scramble for existence, and so fore-doomed them to the lot of hewers of wood and drawers of water.

The ardent student of sociology, who believes that the progress of the human race through the various economic stages of communism, chattel slavery, feudalism, and wage-slavery, has been but a preparation for the higher ordered society of the future; that the most industrially advanced countries are but, albeit often unconsciously, developing the social conditions which, since the breakup of universal tribal communism, have been rendered historically necessary for the inauguration of a new and juster economic order, in which social, political and national antagonism will be unknown, will perhaps regard the Irish adherence to clan ownership at such a comparatively recent date as the Seventeenth Century as an evidence of retarded economical development, and therefore a real hindrance to progress. But the sympathetic student of history, who believes in the possibility of a people by political intuition anticipating the lessons afterwards revealed to them in the sad school of experience, will not be indisposed to join with the ardent Irish patriot in his lavish expressions of admiration for the sagacity of his Celtic forefathers, who foreshadowed in the democratic organization of the Irish clan the more perfect organization of the free society of the future.

Whichever be the true interpretation of Irish history, one fact at least stands out clear and undeniable, viz., that the conflict between the rival systems of land ownership was the pivot around which centered all the struggles and rebellions of which that history has been so prolific. The Irish regarded with inveterate hostility their English rulers, at all times set little store upon promises of incorporation within the pale of the constitution, and rose with enthusiasm under their respective rebel chiefs, because they regarded this as the all-important question, because in their eyes English rule and Dublin parliaments were alike identified as the introducers and upholders of the system of feudalism and private ownership of land, as opposed to the Celtic system of clan or common ownership, which they regarded, and, I think, rightly, as the pledge at once of their political and social liberty.

The English Government were also astute enough to perceive that the political or national subjection of Ireland was entirely valueless to the conquerors while the politically subjected nation remained in possession of economic freedom. Consequently, we find that the first stipulation made to the Irish tribe upon its submission always provided that the lands of the tribe should be regarded as the private property of the chief; that he should therefore accept them as a grant from the crown, from which he should in future hold them; that he should drop his Irish title, which proclaimed him the freely elected chief of a free community, and should instead accept an English title, such as duke or earl, and in all things conform to English ideas of civilization and social order. All these stipulations were in the last degree repugnant to Irish ideas. The chief, as Mill has justly observed, was but the managing member of the tribal association, although in the stress of constant warfare they usually limited their choice to the members of one or two families; yet the right of election was never abdicated by the tribesmen. Whenever the seductions of English gold overmastered the patriotism of an Irish chief, and succeeded in inducing his acceptance of the alien property system and the alien title (as in the case of Art O'Neil and Nial Garbh O'Donnell, the Queen's O'Reilly and the Queen's Maguire), they immediately elected another chief in his stead; and from that moment the unfortunate renegade became an outlaw from his own people, and could only appear in his native territory under an escort of English spears.

The Irish system was thus on a par with those conceptions of social rights and duties which we find the ruling classes today denouncing so fiercely as 'Socialistic.' It was apparently inspired by the democratic principle that property was intended to serve the people, and not by the principle so universally acted upon at present, viz., that the people have no other function in existing than to be the bondslaves of those who by force or by fraud have managed to possess themselves of property. They did not, indeed, regard all forms of productive property as rightfully belonging to the community; but when we remember that the land alone was at that time of importance, all other forms of property being insignificant by comparison, we see that they were as Socialistic as the industrial development of their time required. The English civilization against which they fought was, on the other hand, thoroughly individualistic; and, as it triumphed, we are reaping the fruits to-day in the industrial disputes, the agricultural depressions, the poorhouses, and other such glorious institutions in Church and State as we are permitted the luxury of enjoying in common with our fellow-subjects in this 'integral portion of the British Empire.' The results of the change on the national life of Erin are well illustrated in the scornful words in which Aubrey De Vere apostrophises the 'new race' of exploiters which then arose:

The chiefs of the Gael were the people embodied;
  The chiefs were the blossoms, the people the root.
Their conquerors, the Normans, high-souled and high-blooded,
  Grew Irish at last from the scalp to the foot.
And ye, ye are hirelings and satraps, not nobles—

Your slaves they detest you, your masters, they scorn.
The river lives on, but the sun-painted bubbles
Pass quickly, to the rapids incessantly borne.

Ireland Under British Rule

The break-up of the Kilkenny Confederation in 1649 and the consequent dispersion of the Irish clans was the immediate cause of that confusion of thought and apparent lack of directness in aim which down to our day has characterized all modern Irish politics. Deprived of any form of political or social organization which might serve as an effective basis for its practical realization, the demand for the common ownership of the land naturally fell into abeyance until such time as the conquest of some form of political freedom should enable the dispossessed Irishry to substitute for the lost tribal association the fuller and broader conception of an Irish nation as the natural repository and guardian of the people's heritage. But when the fusing process of a common subjection had once more welded the heterogeneous elements of Irish society into one compact nationality it was found that in the intervening period a new class had arisen in the land—a class which, while professedly ultra-nationalistic in its political aims, had nevertheless so far compounded with the enemy as to accept the alien social system, with its accompanying manifestation, the legal dispossession and economic dependence of the vast mass of the Irish people, as part of the natural order of society.

The Irish middle class, who then by virtue of their social position and education stepped to the front as Irish patriot leaders, owed their unique status in political life to two entirely distinct and apparently antagonistic causes. Their wealth they derived from the manner in which they had contrived to wedge themselves into a place in the commercial life of the 'Saxon enemy,' assimilating his ideas and adopting his methods, until they often proved the most ruthless of the two races in pushing to its furthest limits their powers of exploitation. Their political influence they derived from their readiness at all times to do lip service to the cause of Irish nationality, which in their phraseology meant simply the transfer of the seat of government from London to Dublin, and the consequent transfer to their own or their relatives' pockets of some portion of those legislative fees and lawyers' pickings then, as at present, expended among the Cockneys. With such men at the helm it is no wonder that the patriot parties of Ireland have always ended their journey upon the rock of disaster. Beginning by accepting a social system abhorrent to the best traditions of a Celtic people, they next abandoned as impossible the realization of national independence. By the first act they set the seal of their approval upon a system founded upon the robbery of their countrymen, and by the second they bound up the destinies of their country with the fate of an Empire in the humiliation of whose piratical rulers lies the Irish people's only chance of national and social redemption.

As compensation for this gross betrayal the middle-class politicians offer—Home Rule. To exactly analyze what Home Rule would confer on Ireland is a somewhat difficult task, since every one interprets the 'thing' in his own way and according to his own peculiar bent. Perhaps the safest way, and at any rate the one least open to objection, will be to regard as Home Rule the Bill introduced by Mr. Gladstone. As this scheme represents the utmost that the statesmanlike prowess of Mr. Parnell, with a solid phalanx of eighty-six members behind him, could wrest from the fear or favor of English Liberalism, it is surely safe enough to assume that no other merely political body from Ireland is ever likely to improve upon this concession by any alliance with either of the great factions who watch over the interests of the English propertied class. Home Rule proposed to establish in Ireland a domestic legislature, that would be carefully divested of all those powers and attributes which by the common consent of civilized peoples are regarded as properly belonging to the sphere and functions of government; that would have no power in controlling diplomacy, post-office, commerce, telegraphs, coinage, customs and excise, weights and measures, copyrights and patents, succession to the Crown, or army, navy, militia or Volunteers.

The only conceivable result of such a state of affairs would have been to create in Ireland a host of place-hunters and government officials who, secure in the enjoyment of a good income themselves, would have always acted as a barrier between the people and their oppressors. As a method whereby the English legislature might have been relieved of some of its duties at home, and thus left more free to pursue its policy of plunder and aggression abroad, it ought to have delighted the heart of the Jingo politicians. That they were too dunderheaded to see their opportunity is a mercy for which far-seeing Irish democrats can never be sufficiently thankful.

The second Home Rule Bill was slightly more democratic than the first, therefore the Government made no effort to force it upon the Upper House. The English Liberal Party—the most treacherous political party in Europe—has always had two favorite devices for destroying obnoxious proposals of reform. First: Unscrupulous slander and opposition; Second: Theoretical acceptance of the principle of reform, but indefinite postponement of its practical realization, continued on one pretext or another until the hearts of the reformers are broken and their organization disrupted. The first was defeated by the genius of Parnell, how well the second method has succeeded let the present political chaos of Ireland testify.

Realizing that, taken on its own merits, Home Rule is simply a mockery of Irish national aspirations, our middle-class leaders have industriously instilled into the public mind the belief that the advent of Home Rule would mean the immediate establishment of manufactures and the opening up of mines, etc., in every part of Ireland. This seems to them the highest possible ideal—an Irish society composed of employers making fortunes and workers grinding out their lives for a weekly wage. But, to say the least, the men who talk in this manner must either be wofully ignorant of the conditions of modern industry, or else, for some private reason of their own, are wilfully deceiving those who believe in them. To establish industry successfully today in any country requires at least two things, neither of which Ireland possesses, and one of which she never can possess. The first is the possession of the wherewithal to purchase machinery and raw material for the equipment of her factories, and the second is customers to purchase the goods when they are manufactured. Now, we find that England, who has had the start in manufacturing over every other nation, who has been extending her commerce and perfecting her machinery for a hundred and fifty years at least, who has created a nation of highly skilled artisans, adept in every form of industrial achievement—England, the wealthiest country in the world, has brought her industries to such a degree of mechanical perfection, that her customers cannot keep her going. She can supply goods of every description much quicker than the world is able to purchase and consume them, and as a direct consequence of this vast producing power, she is compelled every few years to either wholly or partially stop her machinery and close her factories, to discharge her artisan subjects, and compel them to walk about in enforced idleness and semi-starvation until such time as the goods they have produced are purchased and consumed by other people—their customers.

Bear this in mind, and remember also, that Germany, France, Italy, Belgium, Austria, Russia, every state on the continent of Europe and America, India, China and Japan, are all entering into the struggle; that each of them is striving hard, not only to provide what it had formerly relied on England to provide, but also to beat England out of the markets of the world. Remember that for all those countries, the great difficulty is to find customers, that the oldest-established firm in the business—viz., the British Empire—finds that her customers cannot keep her mills and factories going. Remember all this, and then tell me how poor Ireland, exhausted and drained of her life-blood at every pore, with a population almost wholly agricultural and unused to mechanical pursuits, is to establish new factories, and where she is to find the customers to keep them going. She cannot create new markets. This world is only limited after all, and the nations of Europe are pushing their way into its remote corners so rapidly, that in a few years at most, the entire world will have been exhausted as a market for their wares.

Go to the factory towns, to the shipbuilding centres, to the coal mines, to the trade unions, or to the Stock Exchanges of England, the continent of Europe or America, and everywhere you will hear the same cry: 'The supply of cotton and linen goods, of ironwork, of coal and of ships, of goods of every description, is exceeding the demand; we must work short time, we must reduce the worker's wages, we must close our factories—there is [*sic*] not enough customers to keep our machinery going.' In face of such facts, the thoughtful Irish patriot will throw rant aside and freely recognize that it is impossible for Ireland to do what those other countries cannot do, with their greater advantages, viz., to attain prosperity by establishing a manufacturing system in a world-market already glutted with every conceivable kind of commodity. It is well also to remember that even under the most favorable circumstances, even if by some miracle we were able to cover the green fields of Erin with huge, ugly factories, with chimneys belching forth volumes of poisonous smoke and coating the island with a sooty desolation—even then we would quickly find that under the conditions born of the capitalistic system our one hope of keeping our feet as a manufacturing nation, would depend upon our ability to work longer and harder for a lower wage than the other nations of Europe, in order that our middle class may have the opportunity of selling their goods at a lower price than their competitors. This is equivalent to saying that our chance of making Ireland a manufacturing country depends upon us becoming the lowest blacklegs in Europe. Even then the efforts would be doomed to failure, for the advent of the yellow man into the competitive arena, the sudden development of the capitalistic system in China and Japan, has rendered forever impossible the uprise of another industrial nation in Europe.[1]

Again, it is said we need not perhaps establish industry or try it, but we can at least establish peasant proprietary, and

[1] The first edition included the following sentences deleted from this edition: 'But, we are told by some of our leaders, "if we cannot compete with other countries in the world-market, we can at least produce for ourselves." Under no circumstances can we do so without bringing upon ourselves disasters as great as those we wish to escape from. With greater advantages and larger experience in the field than we possess, the capitalists of other countries can easily undersell our goods, even in the home market, and if in order to give our manufacturers a chance we were to adopt protection (impossible under Home Rule), the result would be to immediately increase the price of every kind of goods while no one would benefit except the few capitalists for whose sake our Irish workers would be working harder and longer and paying higher prices than before.'

make every man the owner of his own farm, let every man live, if not under his own vine and fig tree, at least upon his own potato patch. In the first place, I consider such an act to be, even if practicable, one of very questionable justice. To make the land of a country the property of a class, is to my mind equally iniquitous, whether that class number a few hundreds or a few thousands. The land of a country belongs of right to the people of that country, and not to any particular class, nor even to any single generation of the people. The private ownership of land by the landlord class is an injustice to the whole community, but the creation of a peasant proprietary would only tend to stereotype and consecrate that injustice, since it would leave out of account the entire laboring class as well as the dispossessed millions of former tenants who[m] landlord rule had driven into the Irish towns or across the seas.

It is, of course, manifestly impossible to reinstate the Irish people on the lands from which they have been driven, but that fact only lends additional point to the demand for the nationalization of land in the hands of the Irish state. Setting that fact aside, however, have our advocates of peasant proprietary really considered the economic tendencies of the time, and the development of the mechanical arts in the agricultural world? The world is progressive, and peasant proprietary, which a hundred years ago might have been a boon, would now be powerless to save from ruin the agriculture of Ireland. The day of small farmers, as of small capitalists, is gone, and wherever they are still found, they find it impossible to compete with the improved machinery and mammoth farms of America and Australia. Whereas each Irish farm is burdened with the support of its field workers for the entire 365 days in the year, the capitalist farmer of the States hires his 'hands' by the hundred for harvesting operations, and discharges them immediately it is completed, thus reducing to one-fourth the annual wages bill of his workers.

How are our small farmers to compete with a state of matters like this, or like unto that revealed in the report of the American Social Science Association, even as far back as 1878? It tells how science and invention, after devoting so much time to industry, have turned their attention to agriculture, and as a result have effected almost a revolution in that branch of human activity. Ploughs which, driven by horses, plough more than five acres per day, or the extent of many an Irish farm, and steam ploughs which do much more; machines for sowing seeds, with which a boy and horse can do three times the work of a man, and do it much better; reaping machines, with which a man with one or two pairs of horses can do the work of at least sixty men with reaping hooks; reaping machines which not only cut the harvest, but tie it as well, are now so common in England and America as to fail to attract attention, and we hear on good authority of machines which cut, thrash, winnow, and sack it, without the intervention of any other human hands than those of the engineer who tends the machine. In cutting the corn, a man or boy, with a horse and machine, can do the work of twenty men, cutting an acre an hour.

All this, be it remembered, is only possible to the farmer who holds his thousands of acres. The first cost of any one of those machines would be enough to ruin the average small farmer in Ireland, and the result is that while he is painfully laboring on his farm, his American competitor can bring in his harvest, send it thousands of miles by railroad, load it into ships, send it across the Atlantic, and eventually sell it practically at our doors as cheap as, and cheaper than, our home produce. The competition of New Zealand beef and frozen mutton has already inflicted incalculable harm upon the Irish cattle trade, and within the last few months I have received private information of a contract entered into with the Peninsular and Oriental Steamship Company to transport butter from the huge cattle ranches of Australia to any port in Great Britain and Ireland at a price that spells ruin to the dairy farms of these countries. While, then, in order to avoid even the appearance of injustice, we may rigidly respect those 'rights of property' in land our peasant farmers have acquired by purchase, we must recognize that peasant proprietary in itself, offers no hope of a free and unanxious life—not even to the peasant proprietor.

Ireland's Future

Ere we can forecast the future we must understand the present, and bring a just sense of proportion to our review of the history of the past. What, then, are the conditions which govern life in Ireland today, and of what are those conditions the outcome? According to the most eminent authorities who have ever dealt with the subject, the soil of Ireland is capable of sustaining a population many times larger than she has ever borne upon its surface, yet Ireland is in a state of chronic starvation. Every ship that leaves our ports is laden down with harvests for human consumption, while the people whose strong hands have reaped that harvest pine in wretchedness and want, or fly from the shores of this fertile island as from the arid sands of a desert. The landlord class, infatuated with that madness which always precedes destruction, press for their rents to the uttermost farthing wherever they can wheedle or coerce a too compliant legislature and executive to support them in their exactions. The capitalist farmer, driven to the wall by the stress of competition, seeks in vain to maintain his foothold in life by an unceasing struggle with the lord of the soil on one hand and a ruthless oppression of the laborer on the other; the small farmer, bereft entirely of hope for the future, settles despairingly into a state of social wretchedness for which no savage land can furnish a parallel; the agricultural laborer, with his fellow in the towns, takes his strength, his brains, his physical and intellectual capabilities to the market, and offers them to his wealthier fellow-creatures, to be exploited in return for a starvation wage. On all sides anarchy and oppression reign supreme, until one could scarcely wonder if even the most orthodox amongst us were tempted to echo the saying of the Spanish Don Juan Aguila after the battle of Kinsale: 'Surely Christ never died for this people!'

These are the conditions under which life is endured in Ireland today. From what do such conditions spring? There are two things necessary for the maintenance of life in Ireland, as in every other country. They are land and labor. Possessed of these two essentials, the human race has at its command all the factors requisite for the well-being of the species. From the earth labor extracts alike its foods and the mineral wealth with which it contrives to construct and adorn its habitations and prepare its raiment. Therefore the possession of the soil is everywhere the first requisite of life. Granting this as a proposition too self-evident to need any elaborate demonstration, we at once arrive at the conclusion that since the soil is so necessary to our existence the first care of every well-regulated community ought to be to preserve the use of that soil, and the right to freely share in its fruits, to every member of the community, present or prospective, born or unborn.

The moment when the land of a country passes from the care of the community as a public trust, and from being the common property of the entire people becomes the private property of individuals, marks the beginning of slavery for that people and of oppression for that country. With the land held as the property of individuals there are immediately created two antagonistic classes in society—one holding the land and demanding from the other a rent for permission to live upon it, and the other driven by the constant increase of their own numbers to offer larger and larger shares of the produce of their labor as tribute to the first class, who thus become masters of the lives of their fellow-beings. With the land held as the common property of the people an abundant harvest would be eagerly welcomed as an addition to the wealth of the community, guaranteeing against want every one of its members. With the land held as private property the abundant harvest must be sold to satisfy the exactions of the holder of the soil, and as he jingles in his pockets the result of the sale of his tenants' produce the families who reaped it may be perishing of want.

As one crime begets another, so one economic blunder invariably brings in its train a series of blunders, each one more fruitful of disaster than the first. When the production of food for public use was abandoned in favor of production of agricultural produce for private sale and private profit, it was almost inevitable that the production of almost every other necessary of life should be subjected to the same conditions. Thus we find that food, clothes, houses, and furniture are not produced in order that people may be fed, clad, sheltered or made comfortable, but rather in order that the class who have obtained possession of the land, machinery, workshops, and stores necessary for the production of these essentials should be thereby enabled to make a comfortable living at the expense of their fellow creatures. If the landlord and employing class think they can make a rent or profit by allowing the people to feed, clothe or house themselves then the latter are allowed to do so under the direction of the former—when, where, and how the masters please. If, on the contrary, they imagine it will pay them better to refuse that right (as they do in every eviction, strike, or lock-out), then they do refuse that permission, and their countrymen go forth starving, their children die of want before their eyes, and their wives and mothers pine in wretchedness and misery in what their forefathers were wont to call the 'Isle of the Blest.'

By the operation of certain historic causes the workers have been deprived of everything by which they can maintain life, and are thus compelled to seek their livelihood by the sale of their capacity for work, their labor power. The worker thus finds that the most essential condition which he must perform in order that he may possess his life is to sell a part of that life into the service and for the profit of another. Whether he sells it by the hour, the day, the week, or the month is immaterial—sell it he must or else starve.

Now, the worker is a human being, with all the powers and capabilities of a human being within him, just as is a landlord, a capitalist, or any other ornament of society. But when he approaches the capitalist in order to complete that bargain, which means the sale of his life piecemeal in order that he may enjoy it as a whole, he finds that he must carefully divest himself of all claims to be considered as a human being, and offer himself upon the market subject to the same law as governs the purchase or sale of any inanimate, soulless commodity, such as a pair of boots, a straw hat or a frock coat. That is to say, the price he will receive for this piecemeal sale of himself will depend upon how many more are compelled by hunger to make the same horrible bargain.

In like manner with the farmer seeking to rent a farm in the open market. Each competitor seeks to outbid the other, until the rent fixed is usually out of all proportion to the price which will in the future be obtained for the produce of the farm bidden for. The agriculturist finds that in years of universal plenty, when throughout the world the earth brings forth its fruit in teeming profusion, the excess of supply over effective demand operates to lower the price of his farm produce, until it scarcely repays his labor in garnering it, and in times of scarcity, when a good price might be obtained, he has little to sell, his customers have not the wherewithal to buy, and the landlord or the money lender are as relentless as ever in their exactions.

As a remedy for such an array of evils Home Rule stands revealed as a glaring absurdity. The Home Rule parties either ignore the question altogether or else devote their attention to vain attempts to patch up the system with schemes of reform which each day tends to discredit more and more. The tenant who seeks in the Land Court for a judicial valuation of his holding finds that in face of the steady fall in agricultural prices (assisted by preferential railway rates in favour of foreign produce) the 'fair' rent of one year becomes the rack-rent of another, and the tenant who avails himself of the purchase clauses of the Land Acts finds that he has only escaped from the personal tyranny of a landlord to have his veins sucked by the impersonal power of the money lender.

Confronted with such facts the earnest Irish worker turns in dismay and joins his voice to that of the uncompromising Nationalist in seeking from the advocate of an Irish Socialist Republic the clue to the labyrinthine puzzle of modern economic conditions. The problem is a grave and difficult one, alike from the general ignorance of its controlling conditions and because of the multiplicity of vested interests which must be attacked and overthrown at every forward step towards its solution. The solution herein set forth is therefore not guaranteed to be absolutely perfect in all its details, but only to furnish a rough draft of a scheme of reform by means of which the ground may be prepared for that revolutionary change in the structure of society which can alone establish an approximation to an ideally just social system.

The agriculture of Ireland can no longer compete with the

scientifically equipped farmers of America, therefore the only hope that now remains is to abandon competition altogether as a rule of life, to organize agriculture as a public service under the control of boards of management elected by the agricultural population (no longer composed of farmers and laborers, but of free citizens with equal responsibility and equal honor), and responsible to them and the nation at large, and with all the mechanical and scientific aids to agriculture the entire resources of the nation can place at their disposal. Let the produce of Irish soil go first to feed the Irish people, and after a sufficient store has been retained to insure of that being accomplished, let the surplus be exchanged with other countries in return for those manufactured goods Ireland needs but does not herself produce. Thus we will abolish at one stroke the dread of foreign competition and render perfectly needless any attempt to create an industrial hell in Ireland under the specious pretext of 'developing our resources.'

Apply to manufacture the same social principle, let the co-operative organization of the workers replace the war of classes under capitalism and transform the capitalist himself from an irresponsible hunter after profit into a public servant, fulfilling a public function and under public control. Recognize the right of all to an equal opportunity to develop to their fullest capacity all the powers and capabilities inherent in them by guaranteeing to all our countrymen and women, the weak as well as the strong, the simple as well as the cunning, the honest equally with the unscrupulous, the fullest, freest, and most abundant human life intelligently organized society can confer upon any of its members.

'But,' you will say, 'this means a Socialist Republic; this is subversive of all the institutions upon which the British Empire is founded—this cannot be realized without national independence.' Well, I trust no one will accuse me of a desire to fan into flame the dying embers of national hatred when I state as my deliberate and conscientious conviction that the Irish democracy ought to strive consistently after the separation of their country from the yoke that links her destinies with those of the British Crown. The interests of labor all the world over are identical, it is true, but it is also true that each country had better work out its own salvation on the lines most congenial to its own people.

The national and racial characteristics of the English and Irish people are different, their political history and traditions are antagonistic, the economic development of the one is not on a par with the other, and, finally, although they have been in the closest contact for seven hundred years, yet the Celtic Irishman is today as much of an insolute [*sic*] problem to even the most friendly English as on the day when the two countries were first joined in unholy wedlock. No Irish revolutionist worth his salt would refuse to lend a hand to the Social Democracy of England in the effort to uproot the social system of which the British Empire is the crown and apex, and in like manner no English Social Democrat fails to recognize clearly that the crash which would betoken the fall of the ruling classes in Ireland would sound the tocsin for the revolt of the disinherited in England.[1]

But on whom devolves the task of achieving that downfall of the ruling classes in Ireland? On the Irish people. But who are the Irish people? Is it the dividend-hunting capitalist with the phraseology of patriotism on his lips and the spoil wrung from sweated Irish toilers in his pockets; is it the scheming lawyer—most immoral of all classes; is it the slum landlord who denounces rackrenting in the country and practises it in the towns; is it any one of these sections who to-day dominate Irish politics? Or is it not rather the Irish Working Class—the

[1] The next two paragraphs read as follows in the first edition: 'But, while awaiting the propitious moment there remains much to be done in the political field – work that can be pushed forward irrespective of Government opposition, work to which the Irish people can devote themselves, in open public organizations while there is a rag of the constitution left. Pending the complete public organization of agriculture let our representatives in Parliament press for the establishment in every rural district of depots for agricultural machinery of the newest and most improved pattern. Let such depots be established at the expense of the state and for the use of the agricultural population to whom the needful machinery for speedy and effective harvesting, etc., shall be supplied on hire at a charge carefully calculated to cover the cost of wear and tear of maintenance and construction alone. Take advantage of every political development to demand the nationalization of Irish railways, and when effected abolish at once the unfair charges by which the railway companies seek to injure home growers in favour of foreign importers.'

only secure foundation on which a free nation can be reared—the Irish Working Class which has borne the brunt of every political struggle, and gained by none, and which is today the only class in all Ireland which has no interest to serve in perpetuating either the political or social forms of oppression—the British Connection or the capitalist system. The Irish Working Class must emancipate itself, and in emancipating itself it must, perforce, free its country. The act of social emancipation requires the conversion of the land and instruments of production from private property into the public or common property of the entire nation. This necessitates a social system of the most absolute democracy, and in establishing that necessary social system the Working Class must grapple with and destroy every vestige of every form of government which could interfere with the most unfettered control by the people of Ireland of all the resources of their country.

On the Working Class of Ireland, therefore, devolves the task of conquering political representation for their class as the preliminary step towards the conquest of political power. This task can only be safely entered upon by men and women who recognize that the first actions of a revolutionary army must harmonize in principle with those likely to be its last, and that, therefore, no revolutionists can safely invite the co-operation of men or classes, whose ideals are not theirs and whom, therefore, they may be compelled to fight at some future critical stage of the journey to freedom. To this category belongs every section of the propertied class, and every individual of those classes who believes in the righteousness of his class position. The freedom of the Working Class must be the work of the Working Class. And let it be remembered that timidity in the slave induces audacity in the tyrant, but the virility and outspokenness of the revolutionist ever frightens the oppressor himself to hide his loathsomeness under the garb of reform. And thus remembering, fight for your class at every point.

Our people are flying to the uttermost ends of the earth; seek to retain them at home by reducing the hours of labor wherever you have the power and by supporting every demand for legislative restriction. Your Irish railways employ thousands of men, whose working hours average twelve per day.

Were they restricted to a forty-eight-hour week of labor, employment would be provided for thousands of Irishmen who at present are driven exiles from their native land. Let your representatives demand an eight-hour bill for railways.[1] Our Irish municipalities and other public bodies controlled by popular vote employ also many thousands of men. What are their hours of labor? On the average ten, and their wages just above starvation point. Insist upon the Irish corporations establishing the eight-hour day in all their works. They at least do not need to fear foreign competition. If you have no vote in the corporation you can at least help to hound off the political platform elsewhere every so-called patriot who refuses to perform this act of justice. Every Irish corporation which declines to institute an eight-hours' working day at a decent wage for its employees has virtually entered into a conspiracy with the British government to expatriate the Irish people, rather than pay an additional halfpenny in the pound on the rates. In all our cities the children of the laboring class are dying off before their time for lack of wholesome nourishing food. As our municipalities and public trusts provide water for the people free of direct payment and charge the cost upon the rates, let them also provide at our schools, free breakfasts, dinners, and teas to the children in attendance there, and pay for it from the same source. No matter what may be the moral character of the parent, let us at least save the helpless children of our race from physical and mental degeneracy, and save our teachers from the impossible task of forcing education upon a child whose brain is enfeebled by the starvation of its body. As the next step in organization, let the corporations and public bodies everywhere throughout the country establish depots for the supply of bread and all the necessaries of life to the people, at cost price and without the intervention of the middleman.[2]

[1] Instead of the foregoing sentence, the first edition read as follows: 'Pledge every Irish representative to support an Eight-Hour Bill for railways; if he refuses you will know that he considers profits as more sacred than patriotism, and would sacrifice his country on the altar of greed.'

[2] One sentence from the first edition is here deleted. It read: 'To save our struggling farmers from the merciless bleeding of our banking system and money-lenders in general, let our representatives in Parliament force

When, in addition to the foregoing reforms, we have demanded the abolition of our hateful poor-house system, and the imposition of a heavy and steeply graduated income tax on all incomes over £400 a year, in order to provide comfortable pensions for the aged, the infirm, and widows and orphans, we will have aroused a new spirit in the people; we will have based our revolutionary movement upon a correct appreciation of the needs of the hour, as well as upon the vital principles of economic justice and uncompromising nationality; we will, as the true revolutionist should ever do, have called into action on our side the entire sum of all the forces and factors of social and political discontent. By the use of the revolutionary ballot we will have made the very air of Ireland as laden with 'treason,' as fully charged with the spirit of revolt, as it is today with the cant of compromise and the mortal sin of flunkeyism; and thus we will have laid a substantial groundwork for more effective action in the future, while to those whom we must remove in our onward march the pledge of our faith in the Social Revolution will convey the assurance that if we crush their profit-making enterprises today, yet when the sun dawns upon our freedom, if they have served their fellow creatures loyally in the hour of strife, they and their children and their children's children will be guaranteed against want and privation for all time by the safest guarantee man ever received, the guarantee backed by all the gratitude, the loyal hearts, the brains and industry of the Irish people, under the Irish Socialist Republic.

---

forward the legislative abolition of our present banking houses and the suppression of all forms of interest mongering, and the establishment in their stead of state banking institutions, with popularly elected boards of directors, issuing loans at rates of interest as low as is consistent with economic soundness.' It will be noted that much of the deleted matter is rather bald reassertion of I.S.R.P. policy statements.

10. THE NEW EVANGEL PREACHED TO IRISH TOILERS

The New Evangel *is of importance as Connolly's own selection of what he took to be the most important of his articles to have appeared in his first paper,* The Workers' Republic. *It was initially published in its entirety in* The Workers' Republic *for March 1901, the paper having become a monthly; the individual initial appearances are dated in the ensuing text. Although some of the themes discussed would have been relevant to Part I, it has seemed desirable to let Connolly's own anthologizing stand, and to have the publication take its place as an evangel, as its name implies, indicating the form of appeal Connolly chose to make to his Irish audience. Although he made further selections from his writings in* The Workers' Republic *this was the only such anthology which he reprinted. It was issued in pamphlet form as a supplement to* The Workers' Republic *for April 1903, and was reissued by him as a 'Harp Library' pamphlet in 1908. It presents no textual problems and is taken from its 1901 publication.*

There is a New Evangel
At this moment preached in France,
And the priests of its great doctrines
Despise the tyrants' glance:
Oh! that holy gospel echoes
From distant sea to sea!
It teaches Men are Brothers,
It teaches all are free.

Joseph Brennan, in *Irish Tribune*, 1848.

STATE MONOPOLY VERSUS SOCIALISM

[*JUNE 10th, 1899*]

One of the most significant signs of our times is the readiness with which our struggling middle class turns to schemes of State or Municipal ownership and control, for relief from the economic pressure under which it is struggling. Thus we find in England demands for the nationalisation of the telephone system, for the extension of municipal enterprise in the use of electricity, for the extension of the parcel system of the Post Office, for the nationalisation of railways and canals. In Ireland we have our middle class reformers demanding state help for agriculture, state purchase of lands, arterial drainage, state construction of docks, piers and harbours, state aid for the fishing industry, state control of the relations between agricultural tenant and landlord, and also nationalisation of railways and canals. There is a certain section of Socialists, chiefly in England, who never tire of hailing all such demands for state activity as a sign of the growth of the Socialist spirit among the middle class, and therefore worthy of all the support the working-class democracy can give. In some degree such a view seems justifiable. The fact that large sections of the capitalist class join in demanding the intervention of the State in industry is a sure sign that they, at least, have lost the overweening belief in the all-sufficiency of private enterprise which characterised their class a generation ago; and that they have been forced to recognise the fact that there are a multitude of things in which the 'brain,' 'self-reliance,' and 'personal responsibility' of the capitalist are entirely unnecessary. To argue that, since in such enterprises the private property-holder is dispensed with, therefore he can be dispensed with in all other forms of industrial activity, is logical enough and we really fail to see in what manner the advocates of capitalist society can continue to clamour for such state ownership as that alluded to—ownership in which the private capitalist is seen to be superfluous, and yet continue to argue that in all other forms of industry the private capitalist is indispensable. For it must be remembered that every function of a useful character performed by the State or Municipality to-day was at one time performed by private individuals for profit, and in conformity with the then generally accepted belief that it could not be satisfactorily performed except by private individuals.

But all this notwithstanding, we would, without undue desire to carp or cavil, point out that to call such demands

'Socialistic' is in the highest degree misleading. Socialism properly implies above all things the co-operative control by the workers of the machinery of production; without this co-operative control the public ownership by the State is not Socialism, it is only State Capitalism. The demands of the middle-class reformers, from the Railway Reform League down, are simply plans to facilitate the business transactions of the capitalist class. State Telephones—to cheapen messages in the interest of the middle class who are the principal users of the telephone system; State Railways—to cheapen carriage of goods in the interest of the middle-class trader; State Construction of piers, docks, etc.,—in the interest of the middle-class merchant; in fact every scheme now advanced in which the help of the State is invoked is a scheme to lighten the burden of the capitalist—trader, manufacturer, or farmer. Were they all in working order tomorrow the change would not necessarily benefit the working class; we would still have in our state industries, as in the Post Office to-day, the same unfair classification of salaries, and the same despotic rule of an irresponsible head. Those who worked most and hardest would still get the least remuneration, and the rank and file would still be deprived of all voice in the ordering of their industry, just the same as in all private enterprises.

Therefore, we repeat, state ownership and control is not necessarily Socialism—if it were, then the Army, the Navy, the Police, the Judges, the Gaolers, the Informers, and the Hangmen, would all be Socialist functionaries, as they are all State officials—but the ownership by the State of all the land and materials for labour, combined with the co-operative control by the workers of such land and materials, would be Socialism.

Schemes of state and municipal ownership, if unaccompanied by this co-operative principle, are but schemes for the perfectioning of the mechanism of capitalist government – schemes to make the capitalist regime respectable and efficient for the purposes of the capitalist; in the second place they represent the class-conscious instinct of the business man who feels that capitalist should not prey upon capitalist, while all may unite to prey upon the workers. The chief immediate sufferers from private ownership of railways, canals, and telephones are the middle class shopkeeping element, and their resentment at the tariffs imposed is but the capitalist political expression of the old adage that 'dog should not eat dog.'

It will thus be seen that an immense gulf separates the 'nationalising' proposals of the middle class from the 'socialising' demands of the revolutionary working class. The first proposes to endow a Class State—repository of the political power of the Capitalist Class—with certain powers and functions to be administered in the common interest of the possessing class; the second proposes to subvert the Class State and replace it with the Socialist State, representing organised society—the Socialist Republic. To the cry of the middle-class reformers, 'Make this, or that, the property of the government,' we reply, 'Yes, in proportion as the workers are ready to make the government their property.'

SOCIALISM AND RELIGION

The Known and the Unknowable [*June 17th, 1899*]

Perhaps upon no point are the doctrines of Socialism so much misunderstood, and so much misrepresented, as in their relation to Religion. When driven into a corner upon every other point at issue; when from the point of view of economics, of politics, or of morality, he is worsted in argument, this question of Religion invariably forms the final entrenchment of the enemy of Socialism—especially in Ireland.

'But it is opposed to Religion,' constitutes the last word, the ultimate shift, of the supporters of capitalism, driven from every other line of defence but stubbornly refusing to yield. 'Socialism is Atheism, and all Socialists are Atheists,' or 'Your Socialism is but a fine name to cover your Atheism in its attacks upon the Church;' all these phrases are so commonly heard in the course of every dispute upon the merits or demerits of the Socialist doctrine that we require no apology for introducing them here in order to point out their illogical character. So far from it being true that Socialism and Atheism are synonymous terms, it is a curious and instructive fact that almost all the prominent propagandists of Freethought in our generation have been, and are, most determined enemies of Socialism. The late Charles Bradlaugh, in his time the most aggressive Freethinker in England, was to the last resolute and uncompromising in his hatred of Socialism; G. W. Foote, the present editor of the *Freethinker*, the national organ of English Secularism, is a bitter enemy of Socialism, and the late Colonel Bob Ingersoll, the chief apostle of Freethought doctrine in the United States, was well known as an apologist of capitalism.

On the continent of Europe many other quite similar cases might be recorded, but those already quoted will suffice, as being those most easily verified by our readers. It is a suggestive and amusing fact that in the motley ranks of the defenders of Capitalism the professional propagandists of Freethought are comrades-in-arms of His Holiness the Pope; the ill-reasoned and inconclusive Encyclicals lately issued against Socialism make of the hierarchy of the Catholic Church belated camp followers in the armies marching under the banners raised by the agnostic exponents of the individualist philosophy. Obviously, even the meanest intelligence can see that there need be no identity of thought between the Freethinker as such, and the Socialist as a Socialist. From what then does the popular misconception arise? In the first instance from the interested attempt of the propertied classes to create such a prejudice against Socialism as might deter the working class from giving ear to its doctrines—an attempt too often successful; and in the second instance, from a misconception of the attitude of the Socialist party towards theological dogma in general. The Socialist Republican Party of Ireland prohibits the discussion of theological or anti-theological questions at its meetings, public or private. This is in conformity with the practice of the chief Socialist parties of the world, which have frequently, in Germany for example, declared Religion to be a private matter, and outside the scope of Socialist action. Modern Socialism, in fact, as it exists in the minds of its leading exponents, and as it is held and worked for by an increasing number of enthusiastic adherents throughout the civilised world, has an essentially material, matter-of-fact foundation. We do not mean that its supporters are necessarily materialists in the vulgar, and merely anti-theological, sense of the term, but that they do not base their Socialism upon any interpretation of the language or meaning of Scripture, nor upon the real or supposed intentions of a beneficent Deity. They as a party neither affirm nor deny those things, but leave it to the individual conscience of each member to determine what beliefs on such questions they shall hold. As a political party they wisely prefer to take their stand upon the actual phenomena of social life as they can be observed in operation amongst us today, or as they can be traced in the recorded facts of history. If any special interpretation of the meanings of Scripture tends to influence human thought in the direction of Socialism, or is found to be on a plane with the postulates of Socialist doctrine, then the scientific Socialist considers that the said interpretation is stronger because of its identity with the teachings of Socialism, but he does not necessarily believe that Socialism is stronger, or its position more impregnable, because of its theological ally. He realises that the facts upon which his Socialist faith are based are strong enough in themselves to withstand every shock, and attacks from every quarter, and therefore, whilst he is at all times willing to accept help from every extraneous source, he will only accept it on one condition, viz., that he is not to be required in return to identify his cause with any other whose discomfiture might also involve Socialism in discredit. This is the main reason why Socialists fight shy of theological dogmas and religions generally; because we feel that Socialism is based upon a series of facts requiring only unassisted human reason to grasp and master in all their details, whereas Religion of every kind is admittedly based upon 'faith' in the occurrence in past ages of a series of phenomena inexplicable by any process of mere human reasoning. Obviously, therefore, to identify Socialism with Religion would be to abandon at once that universal, non-sectarian character which to-day we find indispensable to working-class unity, as it would mean that our members would be required to conform to one religious creed, as well as to one specific economic faith—a course of action we have no intention of entering upon as it would inevitably entangle us in the disputes of the warring sects of the world, and thus lead to the disintegration of the Socialist Party.

Socialism, as a party, bases itself upon its knowledge of facts, of economic truths, and leaves the building up of religious ideals or faiths to the outside public, or to its individual members if they so will. It is neither Freethinker nor Christian, Turk nor Jew, Buddhist nor Idolater, Mahommedan nor Parsee—it is only HUMAN.

THE ECONOMIC BASIS OF POLITICS

The Stomach, not the Brain [*August 12th, 1899*]

Nothing more strikingly illustrates the crude and unscientific theories of the ordinary middle class politician than the desperate attempts at present being made to build up a great political party in Ireland on the lines of the late Home Rule movement. Apparently all sections of the Home Rule party are possessed with the belief that great political movements can be constructed at will, and that an effective, aggressive political force may have its origin, not deep down in the daily life of the people, but in the brains of some half dozen gentlemen in parliament. Viewed from this standpoint the toiling multitudes are mere automata, and the really effective national force is to be found in the men whom the Home Rule press and orators point out to the multitude as 'leaders.' The truth that the political movements of a country spring from the pulsations of its economic life; that all political parties are the instruments of a class, and are great and powerful only in the proportion in which the development of the struggle for existence forces their particular class interest upon the majority of the nation as a dominant factor in their daily life—all this seems to be a quite unheard-of philosophy amongst capitalist politicians.

Yet a slight survey of the history of the world in general, or of Ireland in particular, could not fail to bring the truth of this eminently Socialist doctrine home to the mind of the thoughtful student of events. The great political organisations which have successfully revolutionised the systems or governments under which they lived, have had their origin, not in the brains of mighty leaders, but in the daily and hourly needs of the multitude, and have acquired force and power only in so far as those needs became sharp and pressing enough to goad that sluggard multitude to action. When at such a crisis there arose a man lucky enough, or astute enough, to make himself the mouthpiece of the discontented multitude; to coin its inarticulate groanings into political phraseology, and give its hunger-inspired desire for change an intelligent formulation, then such a man became a 'great leader,' and the organisation following the course he advocated the leading political force. To the minds of the superficial middle class thinkers—always ready to believe that the world turned around their heroes and successful persons as upon its axis—the leaders had created the movements which they led; to the mind of the scientific Socialist the leaders and the movements were both the product of the quickening of intellect caused by social conditions adversely affecting the life of the people at large.

Examine the great revolutionary movements of history and you will find that in all cases they sprang from unsatisfactory social conditions, and had their origin in a desire for material well-being. In other words, the seat of progress and source of revolution is not in the brain, but in the stomach. The fact that this truth has hitherto been obscured, or even denied; that the pioneers of progress uniformly clothed their political demands in the most idealistic language and the most flowery phraseology; or that they constantly appealed for the support of 'all unselfish and generous souls,' rather than to commonplace interests, only proves that we are all too prone to hide even from ourselves the real nature of our impelling desires, and, even when most stubbornly following our grossest instincts, to throw around our actions all the glamour of 'spiritual cravings,' or 'patriotic hopes.'

The power and unconquerable optimism of the Socialist party is due to their recognition of this materialist basis of history, this economic basis of politics. Knowing that their ultimate ideal and immediate demands are in line with the progress of the human race towards prosperity, and that every scheme for better social conditions at all likely to effect its purpose must be of the nature of a step in their direction, Socialists cannot lose courage, because even in the midst of temporary defeat they know that the needs of the workers, who are in the majority, will eventually impel them into line with the Social-Revolutionary forces. From this fact our Irish politicians—and revolutionists—may gain, not comfort perhaps, but wisdom. The history of the American Revolution, the French Revolution, the Irish Volunteers, the risings of 1798, 1848, and the Irish Land League, all bear out our argument upon the economic basis of great political movements.

The American Revolution was a revolt against the action of England in throttling the infant industries of America, and came to a head with a tax upon tea—all 'base' material reasons; the French Revolution was the revolt of an oppressed and famished people against outworn, mediæval landlordism (feudalism), and the vexatious taxes upon industry imposed by a corrupt Court; the Irish Volunteer movement was, in its anti-English aspect, a revolt of the Irish manufacturing class against the restrictions put upon their trade by England,—'FREE TRADE, or else' was the motto hung upon their cannon, and when that one point was gained all the 'patriotic enthusiasm' of the leaders vanished; Grattan termed the Volunteers, upon whose backs he had climbed to political eminence, 'an armed rabble,' and the whole movement collapsed as suddenly as it had arisen—the economic basis being gone the patriotism was no longer evident. 1798 was an abortive Irish edition of the French Revolution—despite the lying twaddle of the present day about the society of United Irishmen being a 'Union of ALL CLASSES,' there is not in history any record of a movement, except the Paris Commune, in which the classes and the masses were so sharply divided; 1848 found its inspiration in the promptings of famine—and its failure in the total incapacity of the doctrinaire Young Irelanders to understand the difference between revolutionary action and 'heroic' posings; the Land League found its inspiration in a partial failure of the crops, and in the newly developed competition of America—and the collapse of the Land League came with reduced rents and partial prosperity.

In every case the social condition of the mass of the people was the determining factor in political activity. Where the mass of the people find existing conditions intolerable, and imagine they see a way out, there will be a great political movement; where the social conditions are not so abnormally acute no amount of political oratory, nor yet co-operation of leaders, can produce a movement.

The great Labour uprising at the Irish Local Government elections of 1898 sprang up spontaneously without a leader, and despite the political parties; when the men who supported it have realised the futility of trying to effect any great improvement in their condition by the action of local bodies, they will seek for a political party which can express their class interests upon a national basis—and seeking it find the Socialist Republican Party, ready and equipped for the task. By our action today we are preparing the ground for more aggressive revolutionary action when the working class of Ireland at last recognise in our principles the embodiment of their hopes; firmly grounded upon our knowledge of the economic basis of all political action, we confidently await the day when the ever-increasing pressure of capitalist society shall bring the workers into our ranks—and the destinies of the nation into our hands.

FATHER FINLAY, S.J., AND SOCIALISM

An Exposition of Social Evolution [*July 1st, 1899*]

Those who seek a comprehensive remedy for the sufferings of the working classes look beyond trades unionism. They perceive that they must modify more profoundly the relations between Labour and Capital; to bridge across the chasm dividing them, and so to abolish that rivalry of interest out of which has grown so much inhumanity to man. One class of reformers propose to effect this change by the absolute abolition of private

> capital—by taking capital, or the material instruments of wealth production, out of the hands of the individuals and classes, and making it the property of the community, vesting it in the State. This scheme—the dream of the Socialist—impossible to work out in practice, hopelessly breaking down wherever it has been tried, violates the fundamental conception of all property. What a free man creates by his labour, that is his property; if it is his property he can do with it what he wills—consume it by present use or reserve it for further production. To forbid him the right to reserve it or use it as capital would be to deny him the right to possess property. From this point of view—as well as from others—Socialism is seen to have much in common with slavery.

The above quotation, from the paper on 'Co-operation' read by Father Finlay, S.J. before the fourth annual general meeting of the Maynooth Union, calls for more than a passing notice, is deserving of more intelligent criticism than our capitalist contemporaries have been able to bring to bear upon it. For this reason we propose to place before our readers a brief statement of our position, in so far at least as it is affected by the assertions contained in the paper quoted from above.

We readily allow that no man in Ireland within the clerical body, and few men in Ireland outside the ranks of the adherents of scientific Socialism, can bring to bear upon questions of political economy, and the effect which theories of political economy have had upon the industrial life of the people, such a wealth of knowledge as the reverend gentleman whose paper we are now discussing. The feeble and ineffective efforts of the Home Rule pressmen to criticise the co-operative movement to which Father Finlay devotes so much of his energy and ability is in itself proof enough that, however efficient our journalistic guides may be as caterers to the palate of a reading public ready to forgive every inconsistency of statement, or colouring of fact, if only it is seasoned with a dash of 'patriotism' or 'true religion,' as helps to the intelligent discussion of an economic question they are worse than useless. The economic theories held by the non-Socialist parties of Ireland today and voiced by their publicists on press and platform, are in fact the theories which prevailed in England more than fifty years ago—during the agitation for the repeal of the Corn Laws, and for Free Trade in general. Such ideas are now regarded throughout the remainder of the world as outworn and obsolete; it is only in Ireland they survive, and in Ireland only among men who having failed to keep step with the intellectual march of the world would fain convince themselves that the intellectual incapacity which shuts them off from sympathy with the thought of the age is the distinguishing birth mark of a true Celt. That the criticism of such persons should be of little effect in adding to our knowledge any important truth on an economic subject is, of course, to be expected, and we do not propose to waste our own or our readers' time in discussing them, but the arguments of Father Finlay naturally carrying more weight, deserve, we repeat, a much more serious study.

To begin with we would like to remind the reverend lecturer that he did not place before his hearers such a clear and definite idea of the true Socialist position as he himself possesses. In a lecture delivered in Dublin, before the Statistical Society, some few years ago he, in dealing with the teachings of Karl Marx— the ablest exponent of Socialism the world has seen, and the founder of that school of thought which embraces all the militant Socialist parties of the world—Father Finlay laid before his hearers an exposition of the evolutionary nature of the Socialist doctrine, its historical derivation and materialistic basis, which is not at all compatible with the crudely false conception of Socialism to be found in the foregoing quotation. Modern Socialism, he showed, is not the product of the brains of any man nor of any number of men; it is the legitimate child of a long, drawn-out historical evolution, and its consummation will only be finally possible when that evolutionary process has attained to a suitable degree of development. As capitalist society—the system of wage-labour and 'free contract' between master and man—was only developed according as the system of feudalism—or serf labour under a hereditary, landowning nobility—broke down owing to the demand for new methods of industry produced by the opening up of new markets through the discovery of America, and the perfection of means of transit and communication, in like manner will Socialism also come when the development of capitalism in its turn renders the burden of a capitalist class unbearable—and the capitalist system unworkable. Socialists point out that the capitalist system depends upon the maintenance of an equilibrium between the producing and consuming powers of the world; that business cannot go on unless the goods produced can find customers; that owing to the rapid development of machinery this equilibrium cannot be maintained; that the productive powers of the world are continually increasing whilst the virgin markets of the world are as continually diminishing; that every new scientific process applied to industry, every new perfecting of machinery, increases the productivity of labour, but as the area of the world remains unaltered the hope of finding new markets for the products of labour grows ever less and less; that a time must come when all the world will be exhausted as a market for the wares of commerce, and yet invention and industrial perfectioning remain as active as ever; that then capitalism—able to produce more in a few months than would supply its customers for years—will have no work for the workers who, constituting the vast majority as they do, will have to choose between certain starvation and revolt for Socialism. That the same economic development which will create the necessity for revolt will also provide the conditions required to make that revolt successful, in so far as it will have forced out of business the multitude of small capitalists, and replaced them by huge companies, stores, and trusts—a unification of industry, requiring only the transference of the right of ownership from the individual to the democratic community to bridge the chasm between capitalism and Socialism. That the private property which the worker should possess in the fruits of his toil is continually confiscated to-day by the capitalist process of industry, and that Socialism by making ALL citizens—society—joint heirs and owners of the tools of production, will restore to the workers that private property of which capitalism deprives them.

Here then is a statement of the aims and principles of modern Socialism. The intelligent reader will observe that this is not a mere piece of speculative philosophy, nor yet the product of disordered brains acted upon by hunger-weakened stomachs. On the contrary it is primarily a scientific analysis of the past and present structure of society—a comprehensive SUMMING UP OF THE FACTS OF HISTORY.

In face of this fact, which we would most respectfully remind Father Finlay he has himself most lucidly explained ere now, what becomes of his statement at Maynooth that Socialism had 'hopelessly broken down wherever it has been tried.' The statement was crudely false, mischievous, and misleading, and Father Finlay would not risk his reputation by repeating it before any audience of scientists in the world. That he thought it quite safe to make such an utterance at Maynooth is an interesting indication of the low estimate in which he held the intellectual grasp of his hearers on the thought of their generation. Socialism has not 'broken down wherever it has been tried,' because, being the fruit of an historical evolution yet to be completed, IT HAS NEVER BEEN TRIED.

If Father Finlay can tell when and where such an industrial order as would be recognised by the Socialist parties of the world as Socialism, has been tried and failed then we will publicly recant our errors. Wanting such information we, and with us an ever-encreasing band of the wage-slaves of capitalism, will continue to prepare for that revolt which shall establish the Socialist Republic.

SOCIALISM AND POLITICAL REFORMERS

[*July 8th, 1899*]

Among the many developments of Socialist activity at which the man in the street is apt to be astonished, perhaps none are more difficult to comprehend at first sight than the implacable hostility shown by the Socialist parties of the world toward the political parties hitherto identified with the agitation for political reform. The uninitiated find it hard to understand why there should be such marked hostility between parties, both of whom place on their programmes planks of political reform seemingly almost identical in character; why the Socialist party, which represents the most revolutionary ideas of our day, should seek the downfall of political reform parties with a zest and eagerness which the most bigoted Conservative could never hope to excel. It is observed that wherever the Socialist party is strong, as in Germany, France, or Belgium, it is the Liberal party—the party of mere political reformers—which has been the first to suffer in loss of prestige and membership, in exact proportion as Socialism has advanced.

Strange though the circumstance may seem to the unreflective mind, it is but what might be expected to result from the appearance upon the political field of a force which, like the Socialist party, had at once a programme of political reform embracing all and more than the old reform parties had striven for, and a programme embodying demands for economic changes which receive no support from middle-class reformers, though a crying necessity of the times. The development of acute economic problems, side by side with the extension of the Franchise—economic problems are, in fact, most acute in the politically freest countries—has borne in upon the minds of the working-class voters the conviction that, except as a means to an end, political freedom is a valueless acquisition for their class. They therefore demand the right to use that political power in the direction of their own class interests, but on making such demand are surprised to see their quondam middle class leaders the first to denounce them and call upon the State to oppose them. When this point has been reached, as in the countries above named and to a lesser degree in England and America, the thoughtful observer of politics can not but see that middle-class parties of reform have outlived their usefulness; that whatever political change is still required to establish the democracy in power can be sought for as well under the banner of the new political force of Socialism as under the old banner of Liberalism, and that this new power by basing its agitation upon the material wants of the producing class gathers to its aid a potential power, in the passion and self-interest of the majority of the nation, which the mere doctrinaires—Liberal, Radical or Republican—could never hope to rally. Therefore political reform parties decay as the Socialist parties thrive; the latter carry the political demands of the former on their banner, side by side with the economic demands of their class, and thus deprived of their sole reason for existence the capitalist reform parties lose their attraction for the multitude—now pressing eagerly onward to the inspiration of a new and better hope.

On the other hand Conservatism is, as a party, secure of an existence as long as the present system lasts. It may be set down as an axiom that there will always be a Conservative party as long as there is tyranny and privilege to conserve. Hence we find the old reform parties shedding their members at both ends—the wealthier section falling over into the ranks of Conservatism, in order to strengthen the only party able to defend their monopolies, and the working class section joining hands with the Socialists as the only party embracing the cause alike of political and industrial liberty. The Socialists are naturally desirous of hastening this process, in order that the political battlefield may be left clear and open for the final struggle between the only two parties possessed of a logical reason for existence—the Conservative party defending the strongholds of monarchy, aristocracy, and capitalism; and the Socialist party storming those strongholds in the interest of human freedom. This consummation can not be realised as long as there exists a political party which, like the Liberals of England and the Continent, and the Home Rule parties of Ireland, attempts to blend the principles of progress and reaction—now blatantly declaring for political freedom, now vigorously defending economic slavery. Therefore the Socialists uniformly seek the discomfiture of Liberalism, regarding it as a buffer between the contending forces of tyranny and freedom; and hence the clear-sighted workmen of the Continent have already reduced that once formidable party to a mere cypher in politics, and will ere long completely wipe it out of existence.

The fact is not without its lesson to us here in Ireland. We too have so-called parties of reform—Home Rule in all its phases is now but a cloak for the designs of the middle class desirous of making terms with the Imperial government it pretends to dislike. It is but capitalist Liberalism, speaking with an Irish accent. As such it is the enemy of every effort at working-class emancipation, and if the workers of Ireland are as alive to the interests of their class as are their brethren on the Continent, they will help build up that Socialist Republican Party which is destined to march over the grave of Home Rule Liberalism to the final assault and destruction of the strongholds of oppression.

11. MICHAEL DAVITT
A TEXT FOR A REVOLUTIONARY LECTURE

Michael Davitt (1846–1906), Irish nationalist, agrarian leader and socialist, played a major part in bringing to life the Irish Land League of 1879–81, which spearheaded the land war whose main long-term effect was the establishment of a peasant proprietorship system in Ireland. He co-operated with Charles Stewart Parnell, but remained outside Parliament; under the influence of the American reformer Henry George (1839–97), author of Progress and Poverty, *he adopted land nationalisation, but in face of opposition did not put the issue to the test, not wishing to break up the unity of the Parnell movement. He attacked Parnell on the latter's conviction in the O'Shea divorce suit, and entered Parliament as an anti-Parnellite after Parnell's death in 1891. He was identified with the growth of the labour movement in Britain, resigned from Parliament in protest against the Boer War, and published a number of books including the moving* Leaves from a Prison Diary *and his account of the land war,* The Fall of Feudalism in Ireland. *In youth he served nine years' imprisonment on a charge connected with his Fenian affiliation; after 1880 he was strongly opposed to the use of force.*

Francis Joseph Christopher Skeffington (1878–1916), as a zealous advocate of women's rights chose his wife's name to be added to his own after marriage. A close friend of Connolly, particularly after the latter's return to Ireland, he opposed the Easter Week Rising on pacifist grounds; nevertheless Connolly from jail designated him as his literary executor, only to learn that Sheehy-Skeffington had been murdered by a British officer during the insurrection. His Michael Davitt *(1908) was something between a biographical study and a 'primer', in his word, of Davitt's life and thought; it was severely attacked by Davitt's widow, whose Catholic piety was repelled by Sheehy-Skeffington's public profession of his abandonment of Catholicism and status as a freethinker. As Connolly shows, it was a somewhat hero-worshipping work; he clearly wished to extend its sales by this notice, but in fact the publishers by an error only printed a few hundred copies. It has recently been reissued by MacGibbon & Kee with an introduction by Professor F. S. L. Lyons (1967). Davitt's role as a labour leader is assessed by Professor T. W. Moody's 'Michael Davitt' in* Leaders and Workers *edited by J. W. Boyle.*[1] *The best account of Sheehy-Skeffington is that by his son Owen in* 1916: The Easter Rising *edited by Owen Dudley Edwards and Fergus Pyle.*[2] *The article that follows appeared as an editorial in* The Harp *(August 1908).*

We have received at this office a copy of a book entitled the life of 'Michael Davitt, Revolutionary, Agitator, and Labor Leader,' by F. Sheehy Skeffington. The book is published in London by Fisher Unwin, and has already evoked a storm of criticism and protests from the various reviewers of Ireland and England, a fact that will not seem in the least extraordinary to those of our readers who will take the trouble to dip into the book itself, as we would strongly advise them to do. For our part we do not intend to place before our readers any mere formal review of the production of Mr. Sheehy Skeffington, but rather to utilise the incident to point the moral which may rightly be drawn from the facts of that stormy period of Irish history during which Michael Davitt was a central public figure. On one point of dissent from the author's appreciation of his hero's qualities will be found centered all the criticism which we would offer were we to devote space to a more extended review. The point is this:

In dealing with the incident of the Parnell Commission Mr. Skeffington says Davitt's conduct 'revealed his possession in the highest degree of great intellectual acuteness, resourcefulness, and knowledge of men.' Our own opinion of Davitt's character as revealed in his whole history is far other. We conceive of him as an unselfish idealist, who in his enthusiasm for a cause gave his name and his services freely at the beck and call of men who despised his ideals and would willingly, but for their need of him, have hung himself as high as Haman. He abhorred clerical dictation in politics, yet when

[1] See Bibliography. [2] MacGibbon & Kee, London, 1968.

the psychological moment arrived to give it a death blow, when it was grappling to destroy the one leader who with himself could rally all the democracy of Ireland—Parnell, Davitt, instead of taking full advantage of the event which threw Parnell into the democratic ranks and uniting with him against clerical interference in politics, foolishly threw away his opportunity, misjudged the whole situation, and fought with all his force and aggressiveness to establish the priesthood in full control of secular affairs in Ireland.

He fought and campaigned for the Labor Cause in England, yet for the sake of harmony in the ranks he also supported and campaigned for a party—the Home Rule party—whose leaders were the bitterest enemies of the newly enfranchised workers of the Irish cities.

Again and again have the industrial proletariat of Ireland closed in grapples with the representatives of Irish capitalism, but never was the voice of Davitt raised in such a fight on behalf of labor. We are convinced that he was quite as sympathetic to the cause of Labor in Ireland as in England, but he had surrendered himself into the control of men who were quite willing to play upon Labor sentiments in England where such sentiments might be made a menace to British aristocracy, but were determined to scotch and oppose such sentiments in Ireland where they might become a menace to themselves. Thus in his later days Davitt became the idol of the revolutionary English democracy, and disliked and distrusted by the revolutionary working class democracy of Ireland. A poor ending for such a career, and solely due to the fact that he did not possess that knowledge of men of which his biographer gives him credit. Honest himself, he believed implicitly in the honesty of others, and became the tool of political crooks and social reactionaries.

But it is as the Father of the Land League that Davitt will live in history, and not in the light of the failure of his later career; and it is with that phase of his activity we wish to deal today. We believe profoundly that a close study of the events of that time would immensely benefit the militant Socialists of all countries.

It would help to demonstrate how the union of the forces

of social discontent with the forces of political agitation converted the latter from a mere sterile parliamentarianism, impotent for good, into a virile force transforming the whole social system, and bringing a political revolution within the grasp of the agitators. It would show how a political majority so strong that it left the socially privileged class absolutely without the political support of the socially subject class yet left untouched the real causes of the social misery of the latter. It would illustrate how a subject nation, kept by the bayonets of foreign army beneath the heel of native tyranny, by transferring the fight from the political battle ground of words to the social and economic battle ground of acts, succeeded in almost conquering its freedom, and in quite humbling the pride of a long dominant class, and by thus demonstrating what could be done and was done by a subject nation warring on the economic field against native and foreign tyrants combined, it would also demonstrate what could be done by the working class of any independent nation should it resolve to make its political activity one instrument and expression of its economic struggles, and its economic struggles in factory, workshop and mine the generating force of its political passions and programs.

As we have again and again pointed out the Irish question is a social question, the whole agelong fight of the Irish people against their oppressors resolves itself in the last analysis into a fight for the mastery of the means of life, the sources of production, in Ireland. Who would own and control the land? The people or the invaders; and if the invaders which set of them, the most recent swarm of land thieves, or the sons of the thieves of a former generation. These were the bottom questions of Irish politics, and all other questions were valued or deprecated in the proportion to which they contributed to serve the interests of some of the factions who had already taken their stand in this fight around property interests. Without this key to the meaning of events, this clue to unravel the actions of 'great men' Irish history is but a welter of unrelated facts, a hopeless chaos of sporadic outbreaks, treacheries, intrigues, massacres, murders and purposeless warfare. With this key all things become understandable and traceable to their primary origin; without this key the lost opportunities of Ireland seem such as to bring a blush to the cheek of the Irish Worker; with this key Irish history is as a lamp to his feet in the stormy paths of to-day.

Yet, plain as this is to the Irish Socialist, it is undeniable that for 100 years, or since the Act of Union of 1800, all Irish political movements ignored this fact, and were conducted by men who did not look below the political surface. These men to arouse the passions of the people invoked the memory of social wrongs such as evictions and famines, but for these wrongs proposed only political remedies such as changes in taxation and transference of the seat of government from one country to another. Hence they accomplished nothing, because the political method of fighting was unrelated to the social subjection at the root of the matter. Political agitators talked of sending men to Westminster to complain of English tyranny, but conducted no campaign against the rackrenting landlord on his estate, and as a result the adhesion of an overwhelming majority of the tenants to the political agitators lightened no economic burdens, stopped no evictions, and accomplished nothing. The Land League stepped in to alter all this, and transferred the real seat of war from the hustings to the estate, from the 'floor of the House of Commons' to the rent office of the landlord and the homestead of the tenant. It instructed the people to resist eviction, to refuse to pay rackrents, to terrorise landgrabbers—the scabs of the agrarian struggle—and to boycott and ostracise all offenders against the welfare of the tenant.

It made adhesion to the cause of the tenants synonymous with the call of Irish patriotism, and thus emphasised the point we have so often labored, viz.—that the Irish question is a social question. As a result of this change of base it revolutionized Irish politics. The men and women who had, with a grin on their faces, cheered the orators who talked of a 'Parliament on College Green' and after cheering went home to scrape together the landlord's rent by denying themselves the comfort and even necessaries of life now listened to the practical talk of men who told them to resist their tyrants at once, and so listening they straightened up mentally and morally and kept their rents in their pockets, held their harvests, kept a grip on their homesteads, laughed in the face of the landlord whom they had hitherto feared, and so broke the back of Irish landlordism. And this great change was the result of bringing the Irish fight down from the cloud land of sentiment on to the hard basis of a fight, day by day, between the producers and the owners for the control of the means of livelihood—or to the basis of a class struggle. That the Land League did not entirely succeed in its mission was due chiefly to one flaw in the original theory of its campaign, viz.—that its promoters not being in agreement as to their ultimate ideal were unable to educate their followers against the fallacy of accepting concessions which divided and disorganised their forces when at the flood tide of success.

That lesson—the lesson of its failure, Socialists have already learned and know how to profit by; the other lesson—the lesson of its strength, is not so widely realised. It is this—the strength and power of the political agitation of the Land League lay in the fact that its representatives were the servants and mouthpieces of a class who were already organised and holding the means of production with a revolutionary intent. They were not asking government to give them possession, they were already in defiant possession and demanding that such possession be legalized. Their base of operation was secondarily at the election booth, primarily on the farm; they thought the organization of an estate against its landlord a thousand times more important than the capture of a parliamentary seat. Rather they knew that the seat would inevitably follow the fate of the estate.

In all this they showed their wisdom. And hence we claim that although the Socialist agitators of to-day in their political activity fulfil well the work of agitators as did the Irish agitators of the past, yet if they would find and utilise to the fullest all the latent revolutionary material and strength they require they must do as the Land League did—take hold of the daily fight in the workshop, and organise it in a revolutionary manner, with a revolutionary purpose and direction.

12. SINN FÉIN AND SOCIALISM

Sinn Féin, an Irish term meaning literally 'we ourselves', was the name of a party founded by the Irish journalist Arthur Griffith (1871–1922); its First National Convention was held in 1905. From this point until 1916 the party was non-violent, favouring contest of parliamentary seats by its members who, on election, would refuse to take their seats; its ultimate aim was cultural and economic as well as political disengagement from Britain, with devolution under a dual monarchy on the Austro-Hungarian model (Griffith published a hortatory book on this theme entitled The Resurrection of Hungary). *Griffith was hostile to labour, but he and Connolly had co-operated in organizing Dublin opposition to the Boer War. Sinn Féin had no electoral success, and tended to lose its more extreme members to the revolutionary republican nationalists. Contrary to widespread myth, the 1916 Rising was not a Sinn Féin action, nor was the party represented in it. After the release of the surviving insurgent leaders it proved practical and convenient for them to take over Griffith's political organization to do their political work. Sinn Féin remained the name of The Irish Republican Army's political arm. Connolly published the following article as the first item in* The Harp *for April 1908; his arrangement of paragraphs, typical for his initial pieces in the journal, has been retained here.*

Sinn Féin.

That is a good name for the new Irish movement of which we hear so much nowadays. Sinn Féin, or in English, Ourselves.

It is a good name and a good motto. The first essential for the success of any party, or of any movement, is that it should believe it carries within its own bosom all the material requisite to achieve its destiny. The moment any organization ceases to believe in the sufficiency of its own powers, the moment its membership begin to put their trust in powers not their own, in that moment that party or that organization enters on its decline.

It has been so with Ireland, it is so with the non-Socialist Working Class.

For over a hundred years Ireland has looked outside her own shores for the means of her redemption. For over a hundred years Ireland through her 'constitutional agitators' has centered her hopes upon the possibility of melting the heart or appealing to the sense of justice of her oppressors. In vain! England – the British Empire, was and is the bourgeoisie personified, the incarnate beast of capitalist property, and her heart was as tender as that of the tiger when he feels his victim helpless in his claws; her sense of justice was as acute as that of the same beast of prey when his jaws are wet with the warm blood of the feast.

For over a hundred years the majority of the Irish people begged for justice, and when ever and anon the hot blood of the best of her children would rise in rebellion at this mendicant posture Ireland turned her face from them and asked the enemy to forgive them.

When her rebel sons and daughters were dead, hunted, imprisoned, hanged or exiled she would weep for them, pray for them, sigh for them, cry for them, and when they were long enough out of the way, erect monuments to them.

But as long as they were virile, active and aggressive, Ireland regarded them only as disturbers who gave the country a bad name.

Not that Ireland was or is alone in that respect. To be execrated when living and deified when dead has been the experience of all champions of Freedom in all the countries and ages of the earth.

This attitude, whether it is exhibited by an oppressed nation or by an oppressed class, is the direct outcome of that frame of mind in either which teaches them to look outside their own ranks for the impulse towards emancipation.

To believe that someone else than the slave is going to free the slave makes the slave impatient and intolerant of every effort at self-liberation on the part of his fellow bondsmen.

Now the course of action implied in the name Sinn Féin, is

the reverse of all that. It teaches the Irish people to rely upon themselves, and upon themselves alone, and teaches them also that dependence upon forces outside themselves is emasculating in its tendency, and has been, and will ever be disastrous in its results.

So far, so good. That is a part of Sinn Féinism I am most heartily in agreement with, and indeed with the spirit of Sinn Féin every thinking Irishman who knows anything about the history of his country must concur.

Even on the question of the Irish language, Gaelic, a question on which most Socialists are prone to stumble, I am heartily in accord. I do believe in the necessity, and indeed in the inevitability, of a universal language, but I do not believe it will be brought about, or even hastened, by smaller races or nations consenting to the extinction of their language. Such a course of action, or rather of slavish inaction, would not hasten the day of a universal language, but would rather lead to the intensification of the struggle for mastery between the languages of the greater powers.

On the other hand a large number of small communities speaking different tongues, are more likely to agree upon a common language as a common means of communication than a small number of great empires, each jealous of its own power and seeking its own supremacy.

I have heard some doctrinaire Socialists arguing that Socialists should not sympathize with oppressed nationalities, or with nationalities resisting conquest. They argue that the sooner these nationalities are suppressed the better, as it will be easier to conquer political power in a few big empires than in a number of small states. This is the language argument over again.

It is fallacious in both cases. It is even more fallacious in the case of nationalities than in the case of languages, because the emancipation of the Working Class will function more through the economic power than through the political state. The first act of the workers will be through their economic organizations seizing the organized industries; the last act the conquest of political power.

In this the working class will, as they needs must, follow in the lines traversed by the capitalist revolutions of Cromwellian England, of Colonial and Revolutionary America, of Republican France, in each of whom the capitalist class had developed their economic power before they raised the banner of political revolt.

The Working Class in their turn must perfect their economic organizations, and when such organizations are in a position to control, seize and operate the industries they will find their political power equal to the task.

But the preparatory work of the revolutionary campaign must lie in the daily and hourly struggles in the workshop, the daily and hourly perfectioning of the industrial organization.

And these two factors for Freedom take no heed to political frontiers, nor to the demarcations of political states. They march side by side with the capitalist; where capitalism brings its machinery it brings the rebels against itself, and all its governments and all its armies can establish no frontier the revolutionary idea cannot pass.

Let the great truth be firmly fixed in your mind that the struggle for the conquest of the political state of the capitalist is not the battle, it is only the echo of the battle. The real battle is being fought out, and will be fought out, on the industrial field.

Because of this and other reasons the doctrinaire Socialists are wrong in this as in the rest of their arguments. It is not necessary that Irish Socialists should hostilise those who are working for the Gaelic language, nor whoop it up for territorial aggrandizement of any nation. Therefore in this we can wish the Sinn Féiners, good luck.

Besides, it is well to remember that nations which submit to conquest or races which abandon their language in favor of that of an oppressor do so, not because of altruistic motives, or because of a love of the brotherhood of man, but from a slavish and cringing spirit.

From a spirit which cannot exist side by side with the revolutionary idea.

This was amply evidenced in Ireland by the attitude of the Irish people towards their language.

For six hundred years the English strove to suppress that mark of the distinct character of the Gael—their language, and failed. But in one generation the politicians did what England had failed to do.

The great Daniel O'Connell, the so-called liberator, conducted his meetings entirely in English. When addressing meetings in Connaught where in his time everybody spoke Gaelic, and over 75 per cent of the people nothing else but Gaelic, O'Connell spoke exclusively in English. He thus conveyed to the simple people the impression that Gaelic was something to be ashamed of—something fit only for ignorant people. He pursued the same course all over Ireland.

As a result of this and similar actions the simple people turned their backs upon their own language, and began to ape 'the gentry.' It was the beginning of the reign of the toady, and the crawler, the seainín and the slave.

The agitator for revenue came into power in the land.

It is not ancient history, but the history of yesterday that old Irish men and women would speak Irish to each other in the presence of their children, but if they caught son or daughter using the language the unfortunate child would receive a cuff on the ear accompanied with the adjuration:

'Speak English, you rascal; speak English like a gintleman!'

It is freely stated in Ireland that when the Protestant evangelizers, soupers they call them at home, issued tracts and Bibles in Irish in order to help the work of proselytising, the Catholic priesthood took advantage of the incident to warn their flocks against reading all literature in Gaelic. Thus still further discrediting the language.

I can not conceive of a Socialist hesitating in his choice between a policy resulting in such self-abasement, and a policy of defiant self-reliance, and confident trust in a people's own power of self-emancipation by a people.

But it is in many of the arguments used by the Sinn Féin speakers that the possibility, nay, the certainty of friction between the Irish Socialist and the adherents of Sinn Féin is likely to arise. Some of the arguments are as ridiculous as the principle itself is reasonable.

Thus the Sinn Féin body of the Argentine Republic, as recorded in the *Gaelic American*, states that Sinn Féin demands freedom for Ireland on the basis of the Act of Renunciation in 1782. This is absurd. The act by which the English Parliament renounced the right to make laws binding on Ireland left untouched the power of oppression, political and economic.

The fight which ended with the Act of Union in 1800 was not a fight for freedom, it was a fight to decide whether the English governing classes or the Irish governing classes should have the biggest share of the plunder of the Irish worker. Whichever side won made no difference to the worker; he was skinned, anyway.

As a cold matter of fact all talk about the 'restoration of our native Parliament' is misreading history. Ireland never had an Irish Parliament—a Parliament representative of the Irish people. The assembly called by the name of an Irish Parliament was in reality as alien to the Irish people as the Council of the Governor-General of India is alien to the Indian people. And some of the laws passed by our so-called native Parliament against the poor Irish peasantry were absolutely revolting in their ferocity and class vindictiveness.

Irish workers will not enthuse worth a cent over a proposal to re-introduce the status of 1782. To paraphrase Fintan Lalor, and I would recommend all thinking Irish workers, men and women, to read Fintan Lalor's masterly argument upon this subject, (price five cents, from the *Harp* office). 'This is not 1782, this is 1908,' and every political or social movement which hopes for success must express itself in terms of present conditions, or on the lines of future developments.

Of a like character are the arguments based upon the achievement of Hungary. As we all know the methods adopted by Hungary to reconquer its Parliament from Austria are the trite illustrations of the Sinn Féin orators. In fact during the early stages of the movement in Ireland before the felicitous name of Sinn Féin was coined the ideas as promulgated got the name of 'the Hungary system.'

I remember one critic declaring that 'the Hungary system was only fit for hungry men.'

When we remember that Hungary is one of the European countries sending the greatest stream of emigrants annually to

America, that the overwhelming majority of the producing classes in Hungary are denied the right to vote by the possessing classes who dominate their Parliament, that the misery of the town and country workers is so great that the country is in a chronic state of rebellion and unrest, and that the military and armed police are more often employed to suppress peaceable demonstrations in Hungary than they are in Ireland we are inclined to wonder if our Sinn Féin orators know these things, or are they only presuming upon the ignorance of the Irish Workers.

Let them advocate their proposals upon the inherent merits of those proposals and they will avoid much criticism; otherwise they will provoke it.

Sinn Féin. Ourselves. I wonder how long it will be until the Working Class realize the full significance of that principle! How long it will be until the Workers realize that the Socialist movement is a movement of the Working Class, and how long until the Socialists realize that the place of every other class in the movement is and must be a subordinate one.

How long it will be until the Socialists realize the folly and inconsistency of preaching to the Workers that the emancipation of the Working Class must be the act of the workers themselves, and yet presenting to those workers the sight of every important position in the party occupied by men not of the Working Class.

We will get the Workers to have trust in their own power to achieve their own emancipation when we demonstrate our belief that there is no task incidental to that end that a worker can not accomplish; when we train the workers to look inward upon their own class for everything required, to have confidence in the ability of their own class to fill every position in the revolutionary army; when, in short, we of the Socialist Working Class take to heart the full meaning of the term Sinn Féin, Ourselves, and apply it to the work of Industrial Reconstruction, the era of the strutters and poseurs will end and we will realize at last what was meant by Marx when he spoke of the revolt of those who

Have Nothing to Lose but their Chains.

PART IV

IMPERIALISM

... freedom and the British Empire cannot co-exist in this country. – James Connolly, in *Irish Work*, December 19th, 1914

13. IMPERIALISM AND SOCIALISM

It may be reasonably questioned whether Connolly would have stood by the whole of the following essay had his opinion of it been obtained in the latter part of his career. It is an unusually harsh application of Marxist teaching to imperialism on a purely theoretical level, with scant reflection on the oppression of the Asiatic peoples destined to suffer under any advance of the white races, whether British or Russian. As such it is in sharp contradiction to the subsequent essay, to say nothing of being belied by Connolly's own lifelong war against imperialism as applied to Ireland. It is very much in the tradition of Karl Kautsky, and is directed against a certain readiness on the part of some English socialists to arrive mysteriously in support of British foreign policy on many occasions while arguing that this was in fulfilment of socialist principles. Such a position from Robert Blatchford (1851–1943), the breezy editor of the popular Clarion, *with its emphasis on the Englishness of socialism, may have been irritating to Connolly but was less alarming than similar views from H. M. Hyndman (1842–1921), the leading English Marxist and leader of the Social Democratic Federation, with whose Scottish wing Connolly himself had been connected. The essay is reprinted here as a reminder of the limitations from which Connolly, in common with other European and American socialists of his time, could suffer by dehumanizing the imperialist question. It was printed in* The Workers' Republic *on November 4th, 1899. Both Blatchford and Hyndman were to support the British war effort in 1914.*

As Socialists—and therefore anxious to at all times throw the full weight of whatever influence we possess upon the side of the forces making most directly for Socialism—we have often been somewhat disturbed in our mind by observing in the writings and speeches of some of our foreign comrades a tendency to discriminate in favour of Great Britain in all the international complications in which that country may be involved over questions of territorial annexation, spheres of influence, etc., in barbarous or semi-civilised portions of the globe. We are, we repeat, disturbed in our mind upon the subject because we ourselves do not at all sympathise with this pro-British policy, but, on the contrary, would welcome the humiliation of the British arms in any one of the conflicts in which it is at present engaged, or with which it has been lately menaced. This we freely avow, but the question then arises: Is this hostility to the British Empire due to the fact of our national and racial subjection by that power, and does it exist in spite of our Socialism, or is it consistent with the doctrines we hold as adherents of the Marxist propaganda, and believers in the Marxist economics.

This is the question we propose briefly to discuss in our article this week. We are led to the discussion of this topic by observing that the English Socialists are apparently divided over the question of the war on the Transvaal; one section of the Social Democratic Federation going strongly for the Boers and against the war; another also declaring against the war, but equally denouncing the Boers; and, finally, one Socialist leader, Mr. Blatchford, editor of the *Clarion* and author of *Merrie England*, coming out bluntly for the war and toasting the health of the Queen, and the 'Success of the British arms.' On the other hand all the journals of the party on the continent of Europe and in America, as far as we are aware, come out in this instance whole-heartedly on the side of the Transvaal and against what the organ of our Austrian comrades fittingly terms England's act of 'blood-thirsty piracy.'

We ask then is there no common ground upon which Socialists can agree to treat all matters of international politics —a common standpoint from which all questions of race or nationality shall be carefully excluded, and every question dealt with from the position of its effect upon the industrial development required to bring the Socialist movement to a head? Nominally all Socialists hold to the international solidarity of Labour, and the identity of the interests of the workers the world over, and during the Franco-German and Spanish-American wars the Socialists of those countries demonstrated that the belief was no mere abstract theory, but a living, concrete fact. But our English friend, Mr. Blatchford, deliberately throws the doctrine to the winds, and declares that 'when England is at war he is English and regards all those who have taken up arms against England as enemies to be fought and beaten.' This is unqualifiedly chauvinist, and as a brutal endorsement of every act of brigandage and murder in which the capitalists of England may involve their country it throws a curious sidelight on the mental make-up of this man—who very nearly shed tears of pity over the wrongs and 'Christ-like appearance' of the Anarchists expelled from the International Socialist Congress in London. Our esteemed comrade, H. M. Hyndman of the Social Democratic Federation, also in an article contributed to the Berlin *Vorwaerts* and reprinted in *Justice* took the position that England ought not to have given way to Russia at Port Arthur, but ought to have fought her and asserted English supremacy in the far East. His reason for so contending being the greater freedom enjoyed under British than under Russian rule.

Mr. Blatchford's chauvinist pronouncement can be ignored as simply a personal predilection, and therefore binding no one, but the opinions of our comrades in the Social Democratic Federation of England hardly stand upon the same footing, but require severer consideration.

That we may not be accused of criticising the attitude of others without stating our own, we hereby place on record our position on all questions of international policy.

Scientific revolutionary Socialism teaches us that Socialism can only be realised when Capitalism has reached its zenith of development; that consequently the advance of nations industrially undeveloped into the capitalistic stage of industry is a thing highly to be desired, since such advance will breed a revolutionary proletariat in such countries and force forward there the political freedom necessary for the speedy success of the Socialist movement; and finally, that as colonial expansion and the conquest of new markets are necessary for the prolongation of the life of capitalism, the prevention of colonial expansion and the loss of markets to countries capitalistically developed, such as England, precipitates economic crises there, and so gives an impulse to revolutionary thought and helps to shorten the period required to develop backward countries and thus prepare the economic conditions needed for our triumph.

That is our position. Arguing from such premises we hold that as England is the most capitalistically developed country in Europe, every fresh conquest of territory by her armies, every sphere of influence acquired in the interests of her commercialists, is a span added to the life of capitalist society; and that every market lost, every sphere of influence captured by the non-capitalist enemies of England, shortens the life of Capitalism by aiding the development of reactionary countries, and hurling back upon itself the socially conservative industrial population of England.

Comrade Hyndman claims that we should oppose Russia because her people are ruled despotically, and favour England because her people are politically free. But that is the reasoning of a political Radical, not the dispassionate analysis of contemporary history we have a right to expect from an economist and a Socialist of Hyndman's reputation. Our comrade quite forgets to apply that materialist philosophy of history which he himself has done so much to popularise in its Marxian form, viz., that the economic system of any given society is the basis of all else in that society—its political superstructure included. If he did so apply it, he would realise that the political freedom of England is born of her capitalism. Her capitalist class required a wage slave class possessing such freedom or mobility of movement as would make them available at short notice wherever the exigencies of capitalism demanded. To gain such absolute freedom of migration a political movement had to be inaugurated placing the capitalist class in a position to break the bonds of serfdom for the labourer. This once achieved the capitalistic concentration of the workers in great centres of population gave to the proletariat the sense of numbers and opportunities of organisation required to complete the work of political enfranchisement. Thus the economic necessities of capitalism always and everywhere beget a measure of political freedom for its slaves.

Russia is not yet a capitalist country, therefore her people bow beneath the yoke of an autocrat. This is only saying that her capitalist class is not strong enough yet to force upon the government laws establishing the conditions most helpful to capitalist development. But every forward move of Russia in the direction of colonial expansion strengthens that capitalist class in Russia and in so doing breeds there the revolutionary working class. On the other hand, if the wishes of comrade Hyndman were to be realised Russian capitalism would be checked in its growth, and the discontent in that country, lacking capitalistic conditions, would resolve itself into a purely agrarian movement. The revolutionary proletariat would remain unborn.

Drive the Russian out of Poland! By all means! Prevent his extension towards Europe! certainly; but favour his extension and his acquisition of new markets in Asia (at the expense of England if need be) if you would see Capitalism hurry onward to its death.

It may be urged that our Irish nationality plays a large part in forming this conception of international politics here set forth. We do not plead guilty, but even if it were so the objection would be puerile. As Socialists we base our political policy on the class struggle of the workers, because we know that the self-interest of the workers lies our way. That the self-interest may sometimes be base does not affect the correctness of our position. In like manner the mere fact that the inherited (and often unreasoning) anti-British sentiment of a chauvinist Irish patriot impels him to the same conclusion as we arrived at as the result of our economic studies does not cause us to shrink from proclaiming our position, but rather leads us to rejoice that our propaganda is thus made all the easier by this none too common identity of aim established as a consequence of what we esteem the strong and irreconcilable hostility between English Imperialism and Socialism.

14. THE COMING REVOLT IN INDIA

ITS POLITICAL AND SOCIAL CAUSES

These articles appeared in The Harp *for January and February 1908. They testify to Connolly's desire to align his socialist mission among the Irish-Americans with the world anti-imperialist struggle. As such he was very much in the tradition of left-wing Irish-American journalism, notably of the Fenian weekly, the New York* Irish World, *founded in 1870, whose socialism was fairly primitive, but which forthrightly allied the cause of freedom in Ireland to that of freedom in India. By* The Harp*'s day, the* Irish World *had grown increasingly clericalist, but it seems almost certain that Connolly was aware of its traditions and former reputation; between 1870 and 1900 it had been the Irish-American paper of by far the highest circulation.*

I

'The educated classes of India may find fault with their exclusion from full political rights ... But it was by force that India was won, and it is for force India must be governed.' – London *Times*, Feb. 1, 1886.

The appearance at the International Socialist Congress at Stuttgart of an Indian delegate, voicing the aspirations of the people of India for freedom, and the news items continually appearing in the capitalist press of sporadic acts of revolt in that country – harbingers of the greater revolt now fermenting throughout that vast empire – justify us in placing before our readers the following brief résumé of conditions in that country in order that it might be more possible for them to intelligently follow events as they develop.

British rule in India, like British rule in Ireland, is a political and social system established and maintained by the conquerors in the interest of the conquered. So runs the legend. But there are not wanting men and women who, strangely enough, maintain that British rule, whether in India or Ireland, is one of the heaviest curses ever inflicted upon an unfortunate people; that its fruits are famine, oppression and pestilence, and that it has but one animating principle wherever found, viz., to extract the utmost possible tribute from the labor of its unfortunate subjects. With that aspect of British rule peculiar to Ireland we are all in a position to be thoroughly acquainted, but there are, unfortunately, many reasons why a like acquaintance with the history and facts of British rule in India is impossible of attainment to the vast majority of our fellow countrymen. Therefore the writer, having had for some time exceptional opportunities of learning the real position of affairs in that country, feels he is doing a service to the cause of freedom and humanity in laying before the readers of the *Harp* a short sketch of the predisposing causes which had led up to the devastating famine which at present holds and the incipient rebellion which threatens the Indian Peninsula. The first point to note is that the reader must in discussing Indian affairs at once rid himself of all the extravagant ideas about the 'wealth of India' with which the reading public have been familiarized through the writings of ignorant English romancers, avaricious English adventurers or unscrupulous English statesmen. India is, in reality, one of the poorest, if not the poorest, of all the countries in the world. Her immense population live from generation to generation in a state of such chronic misery that death from actual hunger excites no comment whatever except when, as in the present famine, their numbers swell so that it is feared even the patient Hindoo may refuse to bear it longer. Thus when we read that the tribute extracted from India by the imperial government in payment of home charges, pensions to retired officials, remittances, contributions to imperial expenditure, etc., reaches an annual total of from 20 to 27 million pounds sterling, the sum, though large in itself, does not at first appear so exorbitant when levied on a population of two hundred million people. It is only when we are aware of the average daily income of the people upon whose labor this tax is levied that we begin to understand how it is that the 'inestimable benefits of British rule' (?) have been so potent a factor in working out the destruction of this people that the failure of a single harvest is enough to bring upon them all the horrors of famine.

The wages of the agricultural laborers of India—where 70 per cent. of the population derive their sole subsistence directly from the cultivation of the soil—are not such as to induce any very extravagant mode of living or to fire the imagination of a glutton. In Bihar, the northwest provinces, the greater portion of the Deccan and Oudh, the average remuneration of the laborer is certainly not more than one anna, six pie, or one and one-half pence (three cents) per day. In some portions of East Bengal the wage sometimes rises to three pence (six cents), or four pence (eight cents) per day—an almost princely remuneration. It should also be remembered that the entire native population is excluded from all share in the government of their country, except in the most menial positions, and that on the other hand the Indian Civil Service is entirely manned by Englishmen, whose salaries are the highest in the world for such services. Thus the poorest people under the sun are taxed to support the wealthiest (and most insolent) official class. It might be interesting, in order to bring the matter more vividly before the reader, to give a few instances of the disparity of means between official England in India and the unfortunate people upon whom it is quartered. The late Professor Fawcett, in an article upon a proposed loan to India, called attention to a few items illustrating the extravagant expenditure of Anglo-Indians when the cost of such extravagance can be saddled upon the Indian people. Two of these items, viz., £1,200 for outfit and passage of a member of the Governor-General's Council, and £2,450 for outfit and passage of the Bishops of Calcutta and Bombay, convey their own lesson so well that no words of mine could possibly add point to their eloquence. Ten million pounds have been spent by the imperial government in erecting for their military garrisons regimental quarters so luxuriously equipped that one Anglo-Indian writer, General Strachey, enthusiastically declared 'our soldiers' barracks are now beyond comparison the finest in the world,' whilst Florence Nightingale, a thoroughly impartial witness, wrote: 'We do not care for the people of India; the saddest sight in the East, nay, probably in the world, is the peasant of our Indian empire.' 'We suppose,' says a young Indian writer, 'it is inseparable from an alien rule that the living of an English soldier should be of primary importance.' And again, 'ten million pounds wrung from the hard earnings of semi-starved dwellers in mud hovels for the rearing of "palatial" barracks. Surely we should pause before we congratulate ourselves on this.' We are constantly informed by all Anglo-Indian writers that the English in India have been mighty instruments of Divine Providence for winning the land from anarchy and oppression, bringing it within the area of civilization and order; and, finally, of introducing its people to all the inestimable benefits of modern civilization.

We Irish are, of course, well enough acquainted with the ways of English officialdom to be able to discount to a certain extent the brightly colored reports of progress emanating from such sources, and they constitute the sole medium by which Indian news is allowed to filter through to the reading public. But it would, nevertheless, be a mistake to suppose that the present writer denies that progress has been made in India under British rule. The only question is, In what degree is that progress due to British rule, and in what degree is it that progress which, under any circumstances, would have been made by an intellectual people with a continuity of literary and philosophic activity stretching back for two thousand years and more? We are told that the English rulers of India were the first to abolish the hideous custom of suttee, by which the Hindoo widow was forced to sacrifice herself on the funeral pyre of her deceased husband.

But an educated Hindoo, Ram Mohun Roy, greatly venerated by his countrymen, had begun a crusade against the custom ten years before the edict was first formulated in 1829. It is more than probable that the exertions of this Indian patriot would eventually have been successful even without English intervention, which at the most, perhaps, hastened the desired consummation.

The vast irrigation works established throughout India are also often alluded to as specimens of the advance of civilization in the East, largely resultant from the paternal efforts of the English government on behalf of its Indian subjects.

Here again the reader is apt to draw erroneous conclusions and picture to himself the government of England laboriously instructing the ignorant Indian natives in the functions and uses, theory and practice of irrigation works. But the remorseless hand of history rudely shatters all belief in the fidelity to truth of any such picture. So far from such irrigation works being the product of English enterprise or genius they are, as a matter of fact, only feeble and halting imitations of the magnificent works and public enterprise of the former Mohammedan rulers whom the English have supplanted. Dr. Spry, writing in 1837, on 'Modern India,' declared:

> It is in the territory of the independent native chiefs and princes that great and useful works are found and maintained.
>
> In our territories the canals, bridges and reservoirs, wells, groves, etc., the works of our predecessors from revenues expressly appropriated to such undertakings, are going fast to decay.

It is noteworthy also that while the former rulers of India neither expected nor accepted any return for the money they voluntarily expended in their irrigation and other public works, the English government could only be induced to embark on such enterprises by the hopes of reaping enormous profits therefrom—hopes which have never been realized. Lord Lawrence in a letter to Lord Cranborne stated that the general opinion held that these works would yield an average profit of 25, 50 or even 100 per cent. To the no small chagrin of the ruling classes of India these high expectations were doomed to disappointment, the full measure of which is revealed in the words of Lord Salisbury, valuable as a no doubt unwilling tribute to British official incompetence and to the superior engineering genius of their predecessors.

'The irrigation works that have been carried out,' he said, 'if they had for their basis the former works of native rulers, have in many instances been a financial success. But ... when we have begun the projects of irrigation for ourselves we have not, I believe, in any instance the desired result of a clean balance sheet.'

Will the reader please contrast this confession of bungling incompetence, allied to a greed to pay dividends, with the conduct of Runjeet Singh, the 'Lion of the Punjab,' whom the English have always vilified as a barbarian and a tyrant, but of whom Marshman tells us that 'he always advanced money free of interest to his peasantry for the purposes of irrigation.' That he was no exception to the rule is amply borne out by the following significant statement in Arnold's *Dalhousie*: 'The Musselman rulers were bold engineers in this respect; not only did they cover India with fine roads, shaded with trees in places which are now tiger walks, but they remembered the Arabic proverb that "water is the earth's wealth." The irrigation works were so benevolently attended to that the fees for wells and artificial reservoirs were always deducted from the produce of every village before the government claim was paid.'[1] In almost every detail of Indian administration the same tale remains to be told.

II

India is regarded by its alien rulers as a huge human cattle farm to be worked solely in the interest of the dominant class of another nation. Whatever is done for the development of its vast internal resources is done not for the benefit of the Indian people but primarily with a view to the dividends which the investing classes of England may draw from such development. The salt tax, a tax upon a first necessary of life, is ten times higher today than it was ever known to be under the Mussulman rulers of India. More than one humane English Governor has confessed his reluctance to increase this tax upon the helpless peasantry, yet it is to-day as high as 1,000 or 1,200 per cent. As in Ireland during the famine years, the Government rated famine-stricken districts for the relief of

[1] Sir Edwin Arnold, *The Marquis of Dalhousie's Administration of British India* (Saunders, Otley & Co., London, 1862).

their own poor, and so crushed into pauperism those who had managed to survive the loss of their potato crop; so in India, whenever the Government extends financial help to a famine-stricken population it seeks to recoup itself for the outlay by an increase in the salt tax. In other words, it gives relief with one hand and with the other increases the taxes upon the food of a famishing people. In the great famine of thirty years ago in Southern India, when it was estimated that no less than six millions of people had perished of hunger, the salt tax was increased by forty-five per cent. The benevolent rulers of India have also, in order to secure this source of income to their exchequer, prohibited under severe penalties all native manufacture of salt, and when the helpless people, unable to buy salt to season their food, endeavored to scrape a condiment from the deposits left by the receding ocean upon the rocks and pebbles of the sea-shore, they were prosecuted for defrauding the revenue. This devotion of the rulers of India to the letter of the law in this respect stands out in marked contrast to their action in another, viz., in squandering in useless frontier expeditions the Famine Relief Fund, which, as its name indicates, was intended for emergencies like the present.

During the nineteenth century India lost no less than sixteen million (16,000,000) people by starvation. All this time she has enjoyed the ameliorative influence of civilization on the British Imperial pattern, and in the full felicity borne of that enjoyment her children have died off like rotten sheep, while the hack apologists of the English governing classes have vied with each other in unctuous laudations of 'our civilizing mission,' and our 'benign rule.'

Yet, in spite of all their anxiety to suppress the truth about India, the official class in whose interests this systematic distortion of facts is practised cannot entirely exclude even from their own organs in the press the awful record of the results of their rule. Here for instance is an extract from the *Indian Pioneer*, an organ of Anglo-Indian officialdom, of 7th February, 1880, which tells its own tale:

The hired laborer is always on the verge of starvation.

> Out of the 109,000,000 in British India, laborers are estimated at 30,000,000. Last year after the heavy rainfall there was frightful mortality from fever, according to the recent sanitary report an increase of 900,000 on the average rate of mortality. There would appear to be a good deal of truth in the opinion of one officer, who reported that *the disease is aggravated by want of food, which at all times prevails amongst the lowest classes.*

Yet that great Home Ruler, Mr. Alfred Webb, not so long ago informed the readers of the *Freeman's Journal* that 'the Indians know their duty to their Sovereign *and are loyal.*' To what?

But, at least, we may be told, India has profited intellectually by her subjection; is not education fostered by the Imperial Government? Yes; it spends on education in India one-fiftieth part of its net revenue there, whereas in England and Scotland alone it spends under the same heading about one twenty-fourth part of the revenue of the United Kingdom. Again, as Irish Nationalists remember that it was the wholesome fear engendered in the English governing classes by the Fenian conspiracy, which led to the disestablishment of the Irish Church, so thoughtful Indians are not likely to forget that the year which saw the establishment of the universities of Bombay, Calcutta and Madras had also seen the smoke and fire of the Indian mutiny.

But has not religion benefited by the British Conquest of India? Well, for every Christian Church in India maintained by the free contributions of Christian people at home the Government establishes brothels for the use of its soldiers, the one frequently in sight of the other. For every Christian made the example of the British garrison from Tommy Atkins upward has made an hundred drunkards. Am I exaggerating? Listen to the words of this Englishman, Mr. Alfred S. Dyer, writing some years ago from Allahabad to the *Christian Commonwealth*:

> If the people of Great Britain, and especially the Christians of Great Britain, do not interfere to stop the mad career of

the handful of sin-supporting politicians who are at present in power in India, there can be no doubt that that career will be stopped by other means ...

As I stood amid the scenes of the mutiny at Cawnpore, and then at Lucknow, and then at Delhi, I realized how easily national judgment can follow national sin, as effect follows cause. I realized it afresh as a few weeks since at Peshawur, the border city of India and Afghanistan, I looked towards the entrance of the Khyber Pass, of disastrous memory, and remembered the tale of the first British Afghan campaign. History uses the convenient word 'emeute' to cover the character of the incident which led to the fatal ending of that unjustifiable enterprise. The truth seems to be that the indignation of the Afghans at the treatment of their women, principally by officers, led to the rising which turned the tide against the licentious English, and led to the retreat to Jellalabad, in which the whole army perished with the exception of one man.

Another so-called 'emeute' similar to that may occur among the hardy race in northernmost India at any time. Licensed sin is in full blast at Peshawur and other cities and places near. At Peshawur, from the door of their compound, the women can see the men, for whose lust they are licensed, paraded for 'divine service.' The people talk about these things. The impurity of the officers, as well as the rank and file, is thrown up in the faces of the missionaries, as two at Peshawur themselves told me.

Religion, in fact, in India, as everywhere else, loses by being identified with the forces of a tyrannical government.

The earlier English East India Company, when it totally prohibited the teaching of Christianity to the natives under its control, did not do as much to prevent its adoption by the Indians as the present governors do when they ostentatiously parade their Sunday religion before a people who have witnessed the immorality of their week-day lives. Even the ordinary administration of law in India in the most peaceful times is saturated with a barbarism unknown elsewhere, and only partly approximated to by the expiring Russian despotism in its present fight against freedom. For instance: According to Sir Henry Cotton, M.P., K.C.S.I., floggings in India are publicly inflicted upon adult male and female offenders, and for petty theft and the like. The last year for which figures are available, 1902, no fewer than 25,186 judicial floggings were inflicted. These are carried out in public. 'The triangles,' he writes, 'are an unpleasant feature outside every Court in India. I have known floggings so severe that the victims have died in the triangles to which they were tied.'

England, in short, has only one use for India. She sees there a spot revealed by an All-wise Providence for the specific purpose of providing comfortable positions and fat salaries and pensions to the younger sons and poor relations of the English moneyed classes. Therefore, as any efforts to entrust the government of India to the children of the soil would necessarily displace those sinecurists from their snug berths and salaries, all suggestions pointing in that direction must be branded as rank heresy, if not political incendiarism. In Java, under the rule of the Dutch, the natives share in the government of their country. In the words of Sir David Wedderburn, 'the Asiatic races are subordinated to their own recognized chiefs, and these are responsible to the Government for the maintenance of order.' Thus the most important official positions are open to the natives. In the independent native States of India, before the Conquest, all posts, according to the Anglo-Indian writer, Marshman, were open to universal competition. What, then is the net result of British rule in India? 'The main evil of our rule,' said Sir T. Munro, Governor of Madras in 1819, 'is the degraded state in which we hold the native,' and as a corollary to this statement one of our contemporary writers, Sir James Caird, informs us from personal investigation that 'in the native States the people are more prosperous than under our rule, and they have not been driven into the evil hands of the sowcars (money-lenders) as our ryots (peasants) have been.' A few months ago famine in all its horrors was once more devastating the country, and once more the native States were exempt from the calamity. The English Government officials for months denied the accuracy of the reports which, despite their vigilance, filtered through to Europe, and then, when the awful truth could no longer be concealed, they, like Pilate of old, called heaven and earth to witness they were guiltless of the blood of this people. And once more they called upon the charitable to contribute to the relief of the destitute, whilst they prepared, horse, foot and artillery, to insure that not one penny of the tribute, the exaction of which has created the destitution, shall be withheld from the British Exchequer, or devoted to the people they have ruined. The people in India require justice, but justice is exactly what they must not expect. Justice is prosaic, dull and unsentimental, and cannot be advertised in Mansion House Funds, or prated about by royal and aristocratic dignities. Charity, however, though utterly useless for the purpose of staying the ravages of famine among a population of thirty-six millions perishing beneath it, yet fulfils the purpose of those who desire to hear their own trumpet blowing and see their names advertised side by side with the elite of society and in company with royalty. Above all, it does not interfere with the ceaseless flow of Indian tribute into the coffers of their conquerors. Therefore, justice India must not expect, but charity (D.V.) she will have. 'Look well at the background of this fine picture, and lo, the reeking shanks and yellow chapless skulls of Skibbereen, and the ghosts of starved Hindoos in dusky millions.'

PART V

MARXIAN SYNDICALISM: THEORY AND PRACTICE

Our demands most moderate are—
We only want the Earth!
—James Connolly, 'Be Moderate' (song)

15. SOCIALISM MADE EASY

Socialism Made Easy *was to be the textbook in which Connolly reconciled the new syndicalist influence on his thought with his older views. Nevertheless, or perhaps because of this, it drew on certain earlier works. The 'workshop talks', as one might expect, had their origin in his informal* Workers' Republic *column 'Home Thrusts', and its later counterpart from* The Harp, *'Harp Strings'. The subsection 'Internationalism' appeared in* The Workers' Republic *on June 17th, 1899, and 'Old Age Pensions' in the issue of June 10th, 1899. The item 'Practical Politics' first appeared in* The Workers' Republic *of September 24th, 1898, and was reworked by Connolly for* Socialism Made Easy. *'Holidays' was reprinted from* The Workers' Republic *of August 12th, 1899, and the untitled passage which follows, dealing with socialism and Christianity, is a much reworked and extended piece from* The Harp *of January 1909. 'Socialism and Nationalism' had appeared under the title 'Let Us Free Ireland' in a collection of 'Home Thrusts' printed as a pamphlet with* The Workers' Republic *in February 1901. In Section II, 'Industrial and Political Unity' and 'Industrial Unionism and Constructive Socialism' appeared in earlier forms in* The Harp *for December and June 1908 respectively. 'The Future of Labor' had had an earlier existence as a lecture for the I.W.W. Propaganda League.*

Socialism Made Easy *was published as a pamphlet in Chicago in 1909 by Charles H. Kerr & Co. Shortly afterwards it was reprinted, minus 'Workshop Talks' (Section I), in Australia under I.W.W. auspices, under the title* The Axe to the Root, *and this title was retained for the Dublin editions of 1921 and 1934, while the earlier title was used for the Glasgow edition of 1916–17 and the Dublin edition of 1968. In view of the lack of favour shown to syndicalism in most parts of the socialist world* Socialism Made Easy *has always been one of the least known of Connolly's writings since the outbreak of war in 1939. The text printed here is that of the Chicago edition of 1909, the only one known to have been passed for press by Connolly.*

FOREWORD

In this work the author presents his own views in his own manner. Hence he employs the first person singular in preference to the impersonal 'we' of journalism or of official production. The articles have been written at various times in Ireland and America and have already attained a wide circulation through being reprinted in various Socialist journals in both countries. Constant requests to the author to have them collected and published in a more permanent and accessible form have induced him to make this selection in the hope that they may be thought not unworthy of a place in at least the fugitive literature of the Socialist movement.

A word as to the plan of the work may not be amiss here. Section 1 is light, satirical, jesting and serious by turns, and follows the usual course of attack and defense, argument and rebuttal, experienced by a Socialist workman in factory, workshop or mine before he has destroyed the prejudices and won the serious consideration of his fellow workers. Section 2 is serious throughout, and is an attempt to deduce from actual every-day experiences and from historical facts the probable correct answer to the question put by the worker when he realizes the necessity of a change, *viz: How must we act? How are we going to do it?*

SECTION I WORKSHOP TALKS

[*Internationalism*]

Socialism is a foreign importation!

I know it because I read it in the papers. I also know it to be the case because in every country I have graced with my presence up to the present time, or have heard from, the possessing classes through their organs in the press, and their spokesmen upon the platform have been vociferous and insistent in declaring the foreign origin of Socialism.

In Ireland Socialism is an English importation, in England they are convinced it was made in Germany, in Germany it is a scheme of traitors in alliance with the French to disrupt the Empire, in France it is an accursed conspiracy to discredit the army which is destined to reconquer Alsace and Lorraine, in Russia it is an English plot to prevent Russian extension towards Asia, in Asia it is known to have been set on foot by American enemies of Chinese and Japanese industrial progress, and in America it is one of the baneful fruits of unrestricted pauper and criminal immigration.

All nations today repudiate Socialism, yet Socialist ideas are conquering all nations. When anything has to be done in a practical direction toward ameliorating the lot of the helpless ones, or towards using the collective force of society in strengthening the hands of the individual it is sure to be in the intellectual armory of Socialists the right weapon is found for the work.

A case in point. There are tens of thousands of hungry children in New York today as in every other large American city, and many well meant efforts have been made to succor them. Free lunches have been opened in the poorest districts, bread lines have been established and charitable organizations are busy visiting homes and schools to find out the worst cases. But all this has only touched the fringe of the destitution, with the additional aggravation that anything passing through the hands of these charitable committees usually costs ten times as much for administration as it bestows on the object of its charity.

Also that the investigation is usually more effectual in destroying the last vestiges of self-respect in its victims than in succoring their needs.

In the midst of this difficulty Superintendent Maxwell of the New York Schools sends a letter to a committee of thirteen charitable organizations which had met together to consider the problem, and in this letter he advocates the method of relieving distress long since initiated by the Socialist representatives in the Municipality of Paris. I quote from the *New York World*:

> A committee of seven was appointed to inquire more fully into the question of feeding school children and to report at a subsequent meeting. School Superintendent Maxwell sent a letter advocating the establishment in New York

> schools with city money of lunch kitchens, these to sell food at actual cost and to give to needy children tickets just like those paid for, to the end that no child might know that his fellow was eating at the expense of the city by the color of his ticket. This is done in Paris.

Contrast this solicitude for the self-respect of the poor children, recognized by Superintendent Maxwell in the plan of these 'foreign Socialists' with the insulting methods of the capitalist 'bread lines' and charitable organizations in general.

But all the same it is too horrible to take practical examples in relieving the distress caused by capitalist society from pestilent agitators who wish to destroy the society whose victims they are succoring, and mere foreigners, too. The capitalist method of parading mothers and children for an hour in the street before feeding them is more calculated to build up the proper degree of pride in the embryo American citizens; and make them appreciate the benefits their fathers and brothers are asked to vote for.

Read this telling how hungry children and mothers stood patiently waiting for a meal on the sidewalk, and whoop it up for pure ecstasy of joy that you are permitted to live in a system of society wherein a great metropolitan daily thought that the fact of five hundred children getting a 'hearty luncheon' was remarkable enough to deserve a paragraph:

> Five hundred ill-fed children who attend the schools on the lower east side got a hearty luncheon yesterday when the first of the children's lunchrooms was opened at Canal and Forsyth streets. Long before noon there was a large gathering of children, some of them accompanied by their mothers, awaiting the opening of the doors.

Well, I am not interested in internationalism. This country is good enough for me.

Is that so? Say: Are you taking a share in the Moscow-Windau-Rydinsk Railway?

'No, where is that?'

My dear friend, where that railway runs has nothing to do with you. What you have to do is simply to take a share, and then go and have a good time whilst the Russian railway workers, whom you do not know, working in a country you never saw, speaking a language you don't understand, earn your dividends by the sweat of their brows.

Curious, ain't it?

We Socialists are always talking about the international solidarity of labor, about the oneness of our interests all over the world, and ever and anon working off our heaving chests a peroration on the bonds of fraternal sympathy which should unite the wage slaves of the capitalist system.

But there is another kind of bond—Russian railway bonds—which join, not the workers, but the idlers of the world in fraternal sympathy, and which creates among the members of the capitalist class a feeling of identity of interest, of international solidarity, which they don't perorate about but which is most potent and effective notwithstanding.

You do not fully recognize the fact that the internationality of Socialism is at most but a lame and halting attempt to create a counterpoise to the internationality of capitalism. Yet so it is.

Here is a case in point. The Moscow-Windau-Rydinsk railway is, as its name indicates, a railway running, or proposed to be run, from one part of Russia to another. You would think that that concerned the Russian people only, and that our patriotic capitalist class, always so ready to declare against working class Socialists with international sympathies, would never look at it or touch it.

You would not think that Ireland, for example—whose professional patriots are forever telling the gullible working men that Ireland will be ruined for the lack of capital and enterprise—would be a good country to find money in to finance a Russian railway.

Yet, observe the fact. All the Dublin papers of Monday, June 12, 1899, contained the prospectus of this far away Russian railway, offered for the investment of Irish capitalists, and offered by a firm of London stockbrokers who are astute enough not to waste money in endeavoring to catch fish in waters where they were not in the habit of biting freely.

And in the midst of the Russian revolution the agents of the Czar succeeded in obtaining almost unlimited treasures in the

United States to pay the expenses of throttling the infant Liberty.

As the shares in Russian railways were sold in Ireland, as Russian bonds were sold in America, so the shares in American mines, railroads and factories are bought and sold on all the stock exchanges of Europe and Asia by men who never saw America in their lifetime.

Now, let us examine the situation, keeping in mind the fact that this is but a type of what prevails all round; you can satisfy yourself on that head by a daily glance at our capitalist papers.

Capital Is International

The shares of Russian railways, African mines, Nicaraguan canals, Chilian gas works, Norwegian timber, Mexican water works, Canadian fur trappings, Australian kanaka slave trade, Indian tea plantations, Japanese linen factories, Chinese cotton mills, European national and municipal debts, United States bonanza farms are bought and sold every day by investors, many of whom never saw any one of the countries in which their money is invested, but who have, by virtue of so investing, a legal right to a share of the plunder extracted under the capitalist system from the wage workers whose bone and sinew earn the dividends upon the bonds they have purchased.

When our investing classes purchase a share in any capitalist concern, in any country whatsoever, they do so, not in order to build up a useful industry, but because the act of purchase endows them with a prospective share of the spoils it is proposed to wring from labor.

Therefore, every member of the investing classes is interested to the extent of his investments, present or prospective, in the subjection of Labor all over the world.

That is the internationality of Capital and Capitalism.

The wage worker is oppressed under this system in the interest of a class of capitalist investors who may be living thousands of miles away and whose very names are unknown to him.

He is, therefore, interested in every revolt of Labor all over the world, for the very individuals against whom that revolt may be directed may—by the wondrous mechanism of the capitalist system—through shares, bonds, national and municipal debts—be the parasites who are sucking his blood also.

That is one of the underlying facts inspiring the internationalism of Labor and Socialism.

[*Old Age Pensions*]

But the Socialist proposals, they say, would destroy the individual character of the worker. He would lean on the community, instead of upon his own efforts.

Yes: Giving evidence before the Old Age Pensions Committee in England, Sir John Dorrington, M.P., expressed the belief that the provision of Old Age Pensions by the State, for instance, would do more harm than good. It was an objectionable principle, and would lead to improvidence.'

There now! You will always observe that it is some member of what an Irish revolutionist called 'the canting, fed classes,' who is anxious that nothing should be done by the State to give the working class habits of 'improvidence,' or to do us any 'harm.' Dear, kind souls!

To do them justice they are most consistent. For both in public and private their efforts are most whole-heartedly bent in the same direction, viz., to prevent improvidence—ON OUR PART.

They lower our wages—to prevent improvidence; they increase our rents—to prevent improvidence; they periodically suspend us from our employment—to prevent improvidence, and as soon as we are worn out in their service they send us to a semi-convict establishment, known as the Workhouse, where we are scientifically starved to death—to prevent improvidence.

Old Age Pensions might do us harm. Ah, yes! And yet, come to think of it, I know quite a number of people who draw Old Age Pensions and it doesn't do them a bit of harm. Strange, isn't it?

Then all the Royal Families have pensions, and they don't seem to do them any harm; royal babies, in fact, begin to draw pensions and milk from a bottle at the same time.

Afterwards they drop the milk, but they never drop the pension—nor the bottle.

Then all our judges get pensions, and are not corrupted thereby—at least not more than usual. In fact, all well-paid officials in governmental or municipal service get pensions, and there are no fears expressed that the receipt of the same may do them harm.

But the underpaid, overworked wage-slave. To give him a pension would ruin his moral fibre, weaken his stamina, debase his manhood, sap his integrity, corrupt his morals, check his prudence, emasculate his character, lower his aspirations, vitiate his resolves, destroy his self-reliance, annihilate his rectitude, corrode his virility—and—and—other things.

[*Practical Politics*]

Let us be practical. We want something pr-r-ractical.

Always the cry of hum-drum mediocrity, afraid to face the stern necessity for uncompromising action. That saying has done more yeoman service in the cause of oppression than all its avowed supporters.

The average man dislikes to be thought unpractical, and so, while frequently loathing the principles or distrusting the leaders of the particular political party he is associated with, declines to leave them, in the hope that their very lack of earnestness may be more fruitful of practical results than the honest outspokenness of the party in whose principles he does believe.

In the phraseology of politics, a party too indifferent to the sorrow and sufferings of humanity to raise its voice in protest, is a moderate, practical party; whilst a party totally indifferent to the personality of leaders, or questions of leadership, but hot to enthusiasm on every question affecting the well-being of the toiling masses, is an extreme, a dangerous party.

Yet, although it may seem a paradox to say so, there is no party so incapable of achieving practical results as an orthodox political party; and there is no party so certain of placing moderate reforms to its credit as an extreme—a revolutionary party.

The possessing classes will and do laugh to scorn every scheme for the amelioration of the workers so long as those responsible for the initiation of the scheme admit as justifiable the 'rights of property'; but when the public attention is directed towards questioning the justifiable nature of those 'rights' in themselves, then the master class, alarmed for the safety of their booty, yield reform after reform—in order to prevent revolution.

Moral—Don't be 'practical' in politics. To be practical in that sense means that you have schooled yourself to think along the lines, and in the grooves those who rob you would desire you to think.

In any case it is time we got rid of all the cant about 'politics' and 'constitutional agitation' in general. For there is really no meaning whatever in those phrases.

Every public question is a political question. The men who tell us that Labor questions, for instance, have nothing to do with politics, understand neither the one nor the other. The Labor Question cannot be settled except by measures which necessitate a revision of the whole system of society, which, of course, implies political warfare to secure the power to effect such revision.

If by politics we understand the fight between the outs and ins, or the contest for party leadership, then Labor is rightly supremely indifferent to such politics, but to the politics which center round the question of property and the administration thereof Labor is not, cannot be, indifferent.

To effect its emancipation Labor must reorganize society on the basis of labor; this cannot be done while the forces of government are in the hands of the rich, therefore the governing power must be wrested from the hands of the rich peaceably if possible, forcibly if necessary.

In the phraseology of the master class and its pressmen the trade unionist who is not a Socialist is more practical than he who is, and the worker who is neither one nor the other but can resign himself to the state of slavery in which he was born, is the most practical of all men.

The heroes and martyrs who in the past gave up their lives for the liberty of the race were not practical, but they were heroes all the same.

The slavish multitude who refused to second their efforts

from a craven fear lest their skins might suffer were practical, but they were soulless serfs, nevertheless.

Revolution is never practical—until the hour of the Revolution strikes. *Then* it alone is practical, and all the efforts of the conservatives and compromisers become the most futile and visionary of human imaginings.

For that hour let us work, think and hope; for that hour let us pawn our present ease in hopes of a glorious redemption; for that hour let us prepare the hosts of Labor with intelligence sufficient to laugh at the nostrums dubbed practical by our slave-lords, practical for the perpetuation of our slavery; for that supreme crisis of human history let us watch, like sentinels, with weapons ever ready, remembering always that there can be no dignity in Labor until Labor knows no master.

[*Confiscation*]

Would you confiscate the property of the capitalist class and rob men of that which they have, perhaps, worked a whole lifetime to accumulate?

Yes, sir, and certainly not.

We would certainly confiscate the property of the capitalist class, but we do not propose to rob anyone. On the contrary, we propose to establish honesty once and forever as the basis of our social relations. This Socialist movement is indeed worthy to be entitled The Great Anti-Theft Movement of the Twentieth Century.

You see, confiscation is one great certainty of the future for every business man outside of the trust. It lies with him to say if it will be confiscation by the Trust in the interest of the Trust, or confiscation by Socialism in the interest of All.

If he resolves to continue to support the capitalist order of society he will surely have his property confiscated. After having, as you say, 'worked for a whole lifetime to accumulate' a fortune, to establish a business on what he imagined would be a sound foundation, on some fine day the Trust will enter into competition with him, will invade his market, use their enormous capital to undersell him at ruinous prices, take his customers from him, ruin his business, and finally drive him into bankruptcy, and perhaps to end his days as a pauper.

That is capitalist confiscation! It is going on all around us, and every time the business man who is not a Trust Magnate votes for capitalism, he is working to prepare that fate for himself.

On the other hand, if he works for Socialism it also will confiscate his property. But it will only do so in order to acquire the industrial equipment necessary to establish a system of society in which the whole human race will be secured against the fear of want for all time, a system in which all men and women will be joint heirs and owners of all the intellectual and material conquests made possible by asociated effort.

Socialism will confiscate the property of the capitalist and in return will secure the individual against poverty and oppression; it, in return for so confiscating, will assure to all men and women a free, happy and unanxious human life. And that is more than capitalism can assure anyone today.

So you see the average capitalist has to choose between two kinds of confiscation. One or the other he must certainly endure. Confiscation by the Trust and consequently bankruptcy, poverty and perhaps pauperism in his old age, or

Confiscation by Socialism and consequently security, plenty and a Care-Free Life to him and his to the remotest generation.

Which will it be?

But it is their property. Why should Socialists confiscate it?

Their property, eh? Let us see: Here is a cutting from the *New York World* giving a synopsis of the Annual Report of the Coats Thread Company of Pawtucket, Rhode Island, for 1907. Now, let us examine it, and bear in mind that this company is the basis of the Thread Trust, with branches in Paisley, Scotland, and on the continent of Europe.

Also bear in mind that it is not a 'horrible example,' but simply a normal type of a normally conducted industry, and therefore what applies to it will apply in a greater or less degree to all others.

This report gives the dividend for the year at 20 per cent per annum. Twenty per cent dividend means 20 cents on the dollar profit. Now, what is a profit?

According to Socialists, profit only exists when all other items of production are paid for. The workers by their labor must create enough wealth to pay for certain items before profit appears. They must pay for the cost of raw material, the wear and tear of machinery, buildings, etc. (the depreciation of capital), the wages of superintendence, their own wages, and a certain amount to be left aside as a reserve fund to meet all possible contingencies. After, and only after, all these items have been paid for by their labor, all that is left is profit.

With this company the profit amounted to 20 cents on every dollar invested.

What does this mean? It means that in the course of five years—five times 20 cents equals one dollar—the workers in the industry had created enough profit to buy the whole industry from its present owners. It means that after paying all the expenses of the factory, including their own wages, they created enough profit to buy the whole building, from the roof to the basement, all the offices and agencies, and everything in the shape of capital. All this in five years.

And after they had so bought it from the capitalists it still belonged to the capitalists.

It means that if a capitalist had invested $1,000 in that industry, in the course of five years he would draw out a thousand dollars, and still have a thousand dollars lying there untouched; in the course of ten years, he would draw two thousand dollars, in fifteen years he would draw three thousand dollars. And still his first thousand dollars would be as virgin as ever.

You understand that this has been going on ever since the capitalist system came into being; all the capital in the world has been paid for by the working class over and over again, and we are still creating it, and recreating it. And the oftener we buy it the less it belongs to us.

The capital of the master class is not their property; it is the unpaid labor of the working class—'the hire of the laborer kept back by fraud.'

[*Holidays*]

Oh, the capitalist has his anxieties, too. And the worker has often a good time.

Sure: Say, where were you for the holidays?

Were you tempted to go abroad? Did you visit Europe? Did you riot, in all the abandonment of a wage slave let loose, among the pleasure haunts of the world?

Perhaps you went to the Riviera; perhaps you luxuriated in ecstatic worship of that glorious bit of Nature's handiwork where the blue waters of the Mediterranean roll in all their entrancing splendor against the shores of classic Italy.

Perhaps you rambled among the vine clad hills of sunny France, and visited the spots hallowed by the hand of that country's glorious history.

Perhaps you sailed up the castellated Rhine, toasted the eyes of bewitching German frauleins in frothy German beer, explored the recesses of the legend haunted Hartz mountains, and established a nodding acquaintance with the Spirit of the Brocken.

Perhaps you traversed the lakes and fjords of Norway, sat down in awe before the neglected magnificence of the Alhambra, had a cup of coffee with Menelik of Abyssinia, smelt afar off the odors of the streets of Morocco, climbed the Pyramids of Egypt, shared the hospitable tent of the Bedouin, visited Cyprus, looked in at Constantinople, ogled the dark-eyed beauties of Circassia, rubbed up against the Cossack in his Ural mountains, or

Perhaps you lay in bed all day in order to save a meal, and listened to your wife wondering how she could make ends meet with a day's pay short in the weekly wages.

And whilst you thus squandered your substance in riotous living, did you ever stop to think of your master—your poor, dear, overworked, tired master?

Did you ever stop to reflect upon the pitiable condition of that individual who so kindly provides you with employment, and does no useful work himself in order that you may get plenty of it?

When you consider how hard a task it was for you to decide

in what manner you should spend your Holiday; where you should go for that ONE DAY, then you must perceive how hard it is for your masters to find a way in which to spend the practically perpetual holiday which you force upon them by your love for work.

Ah, yes, that large section of our masters who have realized that ideal of complete idleness after which all our masters strive, those men who do not work, never did work, and with the help of God—and the ignorance of the people—never intend to work, how terrible must be their lot in life!

We, who toil from early morn till late at night, from January till December, from childhood to old age, have no care or trouble or mental anxiety to cross our mind—except the landlord, the fear of loss of employment, the danger of sickness, the lack of common necessities, to say nothing of luxuries, for our children, the insolence of our superiors, the unhealthy condition of our homes, the exhausting nature of our toil, the lack of all opportunities of mental cultivation, and the ever present question whether we shall shuffle off this mortal coil in a miserable garret, be killed by hard work, or die in the Poorhouse.

With these trifling exceptions we have nothing to bother us; but the boss, ah, the poor, poor boss!

He has everything to bother him. Whilst we are amusing ourselves in the hold of a ship shoveling coal, swinging a hammer in front of a forge, toiling up a ladder with bricks, stitching until our eyes grow dim at the board, gaily riding up and down for twelve hours per day, seven days per week, on a trolley car, riding around the city in all weather with teams or swinging by the skin of our teeth on the iron framework of a skyscraper, standing at our ease OUTSIDE the printing office door listening to the musical click of the linotype as it performs the work we used to do INSIDE, telling each other comforting stories about the new machinery which takes our places as carpenters, harness-makers, tinplate-workers, laborers, etc., in short whilst we are enjoying ourselves, free from all mental worry.

Our unselfish tired-out bosses are sitting at home, with their feet on the table, softly patting the bottom button of their vests.

Working with their brains.

Poor bosses! Mighty brains!

Without our toil they would never get the education necessary to develop their brains; if we were not defrauded by their class of the fruits of our toil we could provide for education enough to develop the mental powers of all, and so deprive the ruling class of the last vestige of an excuse for clinging to mastership, viz., their assumed intellectual superiority.

I say 'assumed,' because the greater part of the brain-work of industry today is performed by men taken from the ranks of the workers, and paid high salaries in proportion as they develop expertness as slave-drivers.

As education spreads among the people the workers will want to enjoy life more; they will assert their right to the full fruits of their labor, and by that act of self-assertion lay the foundation of that Socialist Republic in which the labor will be so easy, and the reward so great, that life will seem a perpetual holiday.

But Socialism is against religion. I can't be a Socialist and be a Christian.

O, quit your fooling! That talk is all right for those who know nothing of the relations between capital and labor, or are innocent of any knowledge of the processes of modern industry, or imagine that men, in their daily struggles for bread or fortunes, are governed by the Sermon on the Mount.

But between workingmen that talk is absurd. We know that Socialism bears upon our daily life in the workshop, and that religion does not; we know that the man who never set foot in a church in his lifetime will, if he is rich, be more honored by Christian society than the poor man who goes to church every Sunday, and says his prayers morning and evening; we know that the capitalists of all religions pay more for the service of a good lawyer to keep them out of the clutches of the law than for the services of a good priest to keep them out of the clutches of the devil; and we never heard of a capitalist, who, in his business, respected the Sermon on the Mount as much as he did the decisions of the Supreme Court.

These things we know. We also know that neither capitalist nor worker can practice the moral precepts of religion, and without its moral precepts a religion is simply a sham. If a religion cannot enforce its moral teachings upon its votaries it has as little relation to actual life as the pre-election promises of a politician have to legislation.

We know that Christianity teaches us to love our neighbor as ourselves, but we also know that if a capitalist attempted to run his business upon that plan his relatives would have no difficulty in getting lawyers, judges and physicians to declare him incompetent to conduct his affairs in the business world.

He would not be half as certain of reaching Heaven in the next world as he would be of getting into the 'bughouse' in this.

And, as for the worker. Well, in the fall of 1908, the *New York World* printed an advertisement for a teamster in Brooklyn, wages to be $12 per week. Over 700 applicants responded. Now, could each of these men love their neighbors in that line of hungry competitors for that pitiful wage?

As each man stood in line in that awful parade of misery could he pray for his neighbor to get the job, and could he be expected to follow up his prayer by giving up his chance, and so making certain the prolongation of the misery of his wife and little ones?

No, my friend, Socialism is a bread and butter question. It is a question of the stomach; it is going to be settled in the factories, mines and ballot boxes of this country and is not going to be settled at the altar or in the church.

This is what our well-fed friends call a 'base, material standpoint,' but remember that beauty, and genius and art and poetry and all the finer efflorescences of the higher nature of man can only be realized in all their completeness upon the material basis of a healthy body, that not only an army but the whole human race marches upon its stomach, and then you will grasp the full wisdom of our position.

That the question to be settled by Socialism is the effect of private ownership of the means of production upon the well-being of the race; that we are determined to have a straight fight upon the question between those who believe that such private ownership is destructive of human well-being and those who believe it to be beneficial, that as men of all religions and of none are in the ranks of the capitalists, and men of all religions and of none are on the side of the workers the attempt to make religion an issue in the question is an intrusion, an impertinence and an absurdity.

Personally I am opposed to any system wherein the capitalist is more powerful than God Almighty. You need not serve God unless you like, and may refuse to serve him and grow fat, prosperous and universally respected. But if you refuse to serve the capitalist your doom is sealed; misery and poverty and public odium await you.

No worker is compelled to enter a church and to serve God; every worker is compelled to enter the employment of a capitalist and serve him.

As Socialists we are concerned to free mankind from the servitude forced upon them as a necessity of their life; we propose to allow the question of all kinds of service voluntarily rendered to be settled by the emancipated human race of the future.

I do not deny that Socialists often leave the church. But why do they do so? Is their defection from the church a result of our attitude towards religion; or is it the result of the attitude of the church and its ministers toward Socialism?

Let us take a case in point, one of those cases that are being paralleled every day in our midst. An Irish Catholic joins the Socialist movement. He finds that as a rule the Socialist men and women are better educated than their fellows; he finds that they are immensely cleaner in speech and thought than are the adherents of capitalism in the same class; that they are devoted husbands and loyal wives, loving and cheerful fathers and mothers, skilful and industrious workers in the shops and office, and that although poor and needy as a rule, yet that they continually bleed themselves to support their cause, and give up for Socialism what many others spend in the saloon.

He finds that a drunken Socialist is as rare as a white blackbird, and that a Socialist of criminal tendencies is such a rara avis that when one is found the public press heralds it forth as a great discovery.

Democratic and republican jailbirds are so common that the public press do not regard their existence as 'news' to anybody, nor yet does the public press think it necessary to say that certain criminals belong to the Protestant or Catholic religions. That is nothing unusual, and therefore not worth printing. But a criminal Socialist—that would be news indeed!

Our Irish Catholic Socialist gradually begins to notice these things. He looks around and he finds the press full of reports of crimes, murders, robberies, bank swindlers, forgeries, debauches, gambling transactions, and midnight orgies in which the most revolting indecencies are perpetrated. He investigates and he discovers that the perpetrators of these crimes were respectable capitalists, pillars of society, and red-hot enemies of Socialism, and that the dives in which the highest and the lowest meet together in a saturnalia of vice contribute a large proportion of the campaign funds of the capitalist political parties.

Some Sunday he goes to Mass as usual, and he finds that at Gospel the priest launches out into a political speech and tells the congregation that the honest, self-sacrificing, industrious, clean men and women, whom he calls 'comrades,' are a wicked, impious, dissolute sect, desiring to destroy the home, to distribute the earnings of the provident among the idle and lazy of the world, and reveling in all sorts of impure thoughts about women.

And as this Irish Catholic Socialist listens to this foul libel, what wonder if the hot blood of anger rushes to his face, and he begins to believe that the temple of God has itself been sold to the all desecrating grasp of the capitalist?

While he is yet wondering what to think of the matter, he hears that his immortal soul will be lost if he fails to vote for capitalism, and he reflects that if he lined up with the brothel keepers, gambling house proprietors, race track swindlers, and white slave traders to vote the capitalist ticket, this same priest would tell him he was a good Catholic and loyal son of the church.

At such a juncture the Irish Catholic Socialist often rises up, goes out of the church and wipes its dust off his feet forever. Then we are told that Socialism took him away from the church. But did it? Was it not rather the horrible spectacle of a priest of God standing up in the Holy Presence lying about and slandering honest men and women, and helping to support political parties whose campaign fund in every large city represents more bestiality than ever Sodom and Gomorrah knew?

These are the things that drive Socialists from the church, and the responsibility for every soul so lost lies upon those slanderers and not upon the Socialist movement.

[*Socialism and Nationalism*]

Well, you won't get the Irish to help you. Our Irish-American leaders tell us that all we Irish in this country ought to stand together and use our votes to free Ireland.

Sure, let us free Ireland!

Never mind such base, carnal thoughts as concern work and wages, healthy homes, or lives unclouded by poverty.

Let us free Ireland!

The rackrenting landlord; is he not also an Irishman, and wherefore should we hate him? Nay, let us not speak harshly of our brother—yea, even when he raises our rent.

Let us free Ireland!

The profit-grinding capitalist, who robs us of three-fourths of the fruits of our labor, who sucks the very marrow of our bones when we are young, and then throws us out in the street, like a worn-out tool, when we are grown prematurely old in his service, is he not an Irishman, and mayhap a patriot, and wherefore should we think harshly of him?

Let us free Ireland!

'The land that bred and bore us.' And the landlord who makes us pay for permission to live upon it.

Whoop it up for liberty!

'Let us free Ireland,' says the patriot who won't touch Socialism.

Let us all join together and cr-r-rush the br-r-rutal Saxon. Let us all join together, says he, all classes and creeds.

And, says the town worker, after we have crushed the Saxon and freed Ireland, what will we do?

Oh, then you can go back to your slums, same as before.

Whoop it up for liberty!

And, says the agricultural workers, after we have freed Ireland, what then?

Oh, then you can go scraping around for the landlord's rent or the money-lenders' interest same as before.

Whoop it up for liberty!

After Ireland is free, says the patriot who won't touch Socialism, we will protect all classes, and if you won't pay your rent you will be evicted same as now. But the evicting party, under command of the sheriff, will wear green uniforms and the Harp without the Crown, and the warrant turning you out on the roadside will be stamped with the arms of the Irish Republic.

Now, isn't that worth fighting for?

And when you cannot find employment, and, giving up the struggle of life in despair, enter the Poorhouse, the band of the nearest regiment of the Irish army will escort you to the Poorhouse door to the tune of 'St. Patrick's Day.'

Oh, it will be nice to live in those days!

'With the Green Flag floating o'er us' and an ever-increasing army of unemployed workers walking about under the Green Flag, wishing they had something to eat. Same as now!

Whoop it up for liberty!

Now, my friend, I also am Irish, but I'm a bit more logical. The capitalist, I say, is a parasite on industry; as useless in the present stage of our industrial development as any other parasite in the animal or vegetable world is to the life of the animal or vegetable upon which it feeds.

The working class is the victim of this parasite—this human leech, and it is the duty and interest of the working class to use every means in its power to oust this parasite class from the position which enables it to thus prey upon the vitals of Labor.

Therefore, I say, let us organize as a class to meet our masters and destroy their mastership; organize to drive them from their hold upon public life through their political power; organize to wrench from their robber clutch the land and workshops on and in which they enslave us; organize to cleanse our social life from the stain of social cannibalism, from the preying of man upon his fellow man.

Organize for a full, free and happy life FOR ALL OR FOR NONE.

SECTION II POLITICAL ACTION OF LABOR

The great strike of the shop employes on the Canadian Pacific Railway has been declared off—lost. While the shopmen were fighting desperately to maintain their organization and decent working conditions, the engineers, firemen, conductors, trainmen, etc., worked with scabs imported from the states and from Europe, and thus by keeping trains moving aided to break the strike. It is only one more illustration of what a vicious, not to say downright criminal, scheme craft autonomy actually is in practice.

Here's another example: After four years of hard fighting from the Mississippi river to the Pacific coast and from the Ohio river to the gulf, the machinists have been compelled to abandon their strikes on the Santa Fe and the L. and N. railways. The engines and cars built and repaired in the railway shops by strike-breakers were hauled over the roads by members of the old brotherhoods without the slightest objections. No wonder that onlookers become disgusted with such 'unionism.' Some union cards cover a multitude of sins.—

MAX HAYES in *International Socialist Review*

Industrial and Political Unity

At meetings throughout this country one frequently hears speakers laboring to arouse the workers to their duty, exclaiming:

'You unite industrially, why then do you divide politically? You unite against the bosses in strikes and lock-outs, and then you foolishly divide when you go to the ballot-box. Why not unite at the ballot-box as you unite in the workshop? Why not show the same unity on the political field as you do on the industrial battlefield?'

At first blush this looks to be an exceedingly apt and forcible form of appeal to our fellow-workers, but when examined more attentively it will be seen that in view of the facts of our industrial warfare this appeal is based upon a flagrant mis-statement of facts. The real truth is that the workers do not unite industrially, but on the contrary are most hopelessly divided on the industrial field, and that their division and confusion on the political field are the direct result of their division and confusion on the industrial field. It would be easy to prove that even our most loyal trade unionists habitually play the game of the capitalist class on the industrial field just as surely as the Republican and Democratic workers do it on the political field. Let us examine the situation on the industrial field and see if it justifies the claim that economically the workers are united, or if it justifies the contention I make that the division of the workers on the political field is but the reflex of the confused ideas derived from the practice of the workers in strikes and lock-outs.

Quite recently we had a great strike of the workers employed on the Subway and Elevated systems of street car service in New York. The men showed a splendid front against the power of the mammoth capitalist company headed by August Belmont, against which they were arrayed. Conductors, motormen, ticket-choppers, platform men, repairers, permanent way men, ticket-sellers—all went out together and for a time paralyzed the entire traffic on their respective system. The company, on the other hand, had the usual recourse to Jim Farley and his scabs and sought to man the trains with those professional traitors to their class. The number of scabs was large, but small in proportion to the men on strike, yet the strike was broken. It was not the scabs, however, who turned the scale against the strikers in favor of the men. That service to capital was performed by good union men with union cards in their pockets. These men were the engineers in the power houses which supplied the electric power to run the cars, and without whom all the scabs combined could not have run a single trip. A scab is a vile creature, but what shall we say of the men who helped the scab to commit his act of treason? The law says that an accessory before the fact is equally guilty of a crime with the actual criminal. What, then, are the trade unionists who supplied the power to scabs to help them break a strike?

They were unconsciously being compelled by their false system of organization to betray their struggling brothers. Was this unity on the industrial field? And is it any wonder that the men accustomed to so scab upon their fellow-workers in a labor struggle should also scab it upon their class in a political struggle? Is it not rather common sense to expect that the *recognition of the necessity for concerted common action of all workers against the capitalist enemy in the industrial battle ground must precede the realization of the wisdom of common action as a class on the political battlefield?* The men who are taught that it is all right to continue working for a capitalist against whom their shop-mates of a different craft are on strike are not likely to see any harm in continuing to vote for a capitalist nominee at the polls even when he is opposed by the candidate of a Labor organization. Political scabbery is born of industrial scabbery; it is its legitimate offspring.

Instances of this industrial disunion could be cited indefinitely. The Longshoremen of the Port of New York went out on strike. They at first succeeded in tying up the ships of the Shipping Trust, great as its wealth is, and in demonstrating the real power of labor when unhampered by contracts with capital. The Shipping Trust was taken by surprise, but quickly recovered, and as usual imported scabs from all over the country. Then was seen what the unity of the working class on the industrial field amounts to under present conditions. As scab longshoremen unloaded the ship, union teamsters with union buttons in their hats received the goods from their hands, loaded them into their wagons, and drove merrily away.

As scab longshoremen loaded a ship union men coaled it, and when the cargo was safely on board union marine engineers set up steam, and union seamen and firemen took it out of the dock on its voyage to its destination. Can men who are trained and taught to believe that such a course of conduct is right and proper be expected to realize the oneness of the interests of the working class as a whole against the capitalist class as a whole, and vote and act accordingly? In short, can their field of vision be so extensive that it can see the brotherhood of all men, and yet so restricted that it can see no harm in a brother labor organization in their own industry being beaten to death by capital?

Contrast this woeful picture of divided and disorganized 'unionism' in America with the following account from the New York *Sun* of the manner in which the Socialist unionists of Scandinavia stand together in a fight against the common enemy, irrespective of 'craft interests' or 'craft contracts':

> A short sojourn in Scandinavia, particularly in Copenhagen and the southern part of Sweden, gives one an object lesson in socialism. In some way or other the socialists have managed to capture all the trade unions in these parts and between them have caused a reign of terror for everybody who is unfortunate enough to own a business of any sort. Heaven help him if he fires one of his helps or tries to assert himself in any way. He is immediately declared in 'blockade.'
>
> This socialist term means practically the same as a boycott. If the offending business man happens to be a retail merchant all workmen are warned off his premises. The drivers for the wholesale houses refuse to deliver goods at his store; the truckmen refuse to cart anything to or from his place, and so on; in fact, he is a doomed man unless he comes to terms with the union. It is worth mentioning that boycotting bulletins and also the names and addresses of those who are bold enough to help the man out are published in leaded type in all the socialistic newspapers. A law to prevent the publication of such boycotting announcements was proposed in the Swedish riksdag this year, but was defeated.
>
> If the boycotted person be a wholesale dealer the proceedings are much the same, or, rather, they are reversed. The retailers are threatened with the loss of the workmen's trade unless they cease dealing with such a firm; the truckmen refuse to haul for it. It has even happened that the scavengers have refused to remove the refuse from the premises. More often, however, the cans are 'accidentally' dropped on the stairs. These scavengers belong to the cities' own forces, as a rule, and receive

> pensions after a certain length of service, but they have all sworn allegiance to the socialistic cause.
>
> In reading the foregoing it is well to remember that practically all the workingmen of such cities—that is, practically all Sweden and Denmark—are union men, i.e., socialists, and are, therefore, able to carry out their threats.

Here we have a practical illustration of the power of Socialism when it rests upon an economic organization, and the effectiveness and far-reaching activity of unionism when it is inspired by the Socialist ideal. Now as an equally valuable object lesson in American unionism, an object lesson in how not to do it, let us picture a typical state of affairs in the machine industry. The moulders' contract with the boss expires and they go out on strike. In a machine shop the moulder occupies a position intermediate between the pattern-maker and the machinist, or, as they are called in Ireland, the engineers. When the moulders go out the boss who has had all his plans laid for months beforehand brings in a staff of scabs and installs them in the places of the striking workers. Then the tragi-comedy begins. The union pattern-maker makes his patterns and hands them over to the scab moulder; the scab moulder casts his moulds and when they are done the union machinist takes them from him and placidly finishes the job. Then having finished their day's work, they go to their union meetings and *vote donations of a few hundred dollars to help the strikers to defeat the boss, after they had worked all day to help the boss to defeat the strikers*. Thus they exemplify the solidarity of labor. When the moulders are beaten the machinists and the patternmakers, and the blacksmiths, and the electricians, and the engineers, and all the rest take their turn of going up against the boss in separate bodies to be licked. As each is taking its medicine its fellows of other crafts in the same shop sympathize with it in the name of the solidarity of labor, and continue to work in the service of the capitalist, against whom the strike is directed, in the name of the sacred contract of the craft union.

When the coal miners of Pennsylvania had their famous

strike in 1902 the railroad brotherhoods hauled in scabs to take their places, and when the scabs had mined coal the same railroad men hauled out this scab-mined coal.

Need I go on to prove the point that industrial division and discord is the order of the day amongst the workers, and that this disunion and confusion on the economic field cannot fail to perpetuate itself upon the political field? Those orators who reproach the workers with being divided on the political field, although united on the industrial, are simply mis-stating facts. The workers are divided on both, and as political parties are the reflex of economic conditions, it follows that industrial union once established will create the political unity of the working class. I feel that we cannot too strongly insist upon this point. Political division is born of industrial division; political scabbery is born of industrial craft scabbery; political weakness keeps even step with industrial weakness. It is an axiom enforced by all the experience of the ages that they who rule industrially will rule politically, and therefore they who are divided industrially will remain impotent politically. The failure of Mr. Gompers to unite politically the forces of the American Federation of Labor was the inevitable outcome of his own policy of division on the industrial battle ground; he reversed the natural process by trying to unite men on class lines whilst he opposed every effort, as in the case of the Brewers, to unite them on industrial lines. The natural lines of thought and action lead from the direct to the indirect, from the simple to the complex, from the immediate to the ultimate. Mr. Gompers ignored this natural line of development and preached the separation into craft organizations, with separate craft interests, of the workers, and then expected them to heed his call to unity on the less direct and immediate battleground of politics. He failed, as even the Socialists would fail if they remained equally blind to the natural law of our evolution into class consciousness. That natural law leads us as individuals to unite in our craft, as crafts to unite in our industry, as industries in our class, and the finished expression of that evolution is, we believe, the appearance of our class upon the political battle ground with all the economic power behind it to enforce its mandates. Until that day dawns our political parties of the working class are but propagandist agencies, John the Baptists of the New Redemption, but when that day dawns our political party will be armed with all the might of our class; will be revolutionary in fact as well as in thought.

To Irish men and women especially, I should not need to labour this point. The historic example of their Land League bequeaths to us a precious legacy of wisdom, both practical and revolutionary, outlining our proper course of action. During Land League days in Ireland when a tenant was evicted from a farm, not only his fellow-tenants but practically the whole country united to help him in his fight. When the evicted farm was rented by another tenant, a land-grabber or 'scab,' every person in the countryside shunned him as a leper, and, still better, fought him as a traitor. Nor did they make the mistake of fighting the traitor and yet working for his employer, the landlord. No, they included both in the one common hostility.

At the command of the Land League every servant and laborer quit the service of the landlord. In Ireland, it is well to remember, in order to appreciate this act of the laborers, that the landlords were usually better paymasters and more generous employers than the tenant farmers. The laborers, therefore, might reasonably have argued that the fight of the tenant farmers was none of their business. But they indulged in no such blindly selfish hair-splitting. When the landlord had declared war upon the tenant by evicting him, the laborers responded by war upon the landlord. Servant boy and servant girl at once quit his service, the carman refused to drive him, the cook to cook for him, his linen remained unwashed, his harvest unreaped, his cows unmilked, his house and fields deserted. The grocer and the butcher, the physician and the schoolmaster were alike hostile to him; if the children of the land-grabber (scab) entered school all other children rose and left; if the land-grabber or his landlord attended Mass everyone else at Mass walked out in a body. They found it hard to get anyone to serve them or feed them in health, to attend them in sickness, or to bury those dear to them in death. It was this relentless and implacable war upon the landowning class and traitors among the tenant class which gave the word 'boycott' to the English language through its enforcement against an Irish landowner, Captain Boycott. It was often horrible, it was always ugly in appearance to the superficial observer, but it was marvelously effective. It put courage and hope and manhood into a class long reckoned as the most enslaved in Europe. It broke the back of the personal despotism of the Irish landlord and so crippled his social and economic power that Irish landed estates from being a favorite form of investment for the financial interests sank to such a position that even the most reckless moneylender would for a time scarce accept a mortgage upon them. That it failed of attaining real economic freedom for the Irish people was due not to any defect in its method of fighting, but rather to the fact that economic questions are not susceptible of being settled within the restricted radius of any one small nation, but are acted upon by influences world-wide in their character.

But how great a lesson for the American worker is to be found in this record of a class struggle in Ireland! The American worker was never yet so low in the social and political scale as the Irish tenant. Yet the Irish tenant rose and by sheer force of his unity on the economic field shattered the power of his master, whilst the American worker remaining divided upon the economic field sinks day by day lower toward serfdom. The Irish tenant had to contend against the overwhelming power of a foreign empire backing up the economic power of a native tyranny, yet he conquered, whilst the American worker able to become the political sovereign of the country remains the sport of the political factions of his masters and the slave of their social power.

The Irish tenant uniting on the economic field felt his strength, and, carrying the fight into politics, simply swept into oblivion every individual or party that refused to serve his class interests, but the American toilers remain divided on the economic field, and hence are divided and impotent upon the political, zealous servants of every interest but their own.

Need I point the moral more? Every one who has the

interests of the working class at heart, every one who wishes to see the Socialist Party command the allegiance of the political hosts of labor, should strive to realize industrial union as the solid foundation upon which alone the political unity of the workers can be built up and directed toward a revolutionary end. To this end all those who work for industrial unionism are truly co-operating even when they least care for political activities.

Industrial Unionism and Constructive Socialism

> There is not a socialist in the world today who can indicate with any degree of clearness how we can bring about the co-operative commonwealth except along the lines suggested by industrial organization of the workers.
>
> Political institutions are not adapted to the administration of industry. Only industrial organizations are adapted to the administration of a co-operative commonwealth that we are working for. Only the industrial form of organization offers us even a theoretical constructive socialist program. There is no constructive socialism except in the industrial field.

The above extract from the speech of a delegate to the National Convention of the Socialist Party, Delegate Stirton, Editor of the *Wage Slave*, of Hancock, Michigan, so well embodies my ideas upon this matter that I have thought well to take them as a text for an article in explanation of the structural form of Socialist Society. In a previous chapter I have analyzed the weakness of the craft or trade union form of organization alike as a weapon of defense against the capitalist class in the everyday conflicts on the economic field, and as a generator of class consciousness on the political field, and pointed out the greater effectiveness for both purposes of an industrial form of organization. In the present article I desire to show how they who are engaged in building up industrial organizations for the practical purposes of to-day are at the same time preparing the framework of the society of the future. It is the realization of that fact that indeed marks the emergence of Socialism as a revolutionary force from the critical to the positive stage. Time was when Socialists, if asked how society would be organized under Socialism replied invariably, and airily, that such things would be left to the future to decide. The fact was that they had not considered the matter, but the development of the Trust and Organized Capital in general, making imperative the Industrial Organizations of Labor on similar lines has provided us with an answer at once more complete to ourselves and more satisfying to our questioners.

Now to analyze briefly the logical consequences of the position embodied in the above quotation.

'Political institutions are not adapted to the administration of industry.'

Here is a statement that no Socialist with a clear knowledge of the essentials of his doctrine can dispute. The political institutions of today are simply the coercive forces of capitalist society, they have grown up out of and are based upon territorial divisions of power in the hands of the ruling class in past ages, and were carried over into capitalist society to suit the needs of the capitalist class when that class overthrew the dominion of its predecessors. The delegation of the function of government into the hands of representatives elected from certain districts, states, or territories represents no real natural division suited to the requirements of modern society but is a survival from a time when territorial influences were more potent in the world than industrial influences, and for that reason is totally unsuited to the needs of the new social order which must be based upon industry. The Socialist thinker when he paints the structural form of the new social order does not imagine an industrial system directed or ruled by a body of men or women elected from an indiscriminate mass of residents within given districts, said residents working at a heterogeneous collection of trades and industries. To give the ruling, controlling and directing of industry into the hands of such a body would be too utterly foolish. What the Socialist does realize is that under a Social Democratic form of Society the administration of affairs will be in the hands of representatives of the various industries of the nation; that the workers in the shops and factories will organize themselves into unions, each union comprising all the workers at a given industry, that said union will democratically control the workshop life of its own industry, electing all foremen, etc., and regulating the routine of labor in that industry in subordination to the needs of society in general, to the needs of its allied trades and to the department of industry to which it belongs. That representatives elected from these various departments of industry will meet and form the industrial administration or national government of the country. In short Social Democracy, as its name implies, is the application to industry, or to the Social life of the nation, of the fundamental principles of democracy. Such application will necessarily have to begin in the workshop, and proceed logically and consecutively upward through all the grades of industrial organization until it reaches the culminating point of national executive power and direction. In other words Social Democracy must proceed from the bottom upward, whereas capitalist political society is organized from above downward; Social Democracy will be administered by a committee of experts elected from the industries and professions of the land; capitalist society is governed by representatives elected from districts, and is based upon territorial division. The local and national governing or rather administrative bodies of Socialism will approach every question with impartial minds armed with the fullest expert knowledge born of experience; the governing bodies of capitalist society have to call in an expensive professional expert to instruct them on every technical question, and know that the impartiality of said expert varies with and depends upon the size of his fee.

It will be seen that this conception of Socialism destroys at one blow all the fears of a bureaucratic state, ruling and ordering the lives of every individual from above, and thus gives assurance that the social order of the future will be an extension of the freedom of the individual, and not a suppression of it. In short it blends the fullest democratic control with the most absolute expert supervision, something unthinkable of any society built upon the political state. To focus the idea properly in your mind you have but to realize how industry to-day transcends all limitations of territory and leaps across rivers, mountains and continents, then you can understand how impossible it would be to apply to such far reaching intricate enterprises the principle of democratic control by the workers through the medium of political territorial divisions.

Under Socialism states, territories or provinces will exist only as geographical expressions, and have no existence as sources of governmental power, though they may be seats of administrative bodies.

Now having grasped the idea that the administrative force of the Socialist Republic of the future will function through unions industrially organized, that the principle of democratic control will operate through the workers correctly organized in such Industrial Unions, and that the political, territorial state of capitalist society will have no place or function under Socialism, you will at once grasp the full truth embodied in the words of this member of the Socialist Party whom I have just quoted, that 'only the industrial form of organization offers us even a theoretical constructive Socialist program.'

To some minds constructive Socialism is embodied in the work of our representatives on the various public bodies to which they have been elected. The various measures against the evils of capitalist property brought forward by, or as a result of the agitation of Socialist representatives on legislative bodies are figured as being of the nature of constructive Socialism. As we have shown the political state of capitalism has no place under Socialism, therefore measures which aim to place industries in the hands of or under the control of such a political state are in no sense steps towards that ideal; they are but useful measures to restrict the greed of capitalism and to familiarize the workers with the conception of common ownership. This latter is indeed their chief function. But the enrollment of the workers in unions patterned closely after the structure of modern industries, and following the organic lines of industrial development is par excellence the swiftest, safest, and most peaceful form of constructive work the Socialist can engage in. It prepares within the framework of capitalist society the working forms of the Socialist Republic, and thus while increasing the resisting power of the worker against present encroachments of the capitalist class it familiarizes him with the idea that the union he is helping to build up is destined to supplant that class in the control of the industry in which he is employed.

The power of this idea to transform the dry detail work of trade union organization into the constructive work of revolutionary Socialism, and thus to make of the unimaginative trade unionist a potent factor in the launching of a new system of society cannot be overestimated. It invests the sordid details of the daily incidents of the class struggle with a new and beautiful meaning, and presents them in their true light as skirmishes between the two opposing armies of light and darkness. In the light of this principle of Industrial Unionism every fresh shop or factory organized under its banner is a fort wrenched from the control of the capitalist class and manned with the soldiers of the Revolution to be held by them for the workers. On the day that the political and economic forces of labor finally break with capitalist society and proclaim the Workers Republic these shops and factories so manned by Industrial Unionists will be taken charge of by the workers there employed, and force and effectiveness thus given to that proclamation. Then and thus the new society will spring into existence ready equipped to perform all the useful functions of its predecessor.

The Future of Labor

In choosing for the subject of this chapter such a title as 'The Future of Labor,' I am aware that I run the risk of arousing expectations that I shall not be able to satisfy. The future of labor is a subject with which is bound up the future of civilization, and therefore a comprehensive treatment of the subject might be interpreted as demanding an analysis of all the forces and factors which will influence humanity in the future, and also their resultant effect.

Needless to say, my theme is a less ambitious one. I propose simply to deal with the problem of labor in the immediate future, with the marshalling of labor for the great conflict that confronts us, and with a consideration of the steps to be taken in order that the work of aiding the transition from Industrial Slavery to Industrial Freedom might be, as far as possible, freed from all encumbering and needless obstacles and expense of time, energy, and money.

But first and as an aid to a proper understanding of my position, let me place briefly before you my reading of the history of the past struggles of mankind against social subjection, my reading of the mental development undergone by each revolting class in the different stages of their struggle, from the first period of their bondage to the first dawn of their freedom. As I view it, such struggles had three well-marked mental stages, corresponding to the inception, development, and decay of the oppressing powers, and as I intend to attempt to apply this theory to the position of labor as a subject class to-day, I hope you will honor me by at least giving me your earnest attention to this conception, and aid by your discussion in determining at which of these periods or stages, the working class, the subject class of to-day, has arrived. My reading then briefly is this: That in the first period of bondage the eyes of the subject class are always turned toward the past, and all its efforts in revolt are directed to the end of destroying the social system in order that it might march backward and re-establish the social order of ancient times—'the good old days.' That the goodness of those days was largely hypothetical seldom enters the imagination of men on whose limbs the fetters of oppression still sit awkwardly.

In the second period the subject class tends more and more to lose sight and recollection of any pre-existent state of society, to believe that the social order in which it finds itself always did exist, and to bend all its energies to obtaining such ameliorations of its lot within existent society as will make that lot more bearable. At this stage of society the subject class, as far as its own aspirations are concerned, may be reckoned as a conservative force.

In the third period the subject class becomes revolutionary, recks little of the past for inspiration, but, building itself upon the achievements of the present, confidently addresses itself to the conquest of the future. It does so because the development of the framework of society has revealed to it its relative importance, revealed to it the fact that within its grasp has grown, unconsciously to itself, a power which, if intelligently applied, is sufficient to overcome and master society at large.

As a classic illustration of this conception of the history of the mental development of the revolt against social oppression, we might glance at the many peasant revolts recorded in European history. As we are now aware, common ownership of land was at one time the basis of society all over the world. Our fathers not only owned their land in common, but in many ways practiced a common ownership of the things produced. In short, tribal communism was at one time the universally existent order. In such a state of society there existed a degree of freedom that no succeeding order has been able to parallel, and that none will be able to, until the individualistic order of to-day gives way to the Industrial Commonwealth, the Workers' Republic, of the future. How that ancient order broke up it is no part of my task to tell. What I do wish to draw your attention to, is that for hundreds, for a thousand years after the break up of that tribal communism, and the reduction to serfdom of the descendants of the formerly free tribesmen, all the efforts of the revolting serfs were directed to a destruction of the new order of things and to a rehabilitation of the old. Take as an example the various peasant wars of Germany, the Jacquerie of France, or the revolt of Wat Tyler and John Ball in England as being the best known; examine their rude literature in such fragments as have been preserved, study their speeches as they have been recorded even by their enemies, read the translations of their songs, and in all of them you will find a passionate harking back to the past, a morbid idealizing of the status of their fathers, and a continued exhortation to the suffering people to destroy the present in order that, in some vague and undefined manner, they might reconstitute the old.

The defeat of the peasantry left the stage clear for the emergence of the bourgeoisie as the most important subject class and for the development of that second period of which I have spoken. Did it develop? Well, in every account we read of the conflicts between the nobility and the burghers in their guilds and cities we find that the aggressive part was always taken by the former and that wherever a revolt took place, the revolting guild merchants and artisans justified their act by an appeal to the past privileges which had been abrogated and the restoration of which formed the basis of their claims, and their only desire if successful in revolt. One of the most curious illustrations of this mental condition is to be found in the *History of the Rise of the Dutch Republic.* by Motley,[1] in which that painstaking historian tells how the Netherlands in their revolt against the Spanish Emperor continued for a generation to base their claims upon the political status of the provinces under a former Emperor, made war upon the Empire with troops levied in the name of the Emperor, and led by officers whose commissions were made out by the rebel provinces in the name of the sovereign they were fighting against. This mental condition lasted in England until the great Civil War, which ended by leaving Charles I without a head, and the bourgeoisie, incarnated in Cromwell, firmly fixed in the saddle; in France it lasted till the Revolution. In both countries it was abandoned, not because of any *a priori* reasoning upon its absurdity nor because some great thinker had evolved a better scheme—but because the growth of the industrial system had made the capitalist class realize that they could at any moment stop the flow of its life-blood, so to speak, and from so realizing it was but a short mental evolution *to frame a theory of political action which proclaimed that the capitalist class was the nation,* and all its enemies the enemies of the nation at large. The last period of that social evolution had been reached, the last mental stage of the transition from feudal ownership to capitalist property.

Now let me apply this reading of history to the development of the working class under capitalism and find out what lessons it teaches us, of value in our present struggle. Passing by the growth of the working class under nascent capitalism, as it belongs more to the period I have just dealt with than to the present subject, and taking up working class history from the

[1] There were several editions that Connolly could have read, published in London by Routledge (1882), Ward, Lock (1883) and Sonnenschein (1889).

point marked by the introduction of machinery to supplant hand labor—a perfectly correct standpoint for all practical purposes—we find in the then attitude of the workers an exemplification of the historical fidelity of our conception. Suffering from the miseries attendant upon machine labor, the displacement of those supplanted and the scandalous overworking of those retained, the workers rioted and rebelled in a mad effort to abolish machinery and restore the era of hand labor. In a word, they strove to revert to past conditions, and their most popular orators and leaders were they who pictured in most glowing terms the conditions prevalent in the days of their fathers.

They were thus on the same mental plane as those mediæval peasants who, in their revolt, were fired by the hope of restoring the primitive commune. And just as in the previously cited case, the inevitable failure of this attempt to reconstruct the past was followed in another generation by movements which accepted the social order of their day as permanent, and looked upon their social status as wage-slaves as fixed and immutable in the eternal order of things. To this category belongs the trade union movement in all its history. As the struggles of the serfs and burghers in the middle ages were directed to no higher aim than the establishing of better relations between these struggling classes and their feudal overlords, as during those ages the division of society into ruling classes of king, lords, and church resting upon a basis of the serfdom of the producers, was accepted by all in spite of the perpetual recurrences of civil wars between the various classes, so, in capitalist society, the trade unionists, despite strikes, lock-outs, and black lists, accepted the employing class as part and parcel of a system which was to last through all eternity.

The rise of Industrial Unionism is the first sign that that—the second stage of the mental evolution of our class—is rapidly passing away. And the fact that it had its inception amongst men actually engaged in the work of trade union organization, and found its inspiration in a recognition of the necessities born of the struggles of the workers, and not in the theories of any political party—this fact is the most cheering sign of the legitimacy of its birth and the most hopeful augury of its future. For we must not forget that it is not the theorists who make history; it is history in its evolution that makes the theorists. And the roots of history are to be found in the workshops, fields, and factories. It has been remarked that Belgium was the cockpit of Europe because within its boundaries have been fought out many of the battles between the old dynasties; in like manner we can say that the workshop is the cockpit of civilization because in the workshop has been and will be fought out those battles between the new and the old methods of production, the issues of which change the face and the history of the world.

I have said that the capitalist class became a revolutionary class when it realized that it held control of the economic heart of the nation. I may add when the working class is in the same position, it will also as a class become revolutionary, it will also give effective political expression to its economic strength. The capitalist class grew into a political party when it looked around and found itself in control of the things needed for the life of the individual and the State, when it saw that the ships carrying the commerce of the nation were its own, when it saw that the internal traffic of the nation was in the hands of its agents, when it saw that the feeding, clothing and sheltering of the ruling class depended upon the activities of the subject class, when it saw itself applied to to furnish finance to equip the armies and fleets of the kings and nobles, in short, when the capitalist class found that all the arteries of commerce, all the agencies of production, all the mainsprings of life in fact, passed through their hands as blood flows through the human heart—then and only then did capital raise the banner of political revolt and from a class battling for concessions became a class leading its forces to the mastery of society at large.

This leads me to the last axiom of which I wish you to grasp the significance. It is this, that the fight for the conquest of the political state is not the battle, it is only the echo of the battle. The real battle is the battle being fought out every day for the power to control industry and the gauge of the progress of that battle is not to be found in the number of voters making a cross beneath the symbol of a political party, but in the number of these workers who enrol themselves in an industrial organization with the definite purpose of making themselves masters of the industrial equipment of society in general.

That battle will have its political echo, that industrial organization will have its political expression. *If we accept the definition of working class political action as that which brings the workers as a class into direct conflict with the possessing class* AS A CLASS, *and keeps them there, then we must realize that* NOTHING CAN DO THAT SO READILY AS ACTION AT THE BALLOT BOX. Such action strips the working class movement of all traces of such sectionalism as may, and indeed must, cling to strikes and lock-outs, and emphasizes the class character of the Labor Movement. IT IS THEREFORE ABSOLUTELY INDISPENSABLE FOR THE EFFICIENT TRAINING OF THE WORKING CLASS ALONG CORRECT LINES THAT ACTION AT THE BALLOT BOX SHOULD ACCOMPANY ACTION IN THE WORKSHOP.

I am convinced that this will be the ultimate formation of the fighting hosts of Labor. The workers will be industrially organized on the economic field and until that organization is perfected, whilst the resultant feeling of class-consciousness is permeating the minds of the workers, the Socialist Party will carry on an independent campaign of education and attack upon the political field, and as a consequence will remain the sole representative of the Socialist idea in politics. But as industrial organization grows, feels its strength, and develops the revolutionary instincts of its members there will grow also the desire for a closer union and identification of the two wings of the army of Labor. Any attempt prematurely to force this identification would only defeat its own purpose, and be fraught with danger alike to the economic and the political wing. Yet it is certain that such attempts will be of continual recurrence and multiply in proportion to the dissatisfaction felt at the waste of energy involved in the division of forces. Statesmanship of the highest kind will be required to see that this union shall take place only under the proper conditions and at the proper moment for effective action. Two things must be kept in mind, viz., that a Socialist Political Party not emanating from the ranks of organized Labor is, as Karl Marx phrased it, simply a Socialist sect, ineffective for the final revolutionary act, but that also the attempt of craft organized unions to create political unity before they have laid the foundation of industrial unity in their own, the economic field, would be an instance of putting the cart before the horse. But when that foundation of industrial union is finally secured then nothing can prevent the union of the economic and political forces of Labor. I look forward to the time when every economic organization will have its Political Committee, just as it has its Organization Committee or its Strike Committee, and when it will be counted to be as great a crime, as much an act of scabbery to act against the former as against any of the latter. When that time comes we will be able to count our effective vote before troubling the official ballot-box, simply by counting our membership in the allied organizations; we will be able to estimate our capacity for the revolutionary act of Social Transformation simply by taking stock of the number of industries we control and their importance relative to the whole social system, and when we find that we control the strategic industries in society, then society must bend to our will—or break. In our organizations we will have Woman Suffrage, whether governments like it or not, we will also have in our own organizations a pure and uncorrupted ballot, and if the official ballot of capitalist society does not purify itself of its own accord, its corruption can only serve to blind the eyes of our enemies, and not to hide our strength from ourselves.

Compare the political action of such a body with that of any party we know. Political parties are composed of men and women who meet together to formulate a policy and programme to vote upon. They set up a political ticket in the hope of getting people, most of whom they do not know, to vote for them, and when that vote is at last cast, it is cast by men whom they have not organized, do not know, and cannot rely upon to use in their own defense. We have proven that such a body can make propaganda, and good propaganda, for socialist principles, but it can never function as the weapon of an industrially organized working class. To it, such a party will always be an outside body, a body not under its direct control, but the political weapon of the *Industrially Organized Working Class will be a weapon of its own forging* and wielded by its own hand. I believe it to be incumbent upon organized Labor to meet the capitalist class upon every field where it can operate to our disadvantage. Therefore I favor direct attacks upon the control of governmental powers through the ballot-box, but I wish to see these attacks supported by the economic organization. In short, I believe that there is no function performed by a separate political party that the economic organization cannot help it perform much better and with greater safety to working class interests. Let us be clear as to the function of Industrial Unionism. That function is to build up an industrial republic inside the shell of the political State, in order that when that industrial republic is fully organized it may crack the shell of the political State and step into its place in the scheme of the universe. But in the process of upbuilding, during the period of maturing, the mechanism of the political State can be utilized to assist in the formation of the embryo Industrial Republic. Or, to change the analogy, we might liken the position of the Industrial Republic in its formative period towards political society, to the position of the younger generation towards the generation passing away. The younger accepts the achievements of the old, but gradually acquires strength to usurp its functions until the new generation is able to abandon the paternal household and erect its own. While doing so, it utilizes to the fullest all the privileges of its position. So the Industrial Unionist will function in a double capacity in capitalist society. In his position as a citizen in a given geographical area, he will use his political voting power in attacks upon the political system of capitalism, and in his position as a member of the Industrial Union he will help in creating the economic power which in the fullness of time will overthrow that political system, and replace it by the Industrial Republic.

My contentions along these lines do not imply by any means that I regard immediate action at the ballot box by the economic organization as essential, although I may regard it as advisable. As I have already indicated, the proletarian revolution will in that respect most likely follow the lines of the capitalist revolutions in the past.

In Cromwellian England, in Colonial America, in Revolutionary France the real political battle did not begin until after the bourgeoisie, the capitalist class, had become the dominant class in the nation. Then they sought to conquer political power in order to allow their economic power to function freely. It was no mere coincidence but a circumstance born of the very nature of things, woven, so to speak, in the warp and woof of fate, that in all the three countries the signal for the revolution was given by the ruling class touching the bourgeoisie in the one part that was calculated to arouse them as a class, and at the same time demonstrate their strength. That one sensitive part was their finance, their ownership of the sinews of war. In England it was over the question of taxes, of ship money, that Hampden first raised the standard of revolt whose last blow was struck at Whitehall when the king's head rolled in the gutter. In America it was over the question of taxes, and again the capitalist class were united, until a new nation was born to give them power. In France it was the failure of the king to raise taxes that led to the convocation of the States General, which assembly first revealed to the French capitalists their power as a class and set their feet upon the revolutionary path. In all three countries the political rebellion was but the expression of the will of a class already in possession of economic power. This is in conformity with the law of human evolution, that the new system can never overthrow the old, until it itself is fully matured and able to assume all the useful functions of the thing it is to dethrone.

In the light of such facts, and judging by such reasoning, we need not exercise our souls over the question of the date of the appearance of the Industrial Organizations of Labor upon the electoral field. Whether we believe, as I believe, that the electoral field offers it opportunities it would be criminal to ignore, or believe, as some do, that electoral action on the part of the economic organizations is at present premature, one thing we can be agreed upon, if we accept the outline of history I have just sketched, viz., that it is necessary to remember that at the present stage of development all actions of our class at the ballot box are in the nature of mere preliminary skirmishes, or educational campaigns and that *the conquest of political power by the working class waits upon the conquest of economic power*, and must function through the economic organization.

Hence, reader, if you belong to the working class your duty is clear. Your union must be perfected until it embraces every one who toils in the service of your employer, or as a unit in your industry. The fact that your employers find it necessary to secure the services of any individual worker is or ought to be that individual's highest and best title to be a member of your union. If the boss needs him you need him more. You need the *open union* and the *closed shop* if you ever intend to control the means and conditions of life. And, as the champion of your class upon the political field, as the ever active propagandist of the idea of the Working Class, as the representative and embodiment of the social principle of the future, you need the Socialist Party. The Future of Labor is bound up with the harmonious development of those twin expressions of the forces of progress; the Freedom of Labor will be born of their happily consummated union.

16. POLITICAL ACTION

The following article, which appeared in The Harp *for July 1908 as an editorial, is so clearly intended as a sequel to* Industrial Unionism and Constructive Socialism *in* Socialism Made Easy *that one finds it hard to account for its omission from that work.*

In our editorial of last month we dealt with the subject of Industrial Unionism, and pointed out that that method of organizing the Working Class provided the only really effective constructive work by which the daily and hourly conflict between the capitalist and the worker could be utilised to generate the steam necessary to carry the Social Revolution through, as well as to provide the forms of administration for the new Industrial Republic. In this issue we propose to say a few words about the structure and functions of Socialist political parties, as such. And as we have not seen anywhere a calm analysis of the different conceptions of political revolutionary action, such as we intend to present, we hope that our readers will extend to us in this instance also the patience and courtesy due and befitting among men and women devoting their lives to the work of emancipation.

The various Socialist parties, the sight of whom contending and attacking each other is so often a source of joy to the capitalist philistine, although they possess a common ideal, and a common concrete object to be worked for do not always possess a common belief in the means by which a political party to attain their end can be created. In this divergence of belief on the question of how to build a revolutionary political party is to be found the real reason for the warring political organisations of Socialism rather than in any divergence of belief in fundamentals. Of course as a rule neither set will admit this; each with all the zealotry of partisans will rather ascribe the existence of another party to the wicked designs of their opponents; if not to the machinations of the capitalist class. But such wildly reckless statements may be safely brushed aside. Whatever unclean or compromising elements may creep into a movement after it becomes popular it is fair to assume that Socialist parties are at their inception not very likely to attract any but the idealist or genuine revolutionist.

There are two distinct and opposing ideas as to how best to build a political party to do the political work of Socialism, and an understanding of these two ideas will serve to enable the reader to grasp the political situation better than listening to any amount of heated debate on the subject by the partisans of either. These two ideas may be briefly stated thus:

I. That the work of the Social Revolution can only be accomplished by men and women with a clear understanding of the economics of capitalism, that therefore a clear and definite program is the first essential, and in the interest of maintaining that definite program of the party it is imperative to expel out of the said party all speakers, writers, or even members who are not in the strictest harmony with its 'clean cut' principles, and

II. That the work of the Social Revolution depends in the last analysis upon the growth of class-consciousness amongst the working class, that therefore the chief task of a Socialist political party is to educate and direct that class consciousness along correct lines, that in order to do so allowance must continually be made for the gradual nature of its development, and for the stages thereof, that therefore it must be made possible for all who have accepted the central principles of common ownership to become members of the party irrespective of their knowledge or lack of knowledge of economics, and that the development of the political struggle of the Socialist movement must be depended upon to clear the minds of the members rather than any process of weeding out.

We think that we are right in outlining these two conceptions of the process of upbuilding a political party as the fundamental, underlying ideas which in practice have produced in the past warring parties of Socialism where harmony was looked for and demanded by the working class. The thoughtful unprejudiced reader will perceive that here is a more fundamental and at the same time more creditable source of disunity than is to be found in the usual allegations of 'dictation and despotism' on the one side, or 'compromise and confusion,' as freely alleged on the other. On the other hand it must be pointed out that, as was almost inevitable human nature being as it is, each of those parties tended to develop traits which seemed to verify the accusations of their opponents.

Dictation and despotism, interfering with the opinions of members on mere matters of party administration very soon followed upon the heels of the attempts of the first party to purify its ranks by expulsion, and compromise for the sake of getting votes at times treads closely in the wake of toleration and broadminded treatment of unfledged recruits.

In Europe the solution of this problem of uniting the political parties of Socialism has been sought in a unity which embraces both schools of thought and while not concealing their utter divergence provides in press and platform a means for discussion, as members, of the things that divide them, and insists that all must recognize the voice of the majority of the party as supreme. To some this may seem as a virtual surrender of its position by the first party, since it abandons its insistence upon the duty of a Socialist party to expel all those who are not 'clear' upon tactics, or are not orthodox.

Thus the S. L. P. when its officers declared for unity, virtually went on record in favor of submitting all differences between Socialists to a majority vote, and admitted that there was no longer any reason for its existence as a party.

In a sense that is true. It is no doubt a vindication of the policy of toleration advocated by the second party. But this is in many cases traceable to other causes also. It is traceable to the fact that within recent years there has grown up in the Socialist movement a change of opinion relative to the functions of a political party. That change was indicated in our editorial in the June issue. Among many of the adherents of the clear cut policy the conviction has gained ground that the political party which exists for the fight at the ballot box is primarily and essentially an agitational and destructive force, and that the real constructive work of the Social Revolution must come from an economic industrial organization. From this conviction two currents of thought have developed. One, that since the economic organization was the constructive one, political action was unnecessary; another, that since the political party was not to accomplish the revolution but only to lead the attack upon the political citadel of capitalism, there no longer existed the same danger in the unclearness of its membership, nor compelling necessity for insisting upon its purification. In other words that Socialism at the ballot box is the dress parade of the army of Labor, Industrial Unionism is the same army with its service clothes on, ready for work.

From all this it is our belief there will evolve, if there has not in principle already evolved, as the fighting army of the workers of this country:

> One Socialist party embracing all shades and conceptions of Socialist political thought.
>
> One Socialist Industrial organization drilling the working class for the supreme mission of their class—the establishment of the Worker's Republic.

Between these two organizations—the advance guard and the main army of labor—there should be no war, and no endorsement. As travellers to a common goal they should not quarrel, and the dear bought experience of the past has taught us that when political organizations endorse economic, tacitly or otherwise, they always exact a heavy price for their action, just as when economic organizations have endorsed political, it always cost the former their soul and their integrity.

Finally, we give it as our opinion that until the economic organisation of the workers has attained a power in control of the workshop and therefore in the nation, equal to that attained by the capitalist class before they raised the revolutionary standard in England, America and France, working class politics are but preliminary skirmishing, and that therefore the broadest, most tolerant political party of Socialism may be made useful as a teacher as long as it is kept distinct from the industrial organization and therefore unable to hamper the movements of the latter when, as the regular army of organised labor, it forms its line of battle for the final attack.

17. INDUSTRIALISM AND THE TRADE UNIONS

As its first words make clear, the article that follows is a sequel to Socialism Made Easy. *It appeared in the* International Socialist Review *for February 1910, that journal being under the direction of Connolly's Chicago publisher, Kerr. Is it necessary to mention that the reference to the Chicago bomb alludes to the bomb-throwing at the Haymarket meeting on May 4th, 1886, for which four innocent anarchists were hanged? Perhaps it is. If so, it might also be advisable to mention that one of them, Albert R. Parsons, died with the words 'Let the voice of the people be heard', and that his anarchist group had been strongly vocal in support of the Irish anti-landlord movement.*

In the second part of my book *Socialism Made Easy*, I have endeavored to establish two principles in the minds of my readers as being vitally necessary to the upbuilding of a strong revolutionary Socialist movement. Those two principles are: First, that the working class as a class cannot become permeated with a belief in the unity of their class interests unless they have first been trained to a realization of the need of industrial unity; second, that the revolutionary act—the act of taking over the means of production and establishing a social order based upon the principles of the working class (labor) cannot be achieved by a disorganized, defeated and humiliated working class but must be the work of that class *after* it has attained to a commanding position on the field of economic struggle. It has been a pleasure to me to note the progress of Socialist thought towards acceptance of these principles, and to believe that the publication of that little work helped to a not inconsiderable degree in shaping that Socialist thought and in accelerating its progress. In the following article I wish to present one side of the discussion which inevitably arises in our Socialist party locals upon the mooting of this question. But as a preliminary to this presentation I would like to decry, and ask my comrades to decry and dissociate themselves from, the somewhat acrid and intolerant manner in which this discussion is often carried on. Believing that the Socialist party is part and parcel of the labor movement of the United States, and that in the growth of that movement to true revolutionary clearness and consciousness it, the Socialist party, is bound to attract to itself and become mentor and teacher of elements most unclear and lacking in class consciousness, we should recognize that it is as much our duty to be patient and tolerant with the erring brother or sister within our ranks as with the rank heathen outside the fold. No good purpose can be served by wildly declaiming against 'intellectuals,' nor yet by intriguing against and misrepresenting 'impossibilists.' The comrades who think that the Socialist party is run by 'compromisers,' should not jump out of the organization and leave the revolutionists in a still more helpless minority, and the comrades who pride themselves upon being practical Socialist politicians should not too readily accuse those who differ with them of being potential disrupters. Viewing the situation from the standpoint of an industrialist I am convinced that both the industrialist and those estimable comrades who cater to the old style trade unions to such a marked degree as to leave themselves open to the suspicion of coquetting with the idea of a 'labor' party, both, I say, have the one belief, both have arrived at the one conclusion, although they have approached that belief and conclusion from such different angles that they appear as opposing instead of aiding, auxiliary forces. That belief which both share in common is that the triumph of Socialism is impossible without the aid of labor organized upon the economic field. It is their common possession of this one great principle of action which impels me to say that there is a greater identity of purpose and faith between those two opposing (?) wings of the Socialist party than either can have with any of the intervening schools of thought. Both realize that the Socialist party must rest upon the economic struggle and the forces of labor engaged therein, and that the Socialism which is not an outgrowth and expression of that economic struggle is not worth a moment's serious consideration.

There, then, we have found something upon which we agree, a ground common to both, the first desideratum of any serious discussion. The point upon which we disagree is: *Can the present form of American trade unions provide the Socialist movement with the economic force upon which to rest?* Or can the A.F. of L. develop towards industrialism sufficiently for our needs? It is the same problem stated in different ways. I propose to state here my reasons for taking the negative side in that discussion.

Let it be remembered that we are not, as some good comrades imagine, debating whether it is possible for a member of the A.F. of L. to become an industrialist, or for all its members, but we are to debate whether the organization of the A.F. of L. is such as to permit of a modification of its structural formation to keep pace with the progress of industrialist ideas amongst its members. Whether the conversion of the membership of the A.F. of L. to industrialism would mean the transformation of that body into an industrial organization or mean the disruption of the Federation and the throwing of it aside as the up-to-date capitalist throws aside a machine, be it ever so costly, when a more perfectly functioning machine has been devised.

At this point it is necessary for the complete understanding of our subject that we step aside for a moment to consider the genesis and organization of the A.F. of L. and the trade unions patterned after it, and this involves a glance at the history of the labor movement in America. Perhaps of all the subjects properly pertaining to Socialist activity this subject has been the most neglected, the least analyzed. And yet it is the most vital. Studies of Marx and popularizing (sic) of Marx, studies of science and popularizing of science, studies of religion and application of same with Socialist interpretations, all these we have without limit, but of attempts to apply the methods of Marx and of science to an analysis of the laws of growth and incidents of development of the organizations of labor upon the economic field the literature of the movement is almost, if not quite, absolutely barren. Our Socialist writers seem in some strange and, to me, incomprehensible manner to have detached themselves from the everyday struggles of the toilers and to imagine they are doing their whole duty as interpreters of Socialist thought when they bless the economic organization with one corner of their mouth and insist upon the absolute hopelessness of it with the other. They imagine, of course, that this is the astutest diplomacy, but the net result of it has been that the organized working class has never looked upon the Socialist party as a part of the labor movement, and the enrolled Socialist party member has never found in American Socialist literature anything that helped him in strengthening his economic organization or leading it to victory.

Perhaps some day there will arise in America a Socialist writer who in his writing will live up to the spirit of the Communist Manifesto that the Socialists are not apart from the labor movement, are not a sect, but are simply that part of the working class which pushes on all others, which most clearly understands the line of march. Awaiting the advent of that writer permit me to remind our readers that the Knights of Labor preceded the A.F. of L., that the structural formation of the Knights was that of a mass organization, that they aimed to organize all toilers into one union and made no distinction of craft, *nor of industry*, and that they cherished revolutionary aims. When the A.F. of L. was organized it was organized as a dual organization, and although at first it professed a desire to organize none but those then unorganized it soon developed opposition to the Knights and proceeded to organize wherever it could find members, and particularly to seek after the enrollment of those who were already in the K. of L. In this it was assisted by the good will of the master class, who naturally preferred its profession of conservatism and identity of interest between Capital and Labor to the revolutionary aims and methods of the Knights. But even this assistance on the part of the master class would not have assured its victory were it not for the fact that its method of organization, *into separate crafts*, recognized a certain need of the industrial development of the time which the K. of L. had failed up to that moment to appraise at its proper significance.

The K. of L., as I have pointed out, organized all workers into one union, an excellent idea for teaching the toilers their ultimate class interests, but with the defect that it made no provision for the treating of special immediate craft interests by men and women with the requisite technical knowledge. The scheme was the scheme of an idealist, too large-hearted and noble-minded himself to appreciate the hold small interests can have upon men and women. It gave rise to all sorts of bickerings and jealousies. The printer grumbled at the jurisdiction of a body comprising tailors and shoemakers over his shop struggles, and the tailors and shoemakers fretted at the attempts of carpenters and bricklayers to understand the technicalities of their disputes with the bosses.

To save the K. of L. and to save the American working class a pilgrimage in the desert of reaction, it but required the advent of some practical student of industry to propose that, instead of massing all workers together irrespective of occupation, they should, keeping their organization intact and remaining bound in obedience to one supreme head, *for administrative purposes only*, group all workers together according to their industries, and subdivide their industries again according to their crafts. That the allied crafts should select the ruling body for the industry to which they belonged, and that the allied industries again should elect the ruling body for the whole organization. This could have been done without the slightest jar to the framework of the organization; it would have recognized all technical differences and specialization of function in actual industry, it would have kept the organization of labor in line with the actual progress of industrial development, and would still have kept intact the idea of the unity of the working class by its common bond of brotherhood, a universal membership card, and universal obligation to recognize that an injury to one was an injury to all. Tentative steps in such a direction were already being taken when the A.F. of L. came upon the scene. The promoters of this organization seizing upon this one plan in the K. of L. organization, specialized its work along that line, and, instead of hastening to save the unity of the working class on the lines above indicated, they made the growing realization of the need of representation of craft differences the entering wedge for disrupting and destroying the earlier organization of that class.

Each craft was organized as a distinct body having no obligation to strike or fight beside any other craft, and making its own contracts with the bosses heedless of what was happening between these bosses and their fellow laborers of another craft in the same industry, building, shop or room. The craft was organized on a national basis, to be governed by the vote of its members throughout the nation, and with a membership card good only in that craft and of no use to a member who desired to leave one craft in order to follow another. The fiction of national unity was and is still paid homage to, as vice always pays homage to virtue, by annual congresses in which many resolutions are gravely debated, to be forgotten as soon as congress adjourns. But the unifying (?) qualities of this form of organization are best revealed by the fact that the main function of the congress seems to be to provide the cynical master class with the, to them, pleasing spectacle of allied organizations fiercely fighting over questions of jurisdiction.

This policy of the A.F. of L. coupled with the unfortunate bomb incident of Chicago, for which the K. of L. received much of the blame, completed the ruin of the latter organization and destroyed the growing unity of the working class for the time being. The industrial union, as typified to-day in the I.W.W.,[1] could have, as I have shown, developed out of the Knights of Labor as logically and perfectly as the adult develops from the child. No new organization would have been necessary, and hence we may conclude that the I.W.W. is the legitimate heir of the native American labor movement, the inheritor of its principles, and the ripened fruit of its experiences. On the other hand the A.F. of L. may truly be regarded as an usurper on the throne of labor, an usurper who occupies the throne by virtue of having strangled its predecessor, and now, like all usurpers, raises the cry of 'treason' against the rightful heir when it seeks to win its own again. It is obvious that the sway of the A.F. of L. in the American labor movement is but a brief interregnum between the passing of the old revolutionary organization and the ascension into power of the new.

[1] Industrial Workers of the World.

But, I fancy I hear some one say, granting that all that is true, may we not condemn the methods by which the A.F. of L. destroyed, or helped to destroy, the Knights of Labor, and still believe that out of the A.F. of L. we may now build up an industrial organization such as we need, such as the K. of L. might have become, and as the I.W.W. aims to be?

This we can only answer by clearly focussing in our mind the A.F. of L. system of organization in actual practice. A carpenter is at work in a city. He has a dispute with the bosses, or all his fellow carpenters have. They will hold meetings to discuss the question of a strike, and finding the problem too big for them they will pass it on to the headquarters, and the headquarters pass it on to the general membership. The general membership, from San Francisco to Rhode Island, and from Podunk to Kalamazoo will have a vote and say upon the question of the terms upon which the Chicago carpenters work, and if said carpenters are called out they will expect all these widely scattered carpenters to support them by financial and moral help. But while they are soliciting and receiving the support of their fellow-carpenters from Dan to Beeshebee they are precluded from calling out in sympathy with them the painters who follow them in their work, the plumbers whose pipes they cover up, the steamfitters who work at their elbows, or the plasterer who precedes them. Yet the co-operation of these workers with them in their strikes is a thousandfold more important than the voting of strike funds which would keep them out on strike—until the building season is over and the winter sets in. In many cities to-day there is a Building Trades Council which is looked upon by many as a beginning of industrialism within the A.F. of L. It is not only the beginning but it is as far as industrialism can go within that body and its sole function is to secure united action in remedying petty grievances and enforcing the observance of contracts, but it does not take part in the really important work of determining hours or wages. It cannot for the simple reason that each of the thirty-three unions in the building industry are international organizations with international officers, and necessitating international referendums before any strikes looking to the fixing of hours or wages, are permissible. Hence, although all the building trades locals in a given district may be satisfied that the time is ripe for obtaining better conditions they cannot act before they obtain the consent of the membership throughout the entire country, and before that is obtained the moment for action is passed. The bond that is supposed to unite the carpenter in New York with the carpenter in Kokomo, Indiana, is converted into a wall of isolation which prevents him uniting, except in the most perfunctory fashion, with the men of other crafts who work beside him. The industrial union and the craft union are mutually exclusive terms. Suppose all the building trades locals of Chicago resolved to unite industrially, to form an industrial union. Every local which became an integral part of said union, pledged to obey its call to action, would by so doing forfeit its charter in the craft union and in the A.F. of L., and outside Chicago its members would be considered as scabs.

The Brewers' Union has been fighting for years to obtain the right to organize *all* brewery employees. It is hindered from doing so, not only by the rules of the A.F. of L., but by the form of organization of that body. Breweries, for instance, employ plumbers. Now if a plumber, so employed, would join the Brewers' Union and obey its call to strike he would be expelled from his craft union, and if ever he lost his job in the brewery would be considered as a scab if he went to work where union plumbers were employed. A craft union cannot recognize the right of another association to call its members out on strike. A machinist works to-day in a machine shop; a few months from now he may be employed in a clothing factory attending to the repairs of sewing machines. If the clothing industry resolves itself into an industrial union and he joins them, as he needs must if he believes in industrialism, he loses his membership in the International Association of Machinists. And if ever he loses his factory job and seeks to return to the machine shop he must either do so as a non-union man or pay a heavy fine if he is permitted to re-enter the I.A. of M. A stationary engineer works to-day at the construction of a new building, three months from now he is in a shipyard, six months from now he is at the mouth of a coal mine. Three different industries, requiring three different industrial unions.

The craft card is good to-day in all of them, but if any of them chose to form industrial unions, and called upon him to join he could only do so on penalty of losing his craft card and his right to strike benefits from his old organization. And if he did join his card of membership in the one he joined would be of no value when he drifted to any of the others. How can the A.F. of L. avoid this dilemma? Industrialism requires that all the workers in a given industry be subject to the call of the governing body, or of the vote of the workers in that industry. But if these workers are organized in the A.F. of L. they must be subject only to the call of their national or international craft body, and if at any time they obey the call of the industry in preference to the craft they are ordered peremptorily back to scab upon their brothers.

If in addition to this organic difficulty, and it is the most insuperable, we take into consideration the system of making contracts or trade agreements on a craft basis pursued by old style unions we will see that our unfortunate brothers in the A.F. of L. are tied hand and foot, handcuffed and hobbled, to prevent their advance into industrialism. During the recent shirt-waist makers' strike in New York when the question was mooted of a similar strike in Philadelphia our comrade Rose Pastor Stokes, according to our Socialist press, was continually urging upon the shirt-waist makers of Philadelphia the wisdom of striking before Christmas, and during the busy season. No more sensible advice could have been given. It was of the very essence of industrialist philosophy. Industrialism is more than a method of organization—it is a science of fighting. It says to the worker: Fight only at the time you select, never fight when the boss wants a fight. Fight at the height of the busy season, and in the slack season when the workers are in thousands upon the sidewalk absolutely refuse to be drawn into battle. Even if the boss insults and vilifies your union and refuses to recognize it take it lying down in the slack season but mark it up in your little note-book, and when work is again rushing and Master Capitalist is pressed for orders squeeze him, and squeeze him till the most sensitive portion of his anatomy, his pocket book, yells with pain. That is the industrialist idea of the present phase of the class war as organized labor should conduct it. But, whatever may have been the case with the shirt-waist makers, that policy so ably enunciated by Comrade Rose Pastor Stokes is utterly opposed to the whole philosophy and practice of the A.F. of L. Contracts almost always expire when there is little demand for labor. For instance the United Mine Workers' contract with the bosses expires in the early summer when they have before them a long hot season with a minimum demand for coal. Hence the expiration of the contract generally finds the coal operators spoiling for a fight, and the union secretly dreading it. Most building trade contracts with the bosses expire in the winter. For example, the Brotherhood of Carpenters in New York, their contract expires in January. A nice time for a fight, in the middle of a northern winter, when all work in their vicinity is suspended owing to the rigors of the climate!

The foregoing will, I hope, give the reader some food for consideration upon the problem under review. That problem is intimately allied with the future of the Socialist party in America. Our party must become the political expression of the fight in the workshop, and draw its inspiration therefrom. Everything which tends to strengthen and discipline the hosts of labor tends irresistibly to swell the ranks of the revolutionary movement, and everything which tends to divide and disorganize the hosts of labor tends also to strengthen the forces of capitalism. *The most dispersive and isolating force at work in the labor movement to-day is craft unionism, the most cohesive and unifying force, industrial unionism.* In view of that fact all objections which my comrades make to industrial unionism on the grounds of the supposedly, or truly anti-political, bias of many members of the I.W.W. is quite beside the mark. That question at the present stage of the game is purely doctrinaire. The use or non-use of political action will not be settled by the doctrinaires who may make it their hobby to-day, but will be settled by the workers who use the I.W.W. in their workshop struggles, and if at any time the conditions of a struggle in shop, factory, railroad or mine necessitate the employment of political action those workers so organized will use it, all theories and theorists to the contrary notwithstanding.

In their march to freedom the workers will use every weapon they find necessary.

As the economic struggle is the preparatory school and training ground for Socialists it is our duty to help guide along right lines the effort of the workers to choose the correct kind of organization to fight their battles in that conflict. According as they choose aright or wrongly so will the development of class consciousness in their minds be hastened or retarded by their every day experience in sharp struggles.

18. THE ISOLATION OF DUBLIN

This and subsequent articles make it very clear how Connolly viewed the great 1913 lockout in syndicalist terms, and insisted that the solution must be by syndicalist means. From this time onward his language, against the old-fashioned craft unions who failed the Dublin workers by refusal to employ the sympathetic strike and boycott, was to be bitter indeed. It has been argued that he as an Irishman kept thereafter a sense of betrayal by British workers; in fact his indignation was much more that of a leader who knew that one big union would solve all of these crises which were being exacerbated by the multitude of well-entrenched unions and officials. Left to themselves, the British workers in his view reveal their solidarity; it is the labour aristocracy which has isolated Dublin. Forward *printed this article on February 7th, 1914.*

I want this week to talk about the 'isolation of Dublin.' Some seven or eight weeks ago the proposal to isolate Dublin was the subject of much controversy in the Labour papers, and much fierce comment in the capitalist press. It is my desire in this week's article to tell how and in what manner the proposal was carried through, and how it is that now Dublin is isolated.

It is not necessary, I presume, to remind our readers of the beginnings of the Dublin struggle. Let us, just for convenience' sake, take up the fight at the moment it became a subject of national action on the part of the British Labour movement.

A public meeting had been proclaimed in Dublin in a brazen illegal manner. For declaring that this proclamation was illegal, and advising their leaders to disregard it and stand to their rights, a number of leaders of the Irish Transport and General Workers' Union had been arrested and imprisoned. A wholesale batoning of the people had followed, and Dublin was the scene of the most unparalleled police brutality.

An appeal was made to the British Trades Union Congress, then happily sitting, and that body in the name of the British working class nobly rose to the occasion, and pledged the credit of the whole British Labour movement to see their Dublin comrades through the fight. As a result, the right of free speech was re-asserted in Dublin, a supply of food was arranged for through the despatch of specially chartered steamers, and a huge amount of money was raised to enable the men and women of Dublin to keep the fight going. Never was seen such enthusiasm in a Labour fight. Trade Unionists, Socialists of all kinds, Anarchists, Industrialists, Syndicalists, all the varying and hitherto discordant elements of the Labour movement found a common platform, were joined together in pursuit of a common object. Now, permit me to underscore that point, and emphasise the great importance. For long years we have been preaching to the Labour movement the necessity of concerted industrial action, telling it that the time was rotten ripe for Industrial Unity, and declaring that as the interests of each were the concern of all, our organisations should be re-arranged with a view to the conserving of their common interests.

We found that to a large extent these ideas were taking root in the minds of the workers, but that to a still larger extent the tacit acceptance of our ideas failed to evoke concerted action built upon these lines. The forces of our enemies were united and wielded with all the precision and relentlessness with which the general staff of an army would wield the battalions and brigades which formed the component parts of that army, but the battalions and brigades of the army of Labour when engaged in battle had no efficient general staff to guide and direct the whole army to the salvation of its individual units; and, worse still, had none of that esprit-de-corps which on the military battle-field would make the desertion of any section to its fate an unthinkable course to the officers of the divisions not engaged. We had seen at London, at Leith and elsewhere that whereas the whole force of the Shipping Federation has been actively engaged in fighting the dockers of these parts, the dockers and seamen of the other parts had maintained the peace, and left their Leith or London brothers to bear alone the full force of the Federation attack, instead of meeting that attack by a movement against the flanks and rear of the Federation in these other parts. We know that although much of this blundering was due to the sectional jealousy of various Union leaders, much was also due to the fact that the conception of common action on a national scale by the whole working class had not yet entered the minds of the rank and file as a whole. Something had been wanting—something that would make the minds of the workers more responsive, more ready to accept the broader idea, and act upon its acceptance. That something Dublin supplied. The dramatic suddenness with which the Dublin fight was thrust upon public attention, the tragic occurrences of the first few days—working class martyrdom, the happy coincidence of a Trade Union Congress, the intervention of British Trade Unionists to assert the right of public meeting for Irish workers—filling the gap in the ranks caused by the failing of Irish Trade Union leaders, the brilliant inspiration of a food ship, and last but not least the splendid heroism of the Dublin men and women showing out against the background of the squalor and misery of their houses. There are times in history when we realise that it is easier to convert a multitude than it ordinarily is to convert an individual, when indeed ideas seem to seize upon the masses as contradistinguished by ordinary times when individuals slowly seize ideas. The propagandist toils on for decades in seeming failure and ignominy, when suddenly some great event takes place in accord with the principles he has been advocating, and immediately he finds that the seed he has been sowing is springing up in plants that are covering the earth. To the idea of working class unity, to the seed of industrial solidarity, Dublin was the great event that enabled it to seize the minds of the masses, the germinating force that gave power to the seed to fructify and cover these islands.

I say in all solemnity and seriousness that in its attitude towards Dublin the Working Class Movement of Great Britain reached its highest point of moral grandeur—attained for a moment to a realisation of that sublime unity towards which the best in us must continually aspire. Could that feeling but have been crystallised into organic expression, could we but have had real statesmen amongst us who, recognising the wonderful leap forward of our class, would have hastened to burn behind us the boats that might make easy a retreat to the old ground of isolation and division, could we have found Labour Leaders capable enough to declare that now that the working class had found its collective soul it should hasten to express itself as befitted that soul and not be fettered by the rules, regulations and codes of organisations conceived in the olden outworn spirit of sectional jealousies, could these things have but been vouchsafed to us, what a new world would now be opening delightfully upon the vision of Labour! Consider what Dublin meant to you all! It meant that the whole force of organised Labour should stand behind each unit of organisation in each and all of its battles, that no company, battalion or brigade should henceforth be allowed to face the enemy alone, and that the capitalist would be taught that when he fought a Union anywhere he must be prepared to fight all Unions everywhere.

For the first days and weeks of the struggle, the Working Classes of Great Britain attained to the height of moral grandeur expressed in that idea, all Labour stood behind Dublin, and Dublin rejoiced. Dublin suffered and agonised, but rejoiced that even in its suffering it was the medium for the apostolate of a rejuvenating idea. How often have I heard the responsive cheers to the question whether they would be prepared to stand by others as these others had stood by them!

And now?

Dublin is isolated. We asked our friends of the Transport Trades to isolate the capitalist class of Dublin, and we asked the other Unions to back them up. But no, they said we would rather help you by giving you funds. We argued that a strike is an attempt to stop the capitalist from carrying on his business, that the success or failure of the strike depends entirely upon the success or non-success of the capitalist to do without the strikers. If the capitalist is able to carry on his business without the strikers, then the strike is lost, even if the strikers receive more in strike pay than they formerly did in wages. We said that if scabs are working a ship and Union men discharge in another part of the boat so loaded, then those Union men are strike breakers, since they help the capitalist in question to carry on his business. That if Union seamen man a boat discharged by scabs, these Union seamen or firemen are by the same reason strike breakers, as also are the railwaymen or carters who assist in transporting the goods handled by the scabs for the capitalist who is fighting his men or women. In other words, we appealed to the collective soul of the workers against the collective hatred of the capitalist.

We asked for no more than the logical development of that idea of working class unity, that the Working Class of Britain should help us to prevent the Dublin capitalists carrying on their business without us. We asked for the isolation of the capitalists of Dublin, and for answer the leaders of the British Labour movement proceed calmly to isolate the Working Class of Dublin. As an answer to those who supported our request for the isolation of Dublin we were told that a much better plan would be to increase the subsidies to enable us to increase strike pay. As soon as this argument had served its purpose, the subsidies fell off, and the 'Dublin Fund' grew smaller and smaller as if by a pre-arranged plan. We had rejected the last terms offered by the employers on the strength of this talk of increased supplies, and as soon as that last attempt at settlement thus fell through, the supplies gradually froze up instead of being increased as we had been promised.

In addition to this the National Union of Railwaymen, whilst in attendance at the Conference on 9th December, had actually in their pockets the arrangements for the re-starting of work on the London and North-Western boat at the North Wall of Dublin, and in the train returning to Dublin the day after the Conference, we read of the line being re-opened. No vote was taken of the men on strike; they were simply ordered back to work by their officials and told that if they did not return, their strike pay would be stopped. The Seamen & Firemen's Union men in Dublin were next ordered to man the boats of the Head Line of steamers then being discharged by free labourers supplied by the Shipping Federation. In both Dublin and Belfast the members refused, and they were then informed that Union men would be brought from Great Britain to take their places. Union men to be brought from England to take the place of members of the same Union who refused to desert their brothers of the Transport Union. We were attempting to hold up Guinness' porter. A consignment was sent to Sligo for shipment there. The local Transport Union official wired me for instructions. I wired to hold it up; his men obeyed, and it was removed from Sligo, railed to Derry, and there put on board by members of Mr. Sexton's Union on ships manned by members of Mr. Havelock Wilson's Union, and discharged in Liverpool by members of Mr. Sexton's Union. Whilst the City of Dublin Steam Packet Company was still insisting upon carrying the goods of our worst enemy, Jacob's (who is still enforcing the agreement denounced by Sir Geo. Askwith), the members of the Seamen & Firemen's Union were ordered to sign on in their boats, although our men were still on strike. We were informed by Mr. Joe Houghton of the Scottish Dockers that his Union would not hold up any boat for us unless joint action was taken by the Transport Workers' Federation. As on a previous occasion, his members at Ayr had worked coal boats belonging to a Belfast firm that was making war upon the Irish Transport Workers' Union, we did not blame Joe very much. He had been disobeyed at Ayr—perhaps he was coerced in Glasgow.

But why go on? Sufficient to say that the Working Class Unity of the first days of the Dublin fight was sacrificed in the interests of sectional officialism. The officials failed to grasp the opportunity offered to them to make a permanent reality of the Union of Working Class forces brought into being by the spectacle of rebellion, martyrdom and misery exhibited by the workers of Dublin. All England and Scotland rose to it; working class officialdom and working class rank and file alike responded to the call of inspiration; it would have raised us all upward and onward towards our common emancipation. But sectionalism, intrigues and old-time jealousies damned us in the hour of victory, and officialdom was the first to fall to the tempter.

And so we Irish workers must again go down into Hell, bow our backs to the lash of the slave driver, let our hearts be seared by the iron of his hatred, and instead of the sacramental wafer of brotherhood and common sacrifice, eat the dust of defeat and betrayal.

Dublin is isolated.

19. INDUSTRIAL UNITY AND POLITICAL DIVISION IN IRELAND

The next article is of significance for a number of reasons. In the light of subsequent developments it is naturally of interest to see Connolly's first public note of warning that Ireland may receive partition as a British answer to her question. It also contains some very telling lines which account for the foundation of the Irish Citizen Army, and it is important to note that Connolly based his conviction of the growth of police brutality on observation of the suffragettes' fate as well as on that of the workers. If Mrs Emmeline Pankhurst, whose rearrest at Glasgow on March 9th, 1914, and transportation by rail to Holloway Gaol was accomplished by a great phalanx of police and detectives, and her daughter Christabel had little enthusiasm for the workers, the other daughter, Sylvia, had identified herself with the Irish strikers' cause by appearing on a platform at the Albert Hall, London, at a meeting for the release of Jim Larkin on November 1st, 1913. Syndicalism might well reach out to embrace the suffragette movement; so at least hoped Connolly. The present article, therefore, which appeared in Forward *on March 21st, 1914, aptly sums up the inter-connection of the Tory rebellion, the women's rebellion and the workers' rebellion, which George Dangerfield was later to see as the basis for the destruction of the Edwardian socio-political structure in his seminal work* The Strange Death of Liberal England.[1]

I have so often animadverted upon the manner in which the Transport Unions of Great Britain have scabbed upon the Irish Transport and General Workers' Union in Dublin that I feel a real pleasure in being able to announce to the readers of *Forward* that a definite movement is now on foot among the same bodies to compel the proprietors of the Ulster Head Line of steamers to reinstate our members in Belfast and Dublin.

The fact that the weakness of our Union owing to the aforementioned scabbing taking place at the end of our struggle had

[1] Constable, London, 1935.

enabled the Shipping Federation to reintroduce the Federation 'slip' among the seamen and firemen upon the steamers in question served no doubt to emphasise the suicidal nature of the conduct I have complained of so bitterly.

The Scottish Union of Dock Labourers, whose Executive I interviewed on Friday, March 6, were the first to promise action, and the other Unions involved are now falling in line. As a result, I am glad to say that I see the probability of a speedy, successful ending of this particular phase of the struggle.

We had a recrudescence of police brutality in Dublin on Friday, March 13. A mass meeting of the unemployed was held in Beresford Place to demand that provision be made for supplying work to the unemployed. Several of the speakers pointed out that every possible hindrance had been put in the way of the men to prevent them registering their names in the Labour Exchange; that the great number of unemployed now in the city was quite abnormal, and was due principally to the number of scabs brought in by the employers during the dispute, and that there were various much-needed schemes of public improvement ready for commencement if the public Boards would only act.

At the conclusion of the Meeting, Captain White announced that he would lead a procession of the unemployed to the Mansion House. Gathering together about thirty of the younger ones he arrayed them in military order, furnishing them with long broom handles used by the stewards to marshal our processions, and the remainder of the crowd falling in behind started off to interview the Lord Mayor. They had not gone two hundred yards when a mail cart driver attempted to drive through the ranks at top speed. Captain White held up his stick to remonstrate with the driver, and in a moment there was a charge of police with batons striking like machines. The crowd was sent flying by the suddenness of the attack, five of the number who attempted resistance being stretched upon the ground, and Captain White arrested after being most unmercifully beaten. He made a fierce resistance, and the uniformed savages clubbed him until their arms must have ached. At present he has forty stitches in his head, and it was no fault of his assailants that his life was not taken.

The Liberal Government is making quite a record for itself as a Government by outrage and coercion. Its attacks upon the women, its brutality towards the men, its general attitude towards all progressive forces—when these forces are weak—have all the marks of a Government saturated with medieval ideas—a Government resolved to stamp out all opposition by carefully calculated exhibitions of brutality. The exhibition of the brutality in the most odious and shameless manner possible is an essential part of the scheme. Indeed, the scheme revolves around the idea that by brute force nakedly exercised, the ideas of progress may be frightened out of existence. Supposing that Captain White had committed an illegal act in impeding the progress of His Majesty's mail, the fact remains that a summons to appear at the police court would have served all the requirements of the law. The Captain is not a fly-by-night, his residence is well known to the police; his standing is such that even on the lowest grounds it would not pay him to evade the law or disobey the summons.

But such a summons would necessarily result in a trial when the whole case would be argued out cold-bloodedly and strictly according to the legal aspects of the conduct of all parties concerned, *i.e.*, the mail van driver, the Captain, the police. But when the arrest is preceded by an unprovoked baton charge, when such a baton charge necessarily would produce an attempt at resistance (since human beings have a natural objection to having their heads broken), then the police are compelled to exaggerate the importance of every incident, to represent a hand lifted in remonstrance as a hand lifted to strike, and to outswear everybody in order to secure a conviction. Then the press gets an opportunity, of which it is eager to take an advantage, to work up excitement upon the incident, and to make it the basis of an attack upon its opponents. Under such circumstances, a fair trial is impossible; it becomes imperative for all the forces of law and order to secure conviction, even by sheer forgery and intimidation.

The circumstances attending the arrest of Mrs. Pankhurst in Glasgow are another exemplification of the policy pursued by the Government in effecting arrests of this nature. No sane man but must admit that Mrs. Pankhurst could easily have been arrested outside the hall, but that would not have produced the terroristic effect aimed at. It was necessary for the purposes of the Government that the arrest should be carried out with every accompanying show of murderous brutality and reckless severity. That this brutality and severity was exercised against women was from the point of view of this Liberal Government rather fortunate than otherwise, since it demonstrated the perfect control over the coercive forces possessed by the capitalist class and its executive. When policemen can be safely relied upon to baton, kick and maltreat women, then it is certain that no mere striker can hope anything from their mercy, and therefore every such outrage is a training in cruelty for the forces upon which capitalism relies for its future defence.

Here in Ireland the proposal of the Government to consent to the partition of Ireland—the exclusion of certain counties in Ulster—is causing a new line of cleavage. No one of the supporters of Home Rule accepts this proposal with anything like equanimity, but rather we are already hearing in Ulster rumours of a determination to resist it by all means. It is felt that the proposal to leave the Home Rule minority at the mercy of an ignorant majority with the evil record of the Orange party is a proposal that should never have been made, and that the establishment of such a scheme should be resisted with armed force if necessary.

Personally I entirely agree with those who think so; Belfast is bad enough as it is; what it would be under such rule the wildest imagination cannot conceive. Filled with the belief that they were after defeating the Imperial Government and the Nationalists combined, the Orangemen would have scant regards for the rights of the minority left at their mercy.

Such a scheme would destroy the Labour movement by disrupting it. It would perpetuate in a form aggravated in evil the discords now prevalent, and help the Home Rule and Orange capitalists and clerics to keep their rallying cries before the public as the political watchwords of the day. In short, it would make division more intense and confusion of ideas and parties more confounded.

Before closing this week, I wish to make a special appeal to readers of *Forward* for some financial help to enable us to pay some little strike pay to the victimised Dublin girls. Hundreds of these are starving; scores are forced to sleep on the floors of slum dwellings, already overcrowded by the families of the friends and acquaintances who give them this poor privilege, and who have themselves been victimised.

They are in dire need, and any sum forwarded for that purpose, and marked 'For Victimised Girls,' will be applied exclusively to their aid. I have every confidence that the readers of *Forward*, who have laboured so splendidly in the past in this respect, will personally and by securing grants from their Unions come to the rescue now of those splendid, whole-hearted, and brave-souled daughters of Erin.

20. OLD WINE IN NEW BOTTLES

'Old Wine in New Bottles' was originally published in the London New Age *of A. R. Orage (1873–1934), himself a major influence on the thought of Jim Larkin. It is Connolly's most detailed statement on the syndicalist implications of the Dublin lockout of 1913 and the reprehensible consequences of the failure of the workers of the British Isles to apply a syndicalist solution to it. 'Old Wine in New Bottles' was republished as Part III of* The Axe to the Root *in the Dublin editions of 1921 and 1934 (**see introductory note to Chapter 15, p. 243**). The 1921 text is that employed here. The* New Age *printed it on April 30th, 1914.*

Scripture tells us in a very notable passage about the danger of putting new wine into old bottles. I propose to say a few words about the equally suicidal folly of putting old wine into new bottles. For I humbly submit that the experiment spoken of is very popular just now in the industrial world, has engaged the most earnest attention of most of the leaders of the working class, and received the practically unanimous endorsement of the Labour and Socialist Press. I have waited in vain for a word of protest.

THE IDEA BEHIND INDUSTRIAL UNIONISM

In the year of grace 1905 a convention of American Labour bodies was held in Chicago for the purpose of promoting a new working-class organisation on more militant and scientific lines. The result of that convention was the establishment of the Industrial Workers of the World—the first Labour organisation to organise itself with the definite ideal of taking over and holding the economic machinery of society. The means proposed to that end—and it is necessary to remember that the form of organisation adopted was primarily intended to accomplish that end, and only in the second degree as a means of industrial warfare under capitalism—was the enrolment of the working class in Unions built upon the lines of the great industries. It was the idea of the promoters of the new organisation that craft interests and technical requirements should be met by the creation of branches, that all such branches should be represented in a common executive, that all united should be members of an industrial Union, which should embrace all branches and be co-extensive with the industry, that all industrial Unions should be linked as members of one great Union, and that one membership card should cover the whole working-class organisation. Thus was to be built up a working-class administration which should be capable of the revolutionary act of taking over society, and whose organisers and officers should in the preliminary stages of organising and fighting constantly remember, and remembering, teach, that no new order can replace the old until it is capable of performing the work of the old, and performing it more efficiently for human needs.

FIGHTING SPIRIT MORE THAN MASS ORGANIZATION

As one of the earliest organisers of that body, I desire to emphasise also that as a means of creating in the working class the frame of mind necessary to the upbuilding of this new order within the old, we taught, and I have yet seen no reason to reconsider our attitude upon this matter, that the interests of one were the interests of all, and that no consideration of a contract with a section of the capitalist class absolved any section of us from the duty of taking instant action to protect other sections when said sections were in danger from the capitalist enemy. Our attitude always was that in the swiftness and unexpectedness of our action lay our chief hopes of temporary victory, and since permanent peace was an illusory hope until permanent victory was secured, temporary victories were all that need concern us. We realised that every victory gained by the working class would be followed by some capitalist development that in course of time would tend to nullify it, but that until that development was perfect the fruits of our victory would be ours to enjoy, and the resultant moral effect would be of incalculable value to the character and to the mental attitude of our class towards their rulers. It will thus be seen that in our view—and now that I am about to point the moral I may personally appropriate it and call it my point of view—the spirit, the character, the militant spirit, the fighting character of the organisation, was of the first importance. I believe that the development of the fighting spirit is of more importance than the creation of the theoretically perfect organisation; that, indeed, the most theoretically perfect organisation may, because of its very perfection and vastness, be of the greatest possible danger to the revolutionary movement if it tends, or is used, to repress and curb the fighting spirit of comradeship in the rank and file.

SUCCESS OF THE SYMPATHETIC STRIKE IN 1911

Since the establishment in America of the organisation I have just sketched, and the initiation of propaganda on the lines necessary for its purpose, we have seen in all capitalist countries, and notably in Great Britain, great efforts being made to abolish sectional division, and to unite or amalgamate kindred Unions. Many instances will arise in the minds of my readers, but I propose to take as a concrete example the National Transport Workers' Federation. Previous to the formation of this body, Great Britain was the scene of the propagandist activities of a great number of irregular and unorthodox bodies, which, taking their cue in the main from the Industrial Workers of the World, made great campaigns in favour of the new idea. Naturally their arguments were in the main directed towards emphasising the absurdity implied in one body of workers remaining at work whilst another body of workers were on strike in the same employment. As a result of this campaign, frowned upon by leading officials in Great Britain, the Seamen's strike of 1911 was conducted on, and resulted in, entirely new lines of action. The sympathetic strike sprang into being; every group of workers stood by every allied group of workers; and a great wave of effective solidarity caught the workers in its grasp and beat and terrified the masters. Let me emphasise the point that the greatest weapon against capital was proven in those days to be the sporadic strike. It was its very sporadic nature, its swiftness and unexpectedness, that won. It was ambush, the surprise attack of our industrial army, before which the well-trained battalions of the capitalist crumpled up in panic, against which no precautions were available.

WEAKNESS OF THE NATIONAL TRANSPORT WORKERS' FEDERATION

Since that time we have had all over these countries a great wave of enthusiasm for amalgamations, for more cohesion in the working-class organisations. In the transport industry all Unions are being linked up until the numbers now affiliated have become imposing enough to awe the casual reader and silence the cavilling objector at Trade Union meetings. But I humbly submit that, side by side with that enlargement and affiliation of organisations, there has proceeded a freezing up of the fraternal spirit of 1911; there is now, despite the amalgamations, less solidarity in the ranks of Labour than was exhibited in that year of conflict and victory.

If I could venture an analysis of the reason for this falling-off in solidarity, I would have to point out that the amalgamations and federations are being carried out in the main by officials absolutely destitute of the revolutionary spirit, and that as a consequence the methods of what should be militant organisations having the broad working-class outlook are conceived and enforced in the temper and spirit of the sectionalism those organisations were meant to destroy.

Into the new bottles of industrial organisation is being poured the old, cold wine of Craft Unionism.

The much-contemned small Unions of the past had at least this to recommend them, viz., that they were susceptible to pressure from the sudden fraternal impulses of their small membership. If their members worked side by side with scabs, or received tainted goods from places where scabs were employed, the shame was all their own, and proved frequently too great to be borne. When it did so we had the sympathetic strike and the fraternisation of the working class. But when the workers handling tainted goods, or working vessels loaded by scabs, are members of a nation-wide organisation, with branches in all great centres or ports, the sense of the personal responsibility is taken off the shoulders of each member and local officials, and the spirit of solidarity destroyed. The local official can conscientiously order the local member to remain at work with the scab, or to handle the tainted goods, 'pending action by the General Executive.'

RECENT EVENTS FORETOLD IN 1914

As the General Executive cannot take action pending a meeting of delegates, and as the delegates at that meeting have to report back to their bodies, and these bodies again to meet, discuss, and then report back to the General Executive, which must meet, hear their reports, and then, perhaps, order a ballot vote of the entire membership, after which another meeting must be held to tabulate the result of the vote and transmit it to the local branches, which must meet again to receive it, the chances are, of course, a million to one that the body of workers in distress will be starved into subjection, bankrupted, or disrupted, before the leviathan organisation will allow their brothers on the spot to lift a finger or drop a tool in their aid. Readers may, perhaps, think that I am exaggerating the danger. But who will think so that remembers the vindictive fine imposed by the N.U.R. upon its members in the North of England for taking swift action on behalf of a persecuted comrade instead of going through all this red tape whilst he was suffering? Or who will think so that knows that Dublin and Belfast members of the Irish Transport Workers' Union have been victimised ever since the end of the lock-out by the Head Line Company, whose steamers have been and are regularly coaled in British ports, and manned by Belfast and British members of the Seamen's and Firemen's Union?

TACTICS THAT WILL WIN

The amalgamations and federations that are being built up to-day are, without exception, being used in the old spirit of the worst type of sectionalism; each local Union or branch finds in the greater organisation of which it is a part a shield and excuse for refusing to respond to the call of brothers and sisters in distress, for the handling of tainted goods, for the working of scab boats. A main reason for this shameful distortion of the Greater Unionism from its true purpose is to be found in the campaign against 'sporadic strikes.'

I have no doubt but that Robert Williams, of the National Transport Workers' Federation, is fully convinced that his articles and speeches against such strikes are and were wise; I have just a little doubt that they were the best service performed for the capitalist by any Labour leader of late years. The big strike, the vast massed battalions of Labour against the massed battalions of capital on a field every inch of which has been explored and mapped out beforehand, is seldom successful, for very obvious reasons. The sudden strike, and the sudden threat to strike suddenly, has won more for Labour than all the great Labour conflicts in history. In the Boer war the long line of communications was the weak point of the British army; in a Labour war the ground to be covered by the goods of the capitalist is his line of communication. The larger it is the better for the attacking forces of Labour. But these forces must be free to attack or refuse to attack, just as their local knowledge guides them. But, it will be argued, their action might imperil the whole organisation. Exactly so, and their inaction might imperil that working-class spirit which is more important than any organisation. Between the horns of that dilemma what can be done? In my opinion, we must recognise that the only solution of that problem is the choice of officers, local or national, from the standpoint of their responsiveness to the call for solidarity, and, having got such officials, to retain them only as long as they can show results in the amelioration of the condition of their members and the development of their Union as a weapon of class warfare.

ADVANCE OR RETREAT

If we develop on those lines, then the creation of a great Industrial Union, such as I have rudely sketched in my opening reminiscence, or the creation of those much more clumsy federations and amalgamations now being formed, will be of immense revolutionary value to the working class; if, on the contrary, we allow officialism of the old, narrow sectional kind to infuse their spirit into the new organisations, and to strangle these with rules suited only to a somnolent working class, then the Greater Unionism will but serve to load us with great fetters. It will but be to real Industrial Unionism what the Servile State would be to our ideal Co-operative Commonwealth.

21. CHANGES

On May 9th, 1914, Forward *printed an article by Connolly which may well be as close as he ever came to giving an apologia for his acceptance of syndicalist ideas. In so doing he made an impressive plea for continued receptivity and constructive open-mindedness on the Left, rejecting the narrowness which would insist on cleaving to the doctrinaire for its own sake. The implications of his argument go well beyond the precise topics he discusses.*

Reading of the May Day celebrations of the past week brought back to my mind in a very vivid fashion a realisation of the changes that have taken place in Socialist propaganda since the inauguration of Labour Day in these countries.

In the earlier period the question of an Eight Hour Working Day was to a large extent a test question on all the May Day Committees, as indeed it also was in the Trade Congresses of that time. Those who were old-time Trade Unionists and adherents of the Liberal or Tory parties stood out for May Day resolutions, demanding simply an 'Eight Hour Working Day,' whilst those who were of the newer school and were inclined to Socialistic ideas quite as vehemently demanded that the wording of the resolution should call for a 'Legislative' or 'Legal Eight Hour Day.' One could indeed tell roughly what proportion the antagonistic schools of Socialists or non-Socialists bore upon any such committee by a study of the wording of the resolution, and tracing the emphasis or lack of emphasis given to the call for legislative action.

The same fight was being fought out in all the Trade Unions, Trades Councils, and Trade Congresses. The question of legislative action to restrict or otherwise regulate the hours of labour divided the sheep from the goats all over the country. Many men, now active propagandists of the Socialist cause, were first launched upon that path by finding themselves as supporters of legislative restriction denounced as Socialists by the old school of individualist Trade Unionists, and being thus thrown into the arms of Socialists developed a sympathetic attitude towards their general teaching.

The more recent recruit to the Socialist ranks can scarcely realise what the position of the movement was at that time when he reads or hears that the passing of a resolution at the British Trade Congress calling for a 'Legal' Eight Hours Working Day was hailed by the Socialist propagandists of that period as a great Socialist victory. Yet so it was. In the ordinary outdoor and indoor Socialist propaganda, the same mental attitude was dominant. If it were now possible to examine the Socialist speeches of that period we would find that an inordinately large proportion of time was given up in them to a belittling of industrial action and to a what was practically an exaggeration of the ease and facility with which the working class could achieve its rights at the ballot box.

This belittling of industrial action and denial of its possibilities formed the main theme of the speeches of so many Socialist orators that it is more than possible that thousands of good earnest Trade Unionists were estranged from a friendly examination of the Socialist cause by what they felt to be something like insidious attacks upon working-class organisation. The Socialist movement at the time was in a nebulous, chaotic state, not only with regard to its organised expression, but also with regard to its growing tactics, and the tendency was for all its speakers to exploit that which for the time being secured the largest audience. Perhaps that is the tendency still. But what I am endeavouring to convey is that consideration of the means towards the end, the tactics to be followed in realising the consummation aimed at formed but a small part of Socialist study. Beyond a general affirmation of a belief in 'Common Ownership,' and in political action as the means of realising that common ownership, few speakers dared to venture. In consequence, the demand for political action became the creed of the Socialist, and in the endeavour to make the propaganda serve the general purpose of advancing the demand for political action, that demand constantly tended to overshadow the general principle of the Socialist movement itself. This stage of Socialist propaganda in Great Britain may be said to have reached its highest point in the General Election, which resulted in the return of a large number of Labour members to Parliament, and the partial reversal of the Taff Vale Decision.

With that victory the propaganda seemed to undergo a radical change. Whether it was because the workers had built too high hopes upon the advent of such a limited number of Labour men into the House of Commons, or because the men elected were destitute of the courage and initiative necessary for their position, or from both causes combined, or from neither, I do not presume to say; but certain it is that there was for a long period a falling off of enthusiasm for the political side of Socialism. Perhaps it would be better to say that there began to dawn a belief that Socialism had really another side, and that a man's belief in the efficacy of legislation was not a real test of the sincerity of his Socialist convictions. Then there came the industrial upheaval of 1911, with its series of brilliant victories won by Labour upon the industrial battle-field, and the growth of an opinion among Socialists totally adverse to political action. For a considerable period this anti-political idea made headway, and we saw its influence making itself felt all over the Socialist world. It is the very antithesis of the opinion I have described as being considered formerly as a true standard by which a Socialist might be judged, yet no one would today argue that because a man held such ideas he could not therefore be rightly classed as a Socialist. In the older days we would have at once brawled[1] such a man as an Anarchist, to-day we are not so sure of his classification. That in itself is a wonderful change in the attitude of the Socialist towards political action.

Because of the slight reverses sustained at a uniform high level of excitement and victory, there is now in many quarters a recrudescence of the older attitude towards industrial battlings. Leaders in plenty, even some engaged in industrial work, are to be found decrying strikes and deprecating all restlessness and rebellion which does not express itself at the ballot box. In some quarters we can even trace what looks suspiciously like a desire to gloat over industrial defeats and to welcome them as

[1] *sic.* A misprint for 'branded'.

evidences of the futility of industrial action, and the super-excellence of politics.

Now having observed this movement around the clock, and observed it from the standpoint of one caught amongst the wheels, I am inclined to ask all and sundry amongst our comrades if there is any necessity for this presumption of antagonism between the industrialist and the political advocate of Socialism. I cannot see any. I believe that such supposed necessity only exists in the minds of the mere theorists or doctrinaires. The practical fighter in the work-a-day world makes no such distinction. He fights, and he votes, he votes and he fights. He may not always, he does not always, vote right; nor yet does he always fight when and as he should. But I do not see that his failure to vote right is to be construed into a reason for advising him not to vote at all; nor yet why a failure to strike properly should be used as a gibe at the strike weapon, and reason for advising him to place his whole reliance upon votes.

I am glad of the experience of the past few years. I am glad that the extremely doctrinaire political attitude towards strikes received a check, and that that check came straight out of the practical experience of the workers in ship, shore, shop and railway. I am glad that the equally doctrinaire attitude of the anti-political people has failed to sweep the working class off its feet. And I trust that out of this experience will be born wisdom, and that such wisdom will enable us to develop a working class action which will combine the political and industrial activities of the workers on militant and aggressive lines.

The development of the power of the modern State should teach us that the mere right to vote will not protect the workers unless they have a strong economic organisation behind them; that the nationalisation or municipalisation of industries but changes the form of the workers' servitude whilst leaving its essence unimpaired, and that in the long run the class in control of the economic forces of the nation will be able to dominate and direct its political powers.

On the other hand, that very development also teaches us that until the workers have perfected their economic power sufficiently to control the economic forces the class actually in control will most relentlessly and scientifically use their political powers to hamper, penalise and if possible destroy the activities of the workers' organisation, and thus prevent the creation of a force sufficient for their suppression.

My reading of history tells me that in all great social changes the revolutionary class always fail of success until it is able to do the work of the class it seeks to destroy, and to do it more efficiently, and when it has so perfected itself that it is able to perform this work, neither gods nor men can stop its onward march to victory. In other words, a new social order cannot supplant the old until it has its own organisation ready to take its place. Within the social order of Capitalism I can see no possibility of building up a new economic organisation fit for the work of superseding the old on Socialist lines, except that new order be built upon the lines of the industries that Capitalism itself has perfected. Therefore I am heart and soul an Industrial Unionist. But because I know that the Capitalist class is alert and unscrupulous in its use of power, I do not propose to leave it the uncontested use of the powers of the State. And because I realise that human nature is a wonderful thing, that the soul of man gives expression to strange and complex phenomena, and that no man knows what powers or possibilities for good or evil lie in humanity, I try to preserve my receptivity towards all new ideas, my tolerance towards all manifestations of social activity.

22. THE PROBLEM OF TRADE UNION ORGANIZATION

Herewith we present the last of our chosen essays presenting Connolly's syndicalism. Published in Foreword *on May 23d, 1914, it demonstrates the degree to which he refined his theory in the light of his practical experience. But it must not be thought that the onset of war rotted away his syndicalism: his first response to the world war was to hope for industrial action to bring the progress of war to a halt. Even after he had decided on violent insurrection he never lost faith in industrial action as fundamentally the most effective form of opposition to the warfare state that could be made, if the workers would but make it.*

Recently I have been complaining in this column and elsewhere of the tendency in the Labour movement to mistake mere concentration upon the industrial field for essentially revolutionary advance. My point was that the amalgamation or federation of unions, unless carried out by men and women with the proper revolutionary spirit was as likely to create new obstacles in the way of effective warfare, as to make that warfare possible. The argument was reinforced by citations of what is taking place in the ranks of the railwaymen and in the transport industry. There we find that the amalgamations and federations are rapidly becoming engines for steam-rollering or suppressing all manifestations of revolutionary activity, or effective demonstrations of brotherhood. Every appeal to take industrial action on behalf of a union in distress is blocked by insisting upon the necessity of 'first obtaining the sanction of the Executive,' and in practice it is found that the process of obtaining that sanction is so long, so cumbrous, and surrounded with so many rules and regulations that the union in distress is certain to be either disrupted or bankrupted before the Executive can be moved. The greater Unionism is found in short to be forging greater fetters for the working class; to bear to the real revolutionary industrial unionism the same relation as the servile State would be to the Co-operative Commonwealth of our dreams.

This argument of mine which to many people may appear as far-fetched, gains new strength from the circumstances related by our friend Robert Williams, of the Transport Workers' Federation, in the weekly report of that body for 9th May. After describing how the Head Line Company played with the above Federation in connection with its protest against the continued victimisation of the members of the Irish Transport Workers' Union, and how he was powerless to effect anything as the other Unions involved still continued to work the scab ships, he goes on to tell of a similar state of affairs in the port of London. The quotation is long, but it is so valuable an instructive lesson to all your readers that I do not hesitate to give it as an ample confirmation of my argument.

> This week, again, there has been a recrudescence of the trouble existing between the Seamen's Union at Tilbury and the Anglo-American Oil Company. This Company has a fleet of oil-tank steamers running between America and various ports in this country.
>
> As a result of the protest made by the crew of the S.S. 'Narragansett' against the chief steward, who acted in the most inhumane manner towards one of the crew who received a severe injury, this Company displaced Union men and took on Shipping Federation scabs. Further than this, they have replaced all Union men by obtaining Federation scabs in ship after ship since the commencement of the trouble. On Sunday last the 'Narragansett' arrived once more at Purfleet, on the lower reaches of the Thames, and the Tilbury Secretary of the Seamen's Union, Mr. E. Potton, naturally commenced to hustle. He communicated with Mr. Harry Gosling, Mr. Havelock Wilson, and the Secretary of this Federation, in order, if possible, to bring pressure upon the Company by preventing the ship from being bunkered.

After consultation with Messrs. Gosling and Wilson, the Secretary telephoned, and further, wrote the Anglo-American Oil Company asking them to confer with one or more of these three, in order to avoid a possible extension of the dispute to the 'coalies' and the tugboatmen, etc. (Purfleet steamers are bunkered from lighters). As in the case of the Head Line, the Secretary specifically drew the attention of the Anglo-American Oil Company to the nature of the complaints, and also sent a written request, following upon a telephone message, by a special messenger for the purpose of saving time. It should be remembered that the bunkers would all be aboard by Tuesday, and this was written on Monday. The Secretary was not very much surprised, however, to receive a reply asking him 'what exactly the complaints are, and on whose behalf they are made.' The reply was strangely in keeping with the replies received from the Head Line Company. The inference is that both these replies received inspiration from the same source.

We are writing these words in the hope that they will be read by all those responsible for the guidance and control of the Transport Workers in all our seaports. On the face of it, it seems that the one course of action was to call off the men who were working this ship. If the Company are asking for a fight, what earthly use is it to fight with a portion of your men, leaving all the others to render service to your enemy? This Company has made an open attack upon all their employees who are members of the Seamen's Union. At the same time the cargo of oil was being pumped into reservoirs ashore by Trade Union engineers, the men employed ashore are members of an affiliated Union in the Federation, the ship is bunkered by members of an affiliated Union, the tugboats and lighters are staffed by members of an affiliated Union, and still we are *powerless*.

We are not so fatuous as to suggest that continuous warfare shall be waged by general strikes whenever a member considers he has a grievance, or whenever an official encounters a difficulty, but we feel that we are

> drifting back to the position we were in prior to 1911. A Federation with 29 Unions as its constituents, but with no ties more binding than the payment of 3d. per member per year, will not, and *cannot*, meet the requirements of modern industry. We are responsible to a quarter of a million men, and the existing methods are utterly incapable of protecting them from the insidious attacks of the employers. The organisation that is afraid of making a massed attack will experience a series of isolated disasters. The workers' organisation secures respect and consideration in proportion to the extent to which it can hamper and embarrass the employers against whom it is pitted.
>
> When co-operation is sought from one Union by another, the men involved say—Consult an official. The official says—Get the consent of my E.C. The Executive officers say—Communicate with the Transport Workers' Federation. The Federation waits on the decision of its own Executive, and by this inconsequent fiddling of time and opportunity, a thousand Romes would have burned to extinction.
>
> The employers move, strike, turn, strike, move, and strike again with the rapidity of a serpent, while we are turning about and contorting with the facility of an alligator. We have at once to determine whether the future is to mean for us efficiency, aptitude, capacity and *life*, or muddle, incompetence, decay and *death*.

Just what is the real remedy for this state of matters, it would be hard to say. But it is at least certain that the organisations I have been speaking of have not discovered the true method of working class organisations. They may be on the road to discovering it; they may also be on the road to foisting upon the working class a form of organisation which will make our last state infinitely worse than our first. It is the old story of adopting the letter but rejecting the spirit. The letter of industrial concentration is now accepted by all trade union officials, but the spirit of working class solidarity is woefully absent. Each union and each branch of each union desires above all things to show a good balance sheet, and that that might be done every nerve is strained to keep their own members at work, and in a condition to pay subscriptions. Hence the pitiful dodges to avoid taking sympathetic action in support of other unions, and hence also the constant victories of the master class upon the industrial field.

I have often thought that we of the working class are too slow, or too loath to take advantage of the experiences of our rulers. Perhaps if upon all questions of industrial or other war we followed more closely after them we would be able to fight them more successfully. Here is one suggestion I make on those lines. I am not welded to it, but I would like to see it discussed:

In the modern State the capitalist class has evolved for its own purposes of offence what it calls a Cabinet. This Cabinet controls its fighting forces, which must obey it implicitly. If the Cabinet thinks the time and opportunity is ripe for war, it declares war at the most favourable moment, *and explains its reasons in Parliament afterwards.*

Can we trust any of our members with such a weapon as the capitalist class trust theirs? I think so. Can we not evolve a system of organisation which will leave to the unions the full local administration, but invest in a Cabinet the power to call out the members of any Union when such action is desirable, and explain their reasons for it afterwards. Such a Cabinet might have the right to call upon all affiliated Unions to reimburse the Union whose members were called out in support of another, but such Unions so supported would be under the necessity of obeying instantly the call of the Cabinet, or whatever might be the name of the board invested with the powers indicated.

Out of such an arrangement the way would be opened for a more thorough organisation of the working class upon the lines of real industrial Unionism. At present we are too much afraid of each other. Whatever be our form of organisation, the spirit of sectionalism still rules and curses our class.

PART VI

LEGITIMACY, SOCIALISM AND WAR

And now, like the proverbial bolt from the blue, war is upon us, and war between the most important, because the most Socialist, nations of the earth. And we are helpless!!! – James Connolly, in *Forward*, August 15th, 1914

23. LAW AND ORDER

The following essay appeared as the editorial in The Workers' Republic *of August 26th, 1899. The terms 'Law' and 'Order' have if anything increased their hypnotic force in the seventy-odd years since its composition, and it has clearly lost little of its immediate relevance during that time. In addition to its obvious implication of hostility to anarchist attitudes, it is at pains to clear socialism of the charges of similarity to anarchism often levelled against it. It is worth noting that Connolly undertook this task in a positive and aggressive fashion, avoiding both a defensive and self-exculpatory tone and any suggestion of directing capitalist ire against the anarchists in a covertly witch-hunting or (in the Irish term) felon-setting way. The distinction between the ideal and the real law gives a link with the future, when Connolly marked the growing repressiveness of capitalism by the degree to which it chipped away at such genuine instruments of universal protection which the Law afforded.*

The statement is often made that Socialists are opposed to Law and Order, and made by men and women who find in the belief implied in the statement a sufficient reason for withholding their support from the aggressive Socialist movement. We do not mean to propitiate that section of our critics by denying our hostility to the governmental powers that be, but we would suggest that a little calm reflection—supplemented by historical inquiry—upon the origin and uses of the terms 'Law' and 'Order' may be of use in determining whether the sanction of legality should be sufficient to protect any social or political institution from attack.

It is worth remembering in this connection that every movement for the improvement of the condition of the human race, every step forward in civilization, has of necessity had to face the opposition of Law, and disturbed the stability of Order. The pioneer of progress has ever been an enemy of Law, and directed all his efforts to the destruction of Order.

The reason is obvious. The human race in its progress upward from savagery has had, at each upward move, to meet the opposition of the class who, thriving upon the misery of their fellows, found their security in the maintenance of the status quo and its attendant evils. This class coming together for mutual support imposed upon their weaker, or less cunning, fellows certain rules and observances calculated to weaken the power of the multitude and augment the privileges of the few. Those rules and observances were called the Law, and in the early stages of human history, as to a lesser extent today, the majority of the race grew into the habit of accepting and even reverencing such rules or Law from the mere fact of their promulgation—especially when such promulgation dated from a period anterior to their own birth as individuals. This blind unreasoning acceptance by the majority of rules made for their own subjection, this passive and spiritless acquiescence in the rightfulness of the social or political condition of the day, is called Order. Every proposal made by the more far-seeing and intelligent to abolish such iniquitous rules is an attack upon Law, and every effort to arouse the multitude from their state of slavish subjection and inspire them with a desire to win better conditions of life, is necessarily aimed at the disturbance of Order. But the habit of thought engendered by the fact of so many generations having lived under the rule of Law—although that Law may have been but the self-preserving ordinances of a tyrannical class—has given to the term 'Law' a commanding influence over the minds of men which even the friends of progress feel compelled to avail themselves of. The first impulse of the average citizen is to yield to the uniforms and trappings with which lawmakers and administrators clothe their offices a reverence and obedience which they would by no means willingly yield to the individuals in their capacity as private citizens; in like manner the ordinances formulated by the Legislative Chamber come to the people invested with a peculiar flavour of pseudo-sanctity which they could never acquire as the mere opinions of the very mediocre gentlemen who usually frame them. Thus the reformer or revolutionist finds the line of least resistance for his party suggested to him by observing this tradition of Law.

Since the people almost involuntarily obey the Law let us capture the law-making machinery, and the new ideas—obnoxious, treasonable, or heretical, and therefore looked upon with suspicion today—will appear to them in all the pomp and panoply of Law, and they will then readily conform to the new conditions. So every discontented party in the State strove to capture the law-making machinery of the State. In this manner every class in Society, from the king to the capitalist, has successively captured political power and when enthroned in possession has legalized its own conception of Society. Each class has had a different method of exploiting Labour, and the fight for governmental power has been a contest in which each rising class above the working class has sought to make its own peculiar manner of appropriating the products of the labour of the workers the only lawful manner. In this fight the mechanism of government has been gradually improved and extended, and its franchises broadened down until the means of acquiring power have at last come within reach of the only remaining subject class—the workers. The direction taken by the revolt of this class—the modern Socialist movement—has thus been determined for it by the previous history of the race; frankly confessing its hostility to Law and Order, but supplementing the avowal by the qualification that it is only against Capitalistic Law and Capitalistic Order that its hostility is directed. Like every other revolting class in the past it aims at the capture of the law-making machinery, in order that in possession of that mechanism of government it may proceed to impose its will upon the nations as an all-compelling law. But it also knows that the conquest of political power by the revolutionary working class must of necessity result in the complete transformation of the very nature of government; that the present forms of government are the reflex of a system of society based upon class rule, and pre-suppose the existence of two separate classes—dominant and subject, coercing and coerced; that whereas every revolting class in the past upon the successful issue of its struggle had still a subject class below it, and therefore maintained all the coercive machinery of government in order to keep that class in its subject position, the emergence of the working class into the light of power and freedom will leave no class in the darkness of subjection; that, therefore, the coercive functions of government will be no longer necessary, and the first duty of the revolutionary working class after the dethronement of class government, and abolition of class robbery, must be to divest the State of its power of political ruler, and place it upon its true basis of industrial administrator.

Then when Law is the self-imposed ordinances of a free people—ordinances self-imposed in the interest of industrial efficiency and general well-being, when Order comes as a result of the harmonious working of a just social system, then Progress will find its adherents in the friends of Law, and the triumph of its ideas without disturbing the stability of Order.

But while Law remains the conservation of all the worst tyrannies imposed by man upon his fellow-man through all our long and bloody history, while Order is but a synonym for the cringing submission of spiritless slaves, the Socialist will remain an enemy of Law, and a disturber of Order.

24. REVOLUTIONARY UNIONISM AND WAR

Just as the British labour elite had frustrated Connolly's hopes of solidarity at the time of the great Dublin lockout and its sequel, so the leadership of European socialism rejected what he believed to be its opportunity for preventing World War I by collective passive resistance. Where British and European socialists were not actively supporting their respective national war efforts, they were proving almost deliberately ineffective in the great majority of cases. Connolly's singling out of the British for particular responsibility for the war might mislead readers into assuming this to be a knee-jerk Irish nationalist response; in fact, it would be truer to say that his British origin dictated this attitude more than his Irish ancestry or domicile, believing as he did that the socialist should, in wartime, counter chauvinism by acknowledging and asserting the war guilt of his own country. He would also have been conscious of writing for an audience in the still neutral U.S.A. where, notoriously, the fact of common language gave British propaganda an enormous advantage in the struggle to win American support in moral and ultimately in military terms. It is worth noting that at the point of writing Connolly was himself without a means of self-expression, since the Irish Worker *had been suppressed in December 1914, and its successors* Irish Work *and* The Worker *had been smothered by official harassment. This article appeared in the* International Socialist Review *for March 1915. It refers in passing to the famous Russian anarchist theoretician Prince Peter Kropotkin (1842–1921), who had enjoyed unusually good relations with socialists and had, for an anarchist, an impressive reputation among them, but who supported the Allies in World War I; and to G. D. Herron, who was an old target of Connolly's; Desmond Ryan*[1] *quotes Connolly from the* Socialist, *June 1904, where Herron and others were described as seeing in socialism 'a means for ventilating their theories on such questions as sex, religion, vaccination, vegetarianism, &c.'*

[1] In *Labour and Easter Week* (Three Candles, Dublin, 1949), p. 60.

Since the war broke out in Europe, and since the Socialist forces in the various countries failed so signally to prevent or even delay the outbreak, I have been reading everything in American Socialist papers or magazines that came to hand, to see if that failure and the reasons therefor, were properly understood among my old comrades in the states.

But either I have not seen the proper publications or else the dramatic side of the military campaigns has taken too firm a hold upon the imagination of Socialist writers to allow them to properly estimate the inner meaning of that debacle of political Socialism witnessed in Europe when the bugles of war rang out upon our ears.

I am going then to try, in all calmness, to relate the matter as it appears to us who believe that *the signal of war ought also to have been the signal for rebellion*, that when the bugles sounded the first note for actual war, their notes should have been taken as the tocsin for social revolution. And I am going to try to explain why such results did not follow such actions. My explanation may not be palpable to some; I hope it will be at least interesting to all.

In the first place let me be perfectly frank with my readers as to my own position now that that possibility has receded out of sight. As the reader will have gathered from my opening remarks, I believe that the Socialist proletariat of Europe in *all* the belligerent countries ought to have refused to march against their brothers across the frontiers, and that such refusal would have prevented the war and all its horrors, even though it might have led to civil war. Such a civil war would not, could not possibly have resulted in such a loss of Socialist life as this international war has entailed and each Socialist who fell in such a civil war would have fallen knowing that he was battling for the cause he had worked for in days of peace, and that there was no possibility of the bullet or shell that laid him low having been sent on its murderous way by one to whom he had pledged the 'life-long love of comrades' in the International Army of Labor.

But seeing that the Socialist movement did not so put the faith of its adherents to the test, seeing that the nations are now locked in this death grapple, and the issue is knit, I do not wish to disguise from any one my belief that there is no hope of peaceful development for the industrial nations of continental Europe whilst England holds the dominance of the sea. The British fleet is a knife held permanently at the throat of Europe; should any nation evince an ability to emerge from the position of a mere customer for British products, and to become a successful competitor of England in the markets of the world, that knife is set in operation to cut that throat.

By days and by nights the British Government watches and works to isolate its competitor from the comity of nations, to ring it around with hostile foes. When the time is propitious, the blow is struck, the allies of England encompass its rival by land, and the fleet of Britain swoops upon its commerce by sea. In one short month the commerce-raiding fleet of Great Britain destroys a trade built up in forty years of slow, peaceful industry, as it has just done in the case of Germany.

Examining the history of the foreign relations of Great Britain since the rise of the capitalist class to power in that country, the continuity of this policy becomes obvious and as marvelous as it is obvious.

Neither religion, nor race affinity nor diversity of political or social institutions availed to save a competitor of England. The list of commercial rivals, or would-be rivals is fairly large and gives the economic key to the reasons for the great wars of England. In that list we find Spain, Holland, France, Denmark and now Germany. England must rule the waves and when the continental nations wished to make at The Hague a law forbidding the capture of merchant vessels during war, England refused her assent. Naturally! It is her power to capture merchant ships during war that enables England to cut the throat of a commercial rival at her own sweet will.

If she had not that power she would need to depend upon her superiority in technical equipment and efficiency, and the uprise in other countries of industrial enterprises able to challenge and defeat her in this world market has amply demonstrated that she has not that superiority any longer.

The United States and Germany lead in crowding England industrially; the former cannot be made a target for the guns of militarist continental Europe, therefore escapes for the time being, as England never fights a white power single-handed. But Germany is caught within the net and has to suffer for her industrial achievements.

The right to capture merchant ships for which England stood out against the public opinion of all Europe is thus seen to be the trump card of England against the industrial development of the world outside her shores—against that complete freedom of the seas by which alone the nations of the world can develop that industrial status which Socialists maintain to be an indispensable condition for Socialist triumph.

I have been thus frank with my readers in order that they may perfectly understand my position and the reasons therefor, and thus to anticipate some of the insinuations that are sure to be levelled against me as one who sympathizes neither with the anti-German hysteria of such comrades as Professor Herron, nor with the suddenly developed belief in the good faith of czars shown by Prince Kropotkin.

I believe the war could have heen prevented by the Socialists; as it was not prevented and the issues are knit, I want to see England beaten so thoroughly that the commerce of the seas will henceforth be free to all nations—to the smallest equally with the greatest.

But *how could this war have been prevented*, which is another way of saying how and why did the Socialist movement fail to prevent it?

The full answer to that question can only be grasped by those who are familiar with the propaganda that from 1905 onwards has been known as 'Industrialist' in the United States and, though not so accurately, has been called 'syndicalist' in Europe.

The essence of that propaganda lay in two principles. To take them in the order of their immediate effectiveness these were: First, that Labor could only enforce its wishes by organizing its strength at the point of production, i.e., the farms, factories, workshops, railways, docks, ships—where the work of the world is carried on the effectiveness of the political vote depending primarily upon the economic power of the workers organized behind it. Secondly, that the process of organizing that economic power would also build the industrial fabric of the Socialist Republic, build the new society within the old.

It is upon the first of these two principles I wish my readers to concentrate their attention in order to find the answer to the question we are asking.

In all the belligerent countries of western and central Europe the Socialist vote was very large; in none of these belligerent countries was there an organized revolutionary industrial organization directing the Socialist vote nor a Socialist political party directing a revolutionary industrial organization.

The Socialist voters having cast their ballots were helpless as voters until the next election; as workers they were indeed in control of the forces of production and distribution, and by exercising that control over the transport service could have made the war impossible. But the idea of thus co-ordinating their two spheres of activity had not gained sufficient lodgment to be effective in the emergency.

No Socialist party in Europe could say that rather than go to war it would call out the entire transport service of the country and thus prevent mobilization. No Socialist party could say so, because no Socialist party could have the slightest reasonable prospect of having such a call obeyed.

The Executive Committee of the Socialist movement was not in control of the labor-force of the men who voted for the Socialist representatives in the legislative chambers of Europe, nor were the men in control of the supply of labor-force in control of the Socialist representatives. In either case there would have been an organized power immediately available against war. Lacking either, the Socialist parties of Europe when they protested against war, had also *fired their last shot* against militarism and were left 'like children crying in the night.'

Had the Socialist party of France been able to declare that rather than be dragged into war to save the Russian czar from the revolutionary consequences which would have followed his certain defeat by Germany, they would declare a railway strike, there would have been no war between France and Germany, as the latter country, saved from the dread of an attack in the West whilst defending itself in the East could not have coerced its Socialist population into consenting to take the offensive against France.

But the French Government knows, the German Government knows, all cool observers in Europe know, that the Socialist and syndicalist organizations of France could not have carried out such a threat even had they made it. Both politically and industrially the revolutionary organizations of France are mere skeleton frameworks, not solid bodies.

Politically large numbers roll together at elections around the faithful few who keep the machinery of the party together; industrially, more or less, large numbers roll together during strikes or lockouts. But the numbers of either are shifting, uncertain and of shadowy allegiance. From such no revolutionary action of value in face of modern conditions of warfare and state organization could be expected. And none came.

Hence the pathetic failure of French Socialism—the Socialist battalion occupying the position of the most tactical importance on the European battlefield. For neither Russia nor Britain could have fought had France held aloof; Russia because of the fear of internal convulsions; Britain, because Britain never fights unless the odds against her foe are overwhelming. And Britain needed the aid of the French fleet.

To sum up then, the failure of European Socialism to avert the war is primarily due to the divorce between the industrial and political movements of Labor. The Socialist voter, as such, is helpless between elections. He requires to organize power to enforce the mandate of the elections, and the *only power he can so organize is economic power*—the power to stop the wheels of commerce, to control the heart that sends the life blood pulsating through the social organisms.

25. OUR DISAPPEARING LIBERTIES

Apart from its interesting contemporary references, the following article is a characteristic expression of the profound anti-militarism of Connolly the ex-soldier and future insurgent Commandant-General. Its sensitive assessment of the impact of an army on civilian life, irrespective of whether its presence be due to defence, quartering or occupation; its emphasis upon economic conscription (Ireland was as yet exempt from legal conscription); and its ringing assertion of human liberties: all distinguish it and lend it permanent relevance to left-wing thought. The final sentences throw the libertarianism of Connolly into sharp relief when considered in conjunction with subsequent theory and practice in socialist spheres. The article appeared on June 5th, 1915, in The Workers' Republic, *by which old name Connolly entitled his last paper. It had commenced publication one week previously.*

One of the commonplaces of the political orator is the saying that 'the price of liberty is eternal vigilance,' a saying which implies that the liberties of mankind are continually endangered from the inroads of unscrupulous enemies against whose attacks we must ever be on the alert. It implies also that the normal state of society is a state of war; that mankind, even amongst the most progressive nations, is ever in danger of seeing its painfully acquired liberties wrested from it and fresh chains substituted, and that consequently they who wish to see progress maintained and the bounds of freedom enlarged must be ever on the watch lest upon some specious excuse they lose in a day what their fathers agonised for generations to win.

This political proverb we seem in peril of forgetting in these troublous times. On every side we see fresh inroads made upon our liberties, but no Irish voice is raised in protest, perhaps no Irish voice dare be raised. But no matter what the risk be, we who essay to voice the hopes and defend the cause of Labour dare not be silent. The needs of the multitude call for expression – it shall not be said they called in vain. If fresh chains are forged for the workers it shall not be said that we by our silence allowed those who trusted us to remain ignorant of the fact that the chains were in preparation.

In the first place we direct attention to the fact that the meanest and cruellest form of conscription is already in active operation in this country. Without consulting anyone as to their opinions upon the justification or otherwise of this war employers are every day giving to their employees the intimation that they must choose between enlistment and starvation. It matters not that the employer may himself be young or vigorous, or have sons young and vigorous, whilst the workman may have a family of little children depending upon him, that employer sits smoking in his office chair and orders the helpless wage-slave to don a uniform he hates, or suffer dismissal and starvation. No greater violation of the right of the individual has ever been known to history. When a man is ordered to take a deadly weapon and proceed to kill a human being with whom he believes he has no grounds of quarrel, personal or national, if the fear of starvation makes him obey that order, then the person issuing that command is guilty of the foulest crime known to humanity—the murder of a human soul. Against such an attack upon the liberty of the individual we protest, and call upon all to protest. Conscription is bad, we hate the thought of it, but conscription is at least openly brutal; this conscription by starvation is foul with the foulness of Hell. We are not alone in this belief. There are thousands who believe in the justness of this war who are sickened with loathing of the means taken to obtain soldiers to carry it on.

Throughout Ireland every day we read of prosecutions under the Defence of the Realm Act in which the triviality of the charges are such as are calculated to bring more contempt than respect upon those responsible. For that we do not repine, nor pretend to repine. But when it appears that the liberty of the most respectable man or woman in this country is absolutely at the mercy of the most disreputable and drunken soldier that ever disgraced a uniform, it is time to call a halt. In many cases we have seen drunken soldiers deliberately pick quarrels with respectable civilians, and after abusing and ill-treating them call upon the police to arrest those whom they had abused and ill-treated. The police always obey, and the magistrates always convict. On the tram, in the streets, in places of amusement or refreshment, nowadays it is a positive danger to be in the proximity of a soldier. Many of these are decent, cleanly enough, but at any time the lowest amongst them may elect to force his gross conversation upon you, and should you resent, the services of the police are called in and a term of imprisonment is certain.

On Sunday whilst the Dublin Labour Day procession was going to the Phoenix Park one of those rowdies attempted to ride a bicycle right through the thickest ranks of the processionists; others on the ground in the Park endeavoured by ribald language and horseplay to stir up trouble wherever they saw groups of policemen convenient to their activities, but fortunately the demonstrators strong in the consciousness of their own power were not moved to active hostility.

We wonder if the governing authorities are really aware of all this. Surely no one can be so fatuous as to imagine that the British Army can be popularised by such methods. If we did believe that this kind of thing had really the support of the government we should not waste our space in chronicling it; it is because we realise that it may spread upward that we speak ere it be too late. Magistrates, and soldiers and policemen and Coalition Cabinets must be made to understand that they all exist in theory for the sake of serving the civilian. If the contrary obtains, if, as seems to be the danger in Ireland, the civilian is subordinated to the soldier, and becomes a dog for all those we have named to kick and abuse, then it will become very difficult indeed to understand wherein lies that constitutional freedom we have lately heard so much about.

The liberty of public meeting is also rapidly becoming a thing of the past in Ireland, as far as it is or may be used for the criticism of the activities of the government or its functionaries; and yet it is this very right of the subject to criticise the governing bodies which is the very essence of freedom in a constitutionally governed country. Without the freedom of the press and the right of public meeting there is no citizenship; there are only the relations of subject and rulers, of slaves and slave-drivers. The question of whether the press is or is not wrong in its criticisms, or whether the public meeting does or does not advocate wise measures or use wise language has no bearing upon the matter. The press criticisms are subject to the judgment of the readers; the public meeting stands or falls with the justice of its cause. To allow either to be judged or punished by those against whom they are directed, is to abolish all constitutional guarantees and to establish the naked rule of force. Against that we protest with all our strength. It is idle to speak of great national emergencies requiring such suppression of liberties. Great national emergencies can only be met by calling upon the reserves of good in our national character, by invoking the aid of all that is best and ennobling. Whatever cause seeks to flourish by stifling criticism and imprisoning thought is a hateful cause, and can only rely upon the support of those natures who turn instinctively to darkness and obscurity.

For all who love the light for the help it brings to the cause of progress the duty is plain. Every one of the liberties our fathers won must be fought for tenaciously! War or no war none of our hard won rights should be, or will be, surrendered without a struggle.

26. WHAT IS OUR PROGRAMME?

Some three months before the commencement of the Easter Week rising Connolly restated his programme in terms which reassert his position with all the qualifications needed for the upheavals engendered by war, and which also sum up much of the theoretical emphases of his career. The article puts the syndicalist method of resistance forward again, but it also acts as an apologia for the insurrection, which by the time of its composition had already been planned, with an early date agreed to. It insists on insurrection as the child of war, and war alone, opposing peace-time rebellion, and it urges the logic whereby Connolly hoped for success, a hope that had totally receded when he took the field. The war therefore led Connolly to take those actions for which he is best remembered; but they were taken only in desperate response to what seemed to be the destruction of his life's work. It was a brave article, as it had to explain his future conduct without revealing it, give a meaning to the present without permanence and justify in terms of continuum a past he feared was largely eroded. It was published in The Workers' Republic *on January 22nd, 1916.*

WHAT IS OUR PROGRAMME?

We are often asked the above question. Sometimes the question is not too politely put, sometimes it is put in frantic bewilderment, sometimes it is put in wrathful objurgation, sometimes it is put in tearful entreaty, sometimes it is put by Nationalists who affect to despise the Labour movement, sometimes it is put by Socialists who distrust the Nationalists because of the anti-Labour record of many of their friends, sometimes it is put by our enemies, sometimes by our friends, and always it is pertinent, and worthy of an answer.

The Labour movement is like no other movement. Its strength lies in being like no other movement. It is never so strong as when it stands alone. Other movements dread analysis and shun all attempts to define their objects. The Labour movement delights in analysing, and is perpetually defining and re-defining its principles and objects. The man or woman who has caught the spirit of the Labour movement brings that spirit of analysis and definition into all his or her public acts, and expects at all times to answer the call to define his or her position. They cannot live on illusions, nor thrive by them; even should their heads be in the clouds they will make no forward step until they are assured that their feet rest upon the solid earth.

In this they are essentially different from the middle or professional classes, and the parties or movements controlled by such classes in Ireland. These always talk of realities, but nourish themselves and their followers upon the unsubstantial meat of phrases; always prate about being intensely practical but nevertheless spend their whole lives in following visions.

When the average non-Labour patriot in Ireland who boasts of his practicality is brought in contact with the cold world and its problems he shrinks from the contact. Should his feet touch the solid earth he affects to despise it as a 'mere material basis,' and strives to make the people believe that true patriotism needs no foundation to rest upon other than the brain storms of its poets, orators, journalists, and leaders.

Ask such people for a programme and you are branded as a carping critic; refuse to accept their judgment as the last word in human wisdom and you become an enemy to be carefully watched; insist that in the crisis of your country's history your first allegiance is to your country and not to any leader, executive, or committee, and you are forthwith a disturber, a factionist, a wrecker.

What is our programme? We at least, in conformity with the spirit of our movement, will try and tell it. Our programme in time of peace was to gather into Irish hands in Irish trade unions the control of all the forces of production and distribution in Ireland. We never believed that freedom would be realised without fighting for it. From our earliest declaration of policy in Dublin in 1896 the editor of this paper has held to the dictum that our ends should be secured 'peacefully if possible, forcibly if necessary.' Believing so, we saw what the world outside Ireland is realising today, that the destinies of the world and the fighting strength of armies are at the mercy of organised Labour as soon as that Labour becomes truly revolutionary. Thus we strove to make Labour in Ireland organised – and revolutionary.

We saw that should it come to a test in Ireland (as we hoped and prayed it might come), between those who stood for the Irish nation and those who stood for the foreign rule, the greatest civil asset in the hand of the Irish nation for use in the struggle would be the control of Irish docks, shipping, railways and production by Unions that gave sole allegiance to Ireland.

We realised that the power of the enemy to hurl his forces upon the forces of Ireland would lie at the mercy of the men who controlled the transport system of Ireland; we saw that the hopes of Ireland as a nation rested upon the due recognition of the identity of interest between that ideal and the rising hopes of Labour.

In Europe today we have seen the strongest governments of the world exerting every effort, holding out all possible sort of inducement, to organised Labour to use its organisation on the side of those governments in time of war. We have spent the best part of our lifetime striving to create in Ireland the working class spirit that would create an Irish organisation of Labour willing to do voluntarily for Ireland what those governments of Europe are beseeching their trade unions to do for their countries. And we have partly succeeded.

We have succeeded in creating an organisation that will willingly do more for Ireland than any trade union in the world has attempted to do for its national government. Had we not been attacked and betrayed by many of our fervent advanced patriots, had they not been so anxious to destroy us, so willing to applaud even the British Government when it attacked us, had they stood by us and pushed our organisation all over Ireland it would now be in our power at a word to crumple up and demoralise every offensive move of the enemy against the champions of Irish freedom. Had we been able to carry out all our plans, as such an Irish organisation of Labour alone could carry them out, we could at a word have created all the conditions necessary to the striking of a successful blow whenever the military arm of Ireland wished to move.

Have we a programme? We are the only people that had

a programme—that understood the mechanical conditions of modern war, and the dependence of national power upon industrial control. What is our programme now? At the grave risk of displeasing alike the perfervid Irish patriot and the British 'competent military authority,' we shall tell it.

We believe that in times of peace we should work along the lines of peace to strengthen the nation, and we believe that whatever strengthens and elevates the working class strengthens the nation. But we also believe that in times of war we should act as in war. We despise, entirely despise and loathe, all the mouthings and mouthers about war who infest Ireland in time of peace, just as we despise and loathe all the cantings about caution and restraint to which the same people treat us in times of war.

Mark well then our programme. While the war lasts and Ireland still is a subject nation we shall continue to urge her to fight for her freedom.

We shall continue, in season and out of season, to teach that the 'far-flung battle line' of England is weakest at the point nearest its heart, that Ireland is in that position of tactical advantage, that a defeat of England in India, Egypt, the Balkans or Flanders would not be so dangerous to the British Empire as any conflict of armed forces in Ireland, that the time for Ireland's battle is NOW, the place for Ireland's battle is HERE. That a strong man may deal lusty blows with his fists against a host of surrounding foes, and conquer, but will succumb if a child sticks a pin in his heart.

But the moment peace is once admitted by the British Government as being a subject ripe for discussion, *that moment our policy will be for peace* and in direct opposition to all talk or preparation for armed revolution. We will be no party to leading out Irish patriots to meet the might of an England at peace. The moment peace is in the air we shall strictly confine ourselves, and lend all our influence to the work of turning the thought of Labour in Ireland to the work of peaceful reconstruction.

That is our programme. You can now compare it with the programme of those who bid you hold your hand now, and thus put it in the power of the enemy to patch up a temporary peace, turn round and smash you at his leisure, and then go to war again with the Irish question settled—in the graves of Irish patriots.

We fear that is what is going to happen. It is to our mind inconceivable that the British public should allow conscription to be applied to England and not to Ireland. Nor do the British Government desire it. But that Government will use the cry of the necessities of war to force conscription upon the people of England, and will then make a temporary peace, and turn round to force Ireland to accept the same terms as have been forced upon England.

The English public will gladly see this done—misfortune likes company. The situation will then shape itself thus: the Irish Volunteers who are pledged to fight conscription will either need to swallow their pledge, and see the young men of Ireland conscripted, or will need to resist conscription, and engage the military force of England at a time when England is at peace.

This is what the diplomacy of England is working for, what the stupidity of some of our leaders who imagine they are Wolfe Tones is making possible. It is our duty, it is the duty of all who wish to save Ireland from such shame or such slaughter to strengthen the hand of those of the leaders who are for action as against those who are playing into the hands of the enemy.

We are neither rash nor cowardly. We know our opportunity when we see it, and we know when it has gone. We know that at the end of this war England will have at least an army of one million men, *or more than two soldiers for every adult male in Ireland.* And these soldiers veterans of the greatest war in history.

We shall not want to fight those men. We shall devote our attention to organising their comrades who return to civil life, to organising them into trade unions and Labour parties to secure them their rights in civil life.

Unless we emigrate to some country where there are men.

PART VII

THE RASCAL AND THE SPAILPIN

There was a man once who published a series of articles and entitled the volume 'Instead of a Book, by a Man too Busy to Write One'. I feel like imitating his good example today. I am too busy to write an article.
– James Connolly, in *Forward*, October 25th, 1913

INTRODUCTION

It is of some importance to remember that, for all of Connolly's genuineness, we must not allow our serious consideration of his political and social writing to blind us to the informal manner in which he habitually enunciated his views. In every paper he edited, and in many to which he was a regular contributor, he ran a column (which normally appeared in every issue) in which he chatted in a relaxed, ironic and easily assimilable manner to his readers. For all of his rejection of the chauvinism of a Robert Blatchford, he was in full agreement with Blatchford on the need for a gently infectious form of communication. Tired workers would accept lessons through laughter which could never penetrate with obvious preaching. If we want a modern parallel here, George Orwell's Tribune *column 'As I Please' might supply it, although Connolly possessed more of a capacity for building bridges to establish direct communication with his audience than the more personally introverted Orwell. Occasionally one of his columns might make a very sustained analysis of some point, although he deliberately preferred to wander from topic to topic with only vague association of ideas. One case of sustained analysis from his informal column is the discussion of Sinn Féin printed as Chapter 12.*

As the editor of journals whose contributors were often few in number, Connolly used many pseudonyms as well as writing editorially and anonymously. But his discursive personal column had only two pseudonyms: 'R. Ascal' in his Scottish days, 'Spailpin' in Ireland and in America. The choice of the latter name is interesting; it is both a direct translation of 'rascal' and the Irish for 'labourer', an association of ideas which is hardly accidental. The stage-Irish 'spalpeen' is normally used with the 'rascal' connotation and the condescension given to a labourer. Connolly was thus enabled to employ pseudonyms of the classically self-belittling kind which granted licence for animadversion at large, while also asserting his working-class identity.

The article printed as Chapter 27 is the third of R. Ascal's regular columns, entitled 'Plain Talk', written for the Edinburgh Labour Chronicle, *a spirited but short-lived monthly. This particular one appeared on December 1st, 1894. Chapter 28 is from the similar column he wrote for* The Workers' Republic *entitled 'Home Thrusts'. It originally appeared in* The Workers' Republic *of July 7th, 1900. Chapter 29 has been included as an unusually fine mixture of economics, exhortation and sardonic humour. Readers who recall how O'Casey satirized the slogan on Irish sobriety and freedom may derive some amusement from the possibility that he first heard it ridiculed by Connolly, whose colleague he was in 1913; one doubts whether he saw this initial attack, published on July 15th, 1900.*

Spailpin's column in The Harp, *'Harp Strings', was longer and more discursive than was possible in the limited space at his disposal in* The Workers' Republic. *Given the high representation accorded hitherto in these pages to Connolly's Irish preoccupations, it has seemed desirable to select a column specifically concerned with the U.S.A.* per se, *reminding Irish-Americans that their zeal to conform to it should not lead them to a hyper-optimistic view of it. The article printed as Chapter 30 appeared at the beginning of the issue for December 1908.*

Since this section emphasizes Connolly's stress on more immediate forms of communication, it has seemed desirable to conclude with his introduction to a book of songs— Songs of Freedom by Irish Authors, *published in Dublin by J. E. C. Donnelly, afterwards publisher of* The Harp. *It appeared in 1907. Its interesting assertion of the urgency of song to the revolutionary movement, as the true expression of the masses, deserves stress in a communications-conscious age whose ideologues still depend too much on dogma and exposition. Whether Connolly at this point is exhibiting the influence of the Catholic doctrine that song can be the union of worship is an interesting speculation. Selections from Connolly's own songs, included in this and other volumes, are not printed here. However advanced his social and political thought, culturally he was highly traditionalist. Some indication of this may be seen by the poem he quotes so favourably in 'Harp Strings' (see Chapter 30). That poem itself doubtless seems highly archaic today, but a shared enjoyment of this sort of nostalgic writing would have established common chords between Connolly and Irish-Americans whose politics initially had little in common with his. His use of this kind of common ground conveys to us the variety of ways in which he sought to establish and build up communication with the audience he hoped to evangelize.*

27. PARTY POLITICIANS – NOBLE, IGNOBLE AND LOCAL

PLAIN TALK

By R. Ascal

The Czar is dead and the elections are over. The new Czar has issued a manifesto, and Bailie M'Donald is now Lord Provost. The peace of Europe is still maintained, the Nihilists are plotting in silence, and Councillor Waterston has been and gone and done it.

A Tory Lord Provost rules over Liberal Edinburgh, and Councillor Sir James Russell sits and sighs and wishes his name was Blaikie.

Edinburgh Town Council attended Divine Service in Hope Park U.P. Church on Sunday, 18th November, *in honour of the Lord Provost*, who is a member of that congregation. I wonder if they meant it.

The Liberals have threatened to oppose Mr Waterston because he voted for Provost M'Donald. Councillor Robertson declared at the Council meeting he was in favour of the honours going round, and would have voted against Sir James Russell had a really capable man been brought forward, but he would not vote for M'Donald.

And yet they all went to church in honour of Lord Provost M'Donald. Otherwise, I presume, they would not have gone at all.

This is the final outcome of the municipal elections: all the old gang are returned to office, and the municipal life of Edinburgh in the ensuing year will be marked by the same scrupulous regard to economy (in wages) and efficiency (in jobbery) to which we have been so well accustomed in the past.

The Social Democrats were defeated. On the authority of the celebrated representative of culture, Mr Francis M'Aweeney, we are told they received 'a crushing blow,' yet a more jubilant lot of men and women it would have been impossible to find on the day after the election.

An opponent passing under the windows of their Committee Room an hour after the result of the poll was declared, on hearing the jubilant speeches and enthusiastic cheering of the Socialists, was constrained to remark to a companion, that the Social Democrats receive a defeat better than their enemies do a victory.

And he was right. Some defeats are better than victories. A defeat endured as the result of contest conducted in a fair and honourable manner is a thousand times more creditable to the defeated party than a victory gained by all the mean and unscrupulous arts of the wirepullers.

The Socialists did not send any carriages for their lady supporters; they did not have committee rooms outside the polling booth, and, waylaying unfortunate voters, rush them in, and then escort them between tall hats and frock coats, to record their votes in favour of the rights of property; they did not tell Irish Catholics that Mr Connolly was a Freethinker, who wanted to overthrow the Church, and then tell old Scotch women of both sexes that Mr Connolly was an Irish Papist who wanted to introduce the Scarlet Woman; they did not seek the support of the Unionists by telling of the letter of recommendation from a leading Edinburgh Unionist; and seek the support of the Home Rulers by calling to their aid every quondam Home Ruler, or leader, who could be induced to sell his name, and voice, and birthright for the ill-smelling pottage of Liberal promises.

The Social Democrats were defeated. But last year the vote polled in George Square Ward for the I.L.P. candidate was only one-thirteenth of the total poll, whereas in St Giles, the vote for the avowed Social Democrat reached one-seventh of the total poll. A great advance, truly.

The official Liberal – backed by all the strength, reputation, and admirable electioneering organisation of the combined Liberal and Nationalist parties, and aided by the avowed support of the most influential Unionists in the ward, with a known man and a lawyer as their candidate, were yet only able to obtain a majority of four to one over a party the most revolutionary and the most recent in public life, with no electioneering organisation, and with a candidate known to earn his bread by following an occupation most necessary in our city life, but nevertheless universally despised by the public opinion of aristocratic Edinburgh.

It is to be hoped that next year the Ward will not be troubled with the presence of another bogus Unionist candidate.

Had there been no Unionist, and had the advanced working-class voters been left free to choose between the revolutionary Social-Democrat and the orthodox Liberal and defender of the rights of property, there is little doubt the result of the poll would not have brought much comfort to the enemies of Socialism.

But hundreds of men, who would otherwise have voted Socialist, cast their votes reluctantly for Mr Mitchell as the candidate most likely to ensure the defeat of the Tory.

They will now have twelve months in which to meditate on the difference between the Liberal Tweedledee and the Tory Tweedledum, and after having so meditated they are invited to record the result of their studies at the polling booth on the first Tuesday of November 1895, if not before.

There is great heartburning in certain Liberal circles in Edinburgh over a matter which does not affect the working-class voter. It is an invitation to an 'At Home,' to be held in the Waterloo Rooms, Glasgow, by Lady Helen Ferguson of Novar.

All the gentlemen whose purses are in the habit of opening for the relief of distressed M.P.s and huckstering politicians in general, together with a few who have remained obdurate in spite of the pathetic appeals of Messrs Donworth and Dillon, are invited to this great social function.

Class the first will be thanked for their splendid devotion to the cause of Liberalism, and class the second will, it is hoped, be so overwhelmed with the magnificent display, and so enchanted by the bright smiles of the delegates from the Ladies' Liberal Association that they will open their hearts and their purses also, and all will be well.

By such means are replenished the Liberal coffers, and the Liberal working-man throws his cap in the air, and when he meets his Socialist comrade asks—'Where is the Tory gold?'

And his Socialist comrade, who has been stinting himself of his glass of beer in order to pay the election expenses of *his* candidate usually scratches his head and wonders also—'Where is the Tory gold?'

Gold of any kind or colour is a very scarce commodity in a Socialist committee room. *N.B.*—Those who do not believe this should come and join us and get a share of the plunder. Entry-money, sixpence; weekly subscription, one penny.—ADVT.

Any orthodox Liberal or Tory politician will tell you that one cause of the great misery among the working-class is to be found in the alarming prevalence of early marriages.

Yet in face of this lamentable fact, we are informed that his Grace the Duke of Argyll, who is 71 years of age, is about to get married to his third wife. As this step may lead to a still further increase in our pauper population, it is to be hoped wiser counsels will prevail and prevent the young couple taking the final disastrous step.

Ambrose Malvern, aged 68, committed suicide by jumping from a hotel window. This young man had married a widow the previous day. So I read in a contemporary. If some one will undertake to send this to his Grace the Duke of Argyll he might yet pause in his headlong career, and the nation be saved from an impending calamity.

Mr William M'Ewan, M.P., gave £50,000 to assist in building a new wing to Edinburgh University. We gave thanks. Edinburgh Town Council, having a love for the beautiful, spent £70,000 in obtaining for the citizens a better view of M'Ewan's £50,000. Again we gave thanks. The first act of the newly-elected Town Council was to accept an estimate for the proposed widening of the North Bridge and refuse to insert in it a clause requiring the payment of the current rate of wages. The labouring people who voted for the return of the old gang to office are still giving thanks.

We are a great people.

I hear the Rev. Mr Jackson, at a meeting in the Albert Hall, on Sunday, 18th November, declared his Socialism was of the kind endorsed by the Trades Union Congress at their recent meeting in Norwich. If this is true the rev. gentleman is eligible for membership of the I.L.P. or S.S.F., and I would advise him to enter into communication with one or other of these bodies, and take his proper place in the communion of the faithful.

But before admission he might, as a public character, be required to give some practical proofs of his sincerity. Not that we would expect him, as a follower of Him of Nazareth, to 'sell all he has and give it to the poor,' as one would-be follower was required to do. Oh, no, our latter-day Christianity is far too 'practical' to adopt such hare-brained theories of restitution as that implied in the aforementioned utterance of their Master.

But a certain colleague of Mr Jackson on the School Board has recently made an effort to deprive the women cleaners employed by that body of their wages, that is of their means of life, during sickness. Will Mr Jackson preach a sermon on the subject, taking for his text the injunction, 'Rob not the poor because he is poor.'

Or will he allow the Edinburgh Socialists the free use of his hall, or church, for the purpose of conducting a fortnight's mission to clergymen. Subject of mission: Instruction in the use of the Divine command, 'Love thy neighbour as thyself.'

Until our reverend friend is prepared to give such practical proofs of his Socialism will he please remember that 'Faith without works is dead.'

The conduct of the Edinburgh School Board, coupled with the conduct of the Town Council in refusing to insert the fair wages clause in a most important contract, should help to clear the cobwebs from the eyes of the intelligent voters and enable them to appreciate the necessity for an infusion of new Socialistic blood into all our public bodies.

For some time to come the work of Socialists on all such bodies will not be so much to pass new laws as to infuse into their administration the spirit of the new life, to use all power to inaugurate the reign of justice, to convert our industrial system from a machine for making profit into an instrument for sustaining life, to transform our politics from the government of men into the wise and well-ordered administration of things, to relegate to the limbo of exploded superstitions the old doctrine of freedom of contract between affluence and starvation, and thus, by constantly placing our doctrines and our efforts upon the same platform as the class interests of the workers, to create such a public feeling in our favour as shall enable us to bridge the gulf between the old order and the new, and lead the people from the dark Egypt of our industrial anarchy, into the Promised Land of industrial freedom.

The return of a Socialist candidate does not then mean the immediate realisation of even the programme of palliatives commonly set before the electors. Nay, such programmes are in themselves a mere secondary consideration, of little weight, indeed, apart from the spirit in which they will be interpreted.

The election of a Socialist to any public body at present, is only valuable in so far as it is the return of a disturber of the political peace.

Until Socialism attains such a foothold in this country as shall enable the Socialists to return a majority to the public bodies which rule the country, every fresh seat captured must simply be regarded as a fresh means of spoiling the little games of the Jabezian philanthropists, financial jobbers, and political thimbleriggers, who thrive on their reputations as Liberal and Tory politicians.

If only for the value of letting the light of public opinion in on the doings of officialdom, we should never relax our efforts until every representative body has its full quota of Socialist members.

While on this matter, it would be as well to keep in mind the fact, that under the Local Government (Scotland) Act, which comes into force in April of 1895, the Poor Law system of this country will be at last placed under democratic control.

The workers will then have an opportunity of humanising this iniquitous system, by placing upon every Parish Council a sufficient number of Social Democrats to counteract the despotic tendencies of our Liberal and Tory taskmasters.

The poor paupers, the war-worn veterans who have fallen in the battle of life, who are imprisoned in those bastiles of poorhouses, may now have the closing years of their lives lightened and brightened by the action of an intelligent Social Democracy.

To every upholder of the present system the poorhouse inmates are a mere burden on the rates, or an intolerable nuisance to honest folk, who are well done for if they are fed and sheltered at all. But to the Social Democrat they are unfortunate victims of an evil social system. They are our brothers and sisters, crushed beneath the wheels of a remorseless competition. They are the effect of which the landlord and capitalist are the cause.

We have so long been accustomed to receive without question the teachings of the master class, that it is no wonder the poorhouse dole and poor-relief should be regarded amongst us as degrading to the recipient instead of to society at large. But it is on society at large, and on its supporters and apologists, the real stigma should rest. Indeed, it would be well for the workers as a whole if they could come to look upon the poor-rates as their first means of relief instead of as their last resource.

Man, as a social animal, has a claim upon the society which gave him birth. This claim is his right to live as long as he is willing to perform his share of the labour necessary to his own maintenance and the maintenance of society at large. This claim involves, in the first place, the right of free access to the means of life; in the second place, the duty of contributing to the support of the weaker members of the community, *i.e.*, children, the sick, infirm, and the aged.

Our Poor Law system is a grudging admission of the truth of this thesis, granted by the classes as an alternative to a troubled social upheaval. It has been surrounded since its inception with every form of insult and degradation their mean and petty minds could devise, until, today, the hideous uniform of the pauper is loathed more than the garb of the convict.

Thus, our masters have striven to debase this institution, whose existence in our midst they feel to be a standing reproach to the devil-take-the-hindmost theory, with which they wish to govern society.

To rescue our Poor Law from their hands, to relieve it from the false ideals with which its administration has been cursed, and to make its administrators in very truth guardians of the poor, this should be the aim of the workers. By so directing their efforts they may create, out of the framework of our Parish Councils, a public body, who, in solicitude for the public welfare and thoughtful provision for the weaker members of our human family, will find the same incentive to effort as the Liberal and Tory politicians find in the grosser pursuit of the glittering spoils of office.

But such a body can only arise out of that higher conception of human rights and duties which will flow from a wide and general acceptance of the principles of enlightened Social Democracy.

28. THE COMING GENERATION

The Coming Generation.

Last week we witnessed in Dublin the first political parade of the coming generation.

Between twenty-five and thirty thousand children turned out and walked in processional order through the streets of the city, to show the world that British Imperialism had cast no glamour over their young minds.

And that in the person of Her Britannic Majesty they recognised only a woman—no better than the mothers who bore them, if as good.

It was a great sight to see the little rebels taking possession of the city—a sight more promising for the future of the country than any we can remember.

Well, the children did their duty. Now are you prepared to do your duty to the children? Listen, my patriotic friend! Every child in that army of processionists—being the children of the poor as they all were, for it is only in the veins of such the stream of patriotism flows pure and undefiled—is destined to become, if it lives, the slave of a master, and will grow up in a world which nowhere recognises its right to life, except on the supposition that it will make a profit for a master.

You rear your child up to love its country, and you support a social system which declares that the child has no right to the country, but must pay for permission to live on it as it is the property of private individuals.

You shout for liberty, and you surrender your children to the mercies of capitalism which will seize them as soon as they leave school, and will devote their little bones, muscles and undeveloped brains to the task of grinding out profits for a boss.

Are you doing your duty? Love Ireland! Yes, if by 'Ireland' you mean not only the earth and the waters, but the men and the women, the boys and the girls—the people of Ireland, in fact.

Ireland without her people is nothing to me, and the man who is bubbling over with love and enthusiasm for 'Ireland,' and can yet pass unmoved through our streets and witness all the wrong and the suffering, the shame and the degradation wrought upon the people of Ireland, aye, wrought by Irishmen upon Irishmen and women, without burning to end it, is, in my opinion, a fraud and a liar in his heart, no matter how he loves that combination of chemical elements which he is pleased to call 'Ireland.'

If you are proud of the children who responded to the call of their country, and passed unheeded the seductions of the tyrant, then bestir yourselves to win for them a right to live in that country, a right to enjoy its beauties, and revel in its abundance, irrespective of the wishes of any employer or landlord.

When Socialism is realised every child in our Irish soil will by the mere fact of its existence be an heir to, and partner in, all the country produces; will have the same right to an assured existence as the citizen has today to his citizenship—in fact that will then be the right of citizenship, the right to live in the country, and the right to enjoy those fruits of labour the country will yield to its children.

That is the reward you should render the children for their love of country; win the country for them and leave it behind you as theirs to enjoy free and unfettered—neither under the heel of foreign tyrant, nor yielding disguised tribute to native slave driver.

You cannot be doing, you are not doing, your duty to the children while you leave them to grow up amidst such surroundings as are to be found in the tenement houses of our city.

You are neglecting your duty as long as you allow your City Hall to be in the power of men who as landlords derive their living from the rents they extort out of the poisonous slums in which they are slowly murdering the children of the working class—those very children you professed to admire on Sunday.

You are traitor to your duty as long as you elect to Parliament the members of a political party which, like the Home

Rule Party, is officered, managed and financed by that same class—the landlords of our city slums.

Ah, be true to your class, to your duty, to our children, and you cannot fail but be worthy of your country, and when next the non-Socialist politicians, or the municipal wirepuller solicits support:

Think of the children who swarm and die
  In loathsome dens where despair is king,
  Like blackened buds of a frosty spring
That wither sunless, remote they lie
  From the love that nurtures each quickening sense,
  While Vice, and Hunger, and Pestilence,
Breast-poisoned nurses, the babies drain dry.

And so thinking, take your place in the ranks of the Socialist Republican Party.

SPAILPIN

29. IRELAND SOBER IS IRELAND FREE?

Strikes.

In Dublin at present we have two very important strikes each affecting hundreds of men.

The Tailors' strike or lockout and the strike of Dockers on the Quays.

In each case we are confronted with the grim fact that in the world today there are but two classes—the Master Class and the Working Class—and that those two classes are at perpetual war with each other.

The Master Class, the dominant ruling class, strives by every means in its power to keep the Working Class in such a state of subjection that the process of spoiling or robbing the worker of his earnings, may go smoothly on with as little risks or dislocation as possible.

The Working Class on the other hand perpetually rises in protest against the incidental details of the robbery, organises to reduce the stealings of the Masters, and ever and anon throws down its tools, and enters on a bloodless insurrection against the conditions of its servitude.

These protests, these organised movements, these unarmed insurrections of labour, these strikes are the inevitable accompaniment of the capitalistic system of society—they are the salient proofs that the Socialist alone knows what he is talking about when he declares that the normal condition of society is not peace, but war; that the Class War is the one, great fact in the modern world.

'Ireland sober is Ireland free,' said Mr George Leahy, President of the Irish Trades Union Congress. How utterly inane and idiotic the saying was should now be apparent to the most unthinking. If all the Tailors and Dockers of Dublin were total abstainers would that alter the fact that in order to obtain a remedy for some paltry grievances these men were compelled to surrender their means of livelihood and leave themselves workless upon the streets.

'There is no antagonism between Capital and Labour,' Mr George Leahy declared also at the same Congress, and, lo! strikes on the Dublin quays, lock-out of the tailoring trade, strikes in Limerick, disputes in half-a-dozen smaller concerns every week, why it looks as if masters and men alike resolved to show the world how little Mr Leahy knows, or how incapable he is of talking common sense.

The Dock Strike has for us certain attractions greater than most industrial disputes in Ireland. The reason being that work on the docks is carried on under thorough capitalist conditions.

There the capitalist system of exploiting labour can be seen better than in most industries in this undeveloped country.

There are no small employers, no working capitalists, no personal relations between masters and men. There is only one connecting link between the employers and the employees, and that link is to be found in the gold, silver, or copper coins the worker draws as the reward for his labour.

The 'Cash Nexus' abhorred of Carlyle is the only point of contact betwixt the dockers and the men who live upon their labour.

Down the quays the workers are not regarded by their masters as human beings—they are only reckoned as so many items in the balance-sheet, and troublesome items at that.

This is Capitalism pure and simple, and to it the workers oppose their organisation—trade unionism pure and simple.

With the accent on the word 'simple.'

The workers on the quay have such voting strength that they can return as their representatives on the City Council practically whoever they like, yet in the North Dock Ward their representatives are a lawyer, a publican, a shipping agent—and Alderman Fleming.

It is hard to classify Alderman Fleming. He is what the Americans style a 'Labour Fakir,' that is to say a man who was once a worker, and has used the labour vote to crawl into a position in a public body where the capitalist class find it to their interest to 'square' him, and use him in order to delude the working class to support capitalist nominees.

That is Fleming.

The dock workers are thus pitted against a powerful combination of interests representing the entire propertied class; and the shipping companies have not only the power of their stored up capital against the poor funds of the men's union, but have also their representatives and friends in the City Council and Parliament, elected by the men themselves.

The masters have the power of money, they have the political power, and they have the municipal power, and in every case they have derived that power from the men against whom they are now using it.

But of course it is better to be thus fought with the weapons you handed to your opponent, than to vote for a Socialist, isn't it?

Under Socialism the docks and the shipping would belong to the nation, and the work would be carried on co-operatively by the dockers in the public interest, under the management of men elected by the dockers. The stevedores, instead of being tyrannical bosses over the men, would be elected from the ranks of the men for their skill in organising effectively the work required, would be the servants of the men, and all labour would be remunerated according to the full value of the work performed.

Strikes would be impossible, because, as the workers would be their own bosses, there would be nobody to strike against. The Municipal Council would be an executive body representing all the industries of the city, and charged with the supervision of the industrial affairs of the population; and with the Municipal Council, and not with any private individuals, would all trades and industries require to deal in all matters affecting trade organisation, labour, and the reward of labour.

But that would be Socialism, and Socialism is an awful thing to contemplate, you know. And so the dockers are left to the leadership of men, some of whom are politicians of the same stripe as their masters, and others of whom told them a few weeks ago that if they were only sober their masters would not oppress them—they and their country would be free!!

SPAILPIN

30. FACETS OF AMERICAN LIBERTY

'Where Liberty is, there is my country.'

So said the enthusiastic 18th century revolutionist. But if he lived nowadays he would have a long search for his country —where Liberty is. The only liberty we know of now, outside the liberty to go hungry, stands in New York Bay, where it has been placed, I am told, in order that immigrants from Europe may get their first and last look at it before setting foot on American soil.

You see, it would be decidedly awkward for our Fourth of July orators to be orating to the newcomers about the blessings of American liberty and then to be asked by some ignorant European to tell where that liberty is to be found.

Some ignorant, discontented unit of the hordes of Europe, for instance, might feel tempted to go nosing around in this great country in search of liberty, and his search might take him into the most awkward places.

He might go down South and see little white American children of seven, eight and nine years of age working in our cotton mills enjoying their liberty to work for a boss at an age when other children are still compelled by tyrannical laws to stay on wrestling with the dreadful problems of reading, 'riting and 'rithmetic.

He might have visited Alabama and seen American citizens out on strike, driven out of their homes by the power of the capitalist mine-owner, and when they erected tents upon private land granted by a charitable farmer for that purpose, he might have seen a Democratic governor order in the state militia to cut down the tents and drive the American workers back to the mine at the point of the bayonet.

He might, being an ignorant European, visit Florida and see men lured from the big cities to the railroad construction camps and kept there on a hunger diet, compelled to endure blows and foulest insults, and when they attempted to escape he might see the power of the state detective force employed to arrest them as if they were criminals and take them back handcuffed to their slavery.

This ignorant representative of the scum of Europe might have visited Colorado in 1904 and seen armed militia invade newspaper offices and imprison printers and journalists alike without legal warrant or pretense at trial, trade union meetings suppressed, duly elected public officials compelled to resign under threat of lynching, respectable men taken out of their beds in the middle of the night and without [being] given a chance to even put their shoes on marched under armed guards across the state lines, hundreds of men thrown into cattle enclosures and kept there for months without trial, and Pinkerton detectives employed to manufacture outrages in order to hang innocent men.

This pilgrim in search of liberty might have learned from the coal miners of Pennsylvania that their state is dotted over east and west with localities where union miners were shot down like dogs whilst peacefully parading the streets or roads in time of strikes, he might have learned that practically every industrial center in the country from Albany, N. Y., to San Francisco, Calif., from New Orleans to Minnesota, has the same tale to tell of the spilling of workmen's blood by the hirelings of the master class, and he might have attended the unemployed demonstration in Union Square, New York, and have seen the free American citizens rapped on the head for daring to ask a job collectively, instead of begging for it individually.

Or this greenhorn might have strolled along West Street, New York, and interviewed some Irish longshoremen, who could tell him that when in Ireland they stayed at home and played cards and bothered the women of the house every time it rained (and in Ireland it rains oftener than it is fair), that they stopped work every time there was a fair day, or a Saint's Day, or a Feast Day, or a Home Rule, Nationalist, Gaelic League or Orange Demonstration, when they stayed up too long at a wake, or wished to go a few miles to attend a wedding.

But that since he became a participant in the freedom of America he has to turn out to his work rain or shine, winter and summer, and be ready to stand in line to be picked out of a gang as he used to pick out pigs at a fair at home, only that the pigs got fed, if they were or were not picked, whereas he and his family are likely to go hungry if he does not keep on the soft side of the boss and get picked. And if he does get picked for a job, he has to stand worse driving and foul abuse than an Irish ass ever received from its driver.

As for holidays—tell it not in Gath. A holiday in Ireland meant rest and recreation for his body and mind; in America a holiday means a rest for his stomach and anxiety for his mind.

I think I can work in a joke here. There was once a hard-working Irish girl who married an enterprising Irish-American. On the day after the wedding she remarked, 'Well, thank God, now I can get a rest for my bones.'

' 'Deed, if you do, Mary,' responded her loving spouse, 'it will be a rest for your jaw-bones.'

(This joke is going to be copyrighted).

After making this pilgrimage through the state possibly our representative of the destitute alien might be impertinent enough to interrupt the Fourth of July orator with the demand to be shown where this American Liberty is.

Then the orator, thanks to Bartholdi, could arise in his dignity and crush the interrupter with the statement that Liberty is to be found outside in the Bay of New York.

It is a waste of time to look inside for what is standing outside. Verb sap, or as we say in the Gaelic, 'An tuigeann tú?' In the classic language of the Bowery, 'Are you next?'

The Liberty we have in Bartholdi's statue is truly typical of liberty in this age and country.

It is placed upon a pedestal out of the reach of the multitudes; it can only be approached by those who have money enough to pay the expense; it has a lamp to enlighten the world, but the lamp is never lit, and it smiles upon us as we approach America, but when we are once in the country we never see anything but its back.

'Tis a great world we live in.

P. H. B., of Shaft, Pa., wrote to the *Harp* in September asking for enlightenment on several points connected with the practical workings of Socialism in the mining industry. The chief points he dealt with were the difficulty of having a system that would insure absolute justice to every individual, and who would do the dirty work, and who would be induced to waste his time in qualifying for a mining engineer when the ordinary miner would be as highly remunerated.

Our friend should remember that Socialists do not suppose that the substitution of common ownership for private ownership will of itself abolish all difficulties or solve all questions of administration. It will not. But it will make the solution of those questions on a just basis easier than it is to-day. In fact, to-day justice is simply not taken into account in such matters. Expediency and profit-making are all that are sought. Yet our friend, like many others, demands of Socialism perfect, absolute, flawless justice down to the minutest detail, and if he cannot be assured of it he will continue to support the capitalist system, although he knows it to be saturated with injustices of the most horrible description.

I presume that he would not ride on a railroad train until he had fully understood all the mechanism of a steam engine, all the principles and practice of steam propulsion, all the complicated appliances of signaling, points, switching and railroad telegraphing.

But that would not be his attitude in reality. No, he would say that he had no doubt there were difficulties in the way of railroading, but that the central principle being right he could trust the associated intelligence of those engaged in the industry to master those difficulties in line with the general principle. That, in fact, has been the general practical attitude of the human race toward all innovations, once the general principle of the new departure was accepted.

Under Socialism, mining, like every other industry, will be democratically administered by the workers in that occupation; foremen, managers, superintendents, etc., will all be elected from and by the rank and file of the workers, and those same workers will also elect the delegates who will represent them on the local and governing bodies of the land. All matters pertaining to the technical efficiency of the mines, and of labor, will be settled either by those experts whom the workers have elected as administrators, by discussion and vote of the men in the union of their industry, or by whatever method their common interest and sense of fairness can devise.

Such positions as mining engineers, or other professions, etc., can be filled by pupils chosen in a competitive examination. There will always be a sufficiency of candidates for any such post of honor, and as the cost of the education for such posts will be borne by the community, and not by the individual aspirant, they need not necessarily entail any disparity of salary.

As for the varying needs of individuals, each individual will require to 'cut his coat according to his cloth,' to use a homely old saying. He whose tastes run to automobiles cannot expect to be strong on books, and he who desires the luxury of travel will have to forego the pleasures of a private garden and a secluded mansion. And so on *ad infinitum.*

Socialism will solve the problem of poverty by abolishing it, but it will not solve all problems, smooth all rough places, nor prevent all mistakes.

Under Socialism men will possibly often mistake their avocations in life, women will marry the wrong men, and men will marry the wrong women.

I know some Socialists say that there will be no marriage question under Socialism, but I do not see that that will necessarily be the case, and I am only concerned with what Socialism will necessarily do. I hold that under Socialism no woman will be compelled to marry a man for a livelihood or for riches, but I hold that it is quite possible that under Socialism a man and woman may imagine that they were destined for each other, love and marry, and after the lapse of years and closer intimacy find they had made a mistake and one came to hate the other.

And when that happens we will have a marriage and divorce question, or a sex question, if you will, and I do not see that the fact that each is economically independent of the other will alter that fact. If the woman desires to be rid of the man whilst the man still loves the woman, or vice versa, we will still have passion, and jealousy, and love, and hatred.

In fact, Socialism will not make us angels upon earth; it will only put a premium upon our better qualities instead of upon our baser, as is done by capitalism today. And that itself would be worth a revolution to realize, or a thousand revolutions.

Under any system of society there will be differences of opinion amongst men and women, and with some natures such differences will be intense and lead to much swinging of literary and verbal cudgels, and metaphorical belaboring with blackthorns.

Talking of blackthorns reminds me of some fine verses I lately came across upon that inspiring subject. Here they are; you can read them while I mop my fevered brow:

LINES TO A BLACKTHORN

You're welcome to my hand, my fine blackthorn,
  That grew in beauty under Erin's skies;
Your blossom sweet, on many a bright May morn,
  Gave added fragrance to the summer's sighs.
Upon your branch the brown-robed linnet sang,
  The goldfinch chattered merrily his lay,
And at your feet the primrose joyous spring
  To welcome your sweet blossoms falling spray.

It moves the fount of memory to tears
  To think this fine 'Kippeen' had root upon
That Irish hillside, where my boyhood years
  In careless glee and innocence sped on,
I hear the lark with pulsing waves of song—
  Sweet herald of the dawn that knew no care—
Across the gulf of Time, again I long
  To feel the rapture of that matin prayer.

And when they cut you down, my fine blackthorn,
  They 'saysoned' you, like bacon in the smoke
Above the ample 'hob,' where night and morn
  The turf fire gave you heart and strength of oak.
And round the fire I hear the welcome cheer
  That burst in limpid music from the heart.
As neighbor entered with 'God save all here,'
  And 'banact lat,' as he would slow depart.

You are welcome to my hand, for like the rod
At Moses' touch bloomed in the desert wild,
I see again dear Erin's verdant sod,
And every flower that on her bosom smiled.
Sure you are nurtured by the same soft rain,
Your veins were warmed by the same bright sun.
And so at your kind touch I live again
The joyous hours with which life's morn begun.
—William J. Dawson.

Another correspondent writes to ask me 'as a practical man' to tell what measures the Socialists would pass and what they would repeal in the city of St. Louis, in the state of Missouri, in the Senate or Congress if they got the victory. 'Tis a tall order.

In the first place I am not a practical man. To be practical under capitalism means that your ideas are consonant with the existence of capitalism. Mine, I trust, are not. My correspondent has not grasped that fact yet; when he does he will realize that to be 'practical' is the last thing I aim at.

I would remind him that the Socialist Party of St. Louis, the Socialist Party of Missouri, and the National organization have each issued platforms which answer his questions, and recommend him to secure copies for his enlightenment. He tells me he wants it answered in the *Harp*, but I desire him to understand that the *Harp* desires only to treat of the general principles of Socialism as a revolutionary movement, and not with any patching up of the old social order.

Personally, I believe that the fact that we still have long platforms and programs is one of the signs of the comparatively backward state of the Socialist movement, of our unripeness for Social Revolution. On the day that we have so far conquered the mind of the workers that we can safely abolish our platforms and concentrate and express our whole fighting principle in one simple phrase capable of being remembered by the average school boy, we will then, and then only, cease to be a propagandist association and become a revolutionary army.

At least so thinks SPAILPIN

31. REVOLUTIONARY SONG

This little book of revolutionary songs is published for a twofold purpose. First, it is in response to the belief of the Editor that no revolutionary movement is complete without its poetical expression. If such a movement has caught hold of the imagination of the masses they will seek a vent in song for the aspirations, the fears and the hopes, the loves and the hatreds engendered by the struggle. Until the movement is marked by the joyous, defiant, singing of revolutionary songs, it lacks one of the most distinctive marks of a popular revolutionary movement, it is the dogma of a few, and not the faith of the multitude. In this belief this small bouquet of songs, culled from a very limited garden, is offered until some one with greater means shall present to the American Working Class a more suitable collection, drawn not from the store of one nation alone, but from the Socialist poetry of the World. The propagandist effect of such a volume of songs with their proper musical setting, would be simply incalculable.

The second purpose of this volume may be readily guessed by a glance at its contents. It will be seen that every song herein contained was written by an Irishman.

This is in no spirit of insularity, but rather is meant as an encouragement to other Irishmen and women, to take their part and do their share in the upbuilding of the revolutionary movement of the Working Class. Most of these songs were written in Ireland, by men actually engaged in the revolutionary struggle of their time, whatever ruggedness may attach to their numbers is due to the fact that they were born in the stress and strain of the fight, and not in the scholarly seclusion of the study.

In conclusion, if this venture meets approval, we will carry our next into the field of recitative poetry, where a rich Irish harvest awaits the gleaner.

EPILOGUE

Connolly's statement at his Court Martial, May 9th, 1916

Connolly developed gangrene in the leg which had been shattered by a dum-dum bullet during the fighting in Easter Week on Thursday, April 27th. His court-martial was therefore delayed, and finally took place in the hospital of Dublin Castle on Tuesday, May 9th. Charges of ill-treatment of prisoners were made during the trial. Irish nationalist tradition had always laid great stress on the speeches of convicted patriots from the dock, and Connolly was at considerable pains to ensure the preservation and publication of his own. He gave it to his daughter Nora when she and his wife visited him on the morning of his execution three days later. She smuggled it out.

To the Field General Court Martial, held at Dublin Castle, on May 9th, 1916.

> [Evidence mainly went to establish the fact that the accused, James Connolly, was in command at the General Post Office, and was also Commandant-General of the Dublin Division. Two of the witnesses, however, strove to bring in alleged instances of wantonly risking the lives of prisoners. The Court held that these charges were *irrelevant* and could not be placed against the prisoner.]

I do not wish to make any defence except against charges of wanton cruelty to prisoners. These trifling allegations that have been made, if they record facts that really happened, deal only with the almost unavoidable incidents of a hurried uprising against long established authority, and nowhere show evidence of set purpose to wantonly injure unarmed persons.

We went out to break the connection between this country and the British Empire, and to establish an Irish Republic.

We believed that the call we then issued to the people of Ireland, was a nobler call, in a holier cause, than any call issued to them during this war, having any connection with the war. We succeeded in proving that Irishmen are ready to die endeavouring to win for Ireland those national rights which the British Government has been asking them to die to win for Belgium. As long as that remains the case, the cause of Irish freedom is safe.

Believing that the British Government has no right in Ireland, never had any right in Ireland, and never can have any right in Ireland, the presence, in any one generation of Irishmen, of even a respectable minority, ready to die to affirm that truth, makes that Government for ever a usurpation and a crime against human progress.

I personally thank God that I have lived to see the day when thousands of Irish men and boys, and hundreds of Irish women and girls, were ready to affirm that truth, and to attest it with their lives if need be.

JAMES CONNOLLY,
Commandant-General, Dublin Division,
Army of the Irish Republic

BIBLIOGRAPHICAL NOTE

The reader who would wish to take his study of Connolly further is advised to turn in the initial instance to the two major volumes of which only an extract from the first has been printed here: *Labour in Irish History* (Maunsel & Co., Dublin, 1910) and *The Reconquest of Ireland* (Maunsel & Co., Dublin, 1915). Both volumes are conveniently published under one cover as *Labour in Ireland* (Maunsel & Co., Dublin, n.d.), while both works are issued separately as inexpensive paperbacks as part of the Irish Socialist Library, a series sponsored by the Irish Communist Party. The latter series also includes *Revolutionary Warfare* (New Books, Dublin and Belfast, 1968), a collection of Connolly's writings on insurrectionary military activity produced by him in the months preceding his own practical exercise in that field. But for detailed and wide-ranging examination there can be no substitute for the three excellent volumes edited by Desmond Ryan. All are selections from Connolly's journalism from 1896 to 1916, and many cross-references, briefer extracts and historiographical citations make them invaluable. Our chief criticism is that occasional deletions have been made, and that such deletions have not been noted in all cases; occasional modernizations have been introduced, such as 'I' for 'the present writer'; and, very rarely, errors have crept into the texts and citations. The three volumes (all published by Three Candles, Dublin) are *Socialism and Nationalism* (1948), *Labour and Easter Week* (1949) and *The Workers' Republic* (1951). We have sought to avoid undue duplication with the Ryan volumes here, so those whom we succeed in sending from our selection to his need not fear to meet too many old friends. There is in addition a popular anthology of Connolly's writings modestly entitled *The Best of Connolly* (Mercier Press, Cork, 1967); it is a paperback and is edited by Proinsias Mac Aonghusa and Liam Ó Réagáin.

Having said all this, it must be added that much of

Connolly's writing still remains only in the original newspapers. To the best of our knowledge, of the documents included in this selection the following have never been reprinted before or, in a few cases, never in their entirety: 3, 4, 5, 6, 7, 8, 11, 12, 14, 16, 19, 23, 27, 28, 29, 30, 31. The Irish Communist Organization, whose confusion with the Irish Communist Party will draw on the offender the wrath of both bodies, has helpfully issued some small pamphlets of selections of 'Connolly's Suppressed Writings', as they insist on terming them. These are often (although not always) articles from *Forward* not included by Ryan; among them is Chapter 22. Of those already published *Yellow Unions in Ireland* and *Press Poisoners in Ireland* (both published by Connolly Books, Belfast) may be mentioned. But neither the resource of the I.C.O. nor this present selection nor any other anthology is a satisfactory substitute for the standard edition of all Connolly's known writings, which ought now to be in preparation.

On Connolly's own life, the best work is C. Desmond Greaves, *The Life and Times of James Connolly* (Lawrence & Wishart, London, 1961). A paperbound reprint has been issued this year. It is a work of vast research, and corrects the record at innumerable points of factual detail. The views expressed are those of an Irish Republican and British Communist; accordingly, Connolly's syndicalism is acknowledged but gets short shrift. But whatever the reader's disagreements with the book, his obligations to it are immense. Owen Dudley Edwards has written a study of Connolly entitled *The Mind of an Activist: James Connolly* (Gill & Macmillan, Dublin, 1971). It seeks to establish Connolly's place in his intellectual generation in Ireland, assesses his relations with Catholicism, and throws some light on his association with Francis Sheehy-Skeffington. It is weak on syndicalism, and on Connolly's evolution as a thinker, tending too much to consider his work as a totality; it is, moreover, directed primarily to an Irish audience, whereas the present work has been conceived for non-Irish readers in the first instance. Its bibliographical references may supplement those in Greaves.

Several of Desmond Ryan's works should be consulted, chiefly his memoir of Connolly, *James Connolly* (Talbot Press, Dublin, 1924), his magnificent autobiography *Remembering Sion* (Arthur Barker, London, 1934), his study of the 1916 Rising (still the best single volume on it), *The Rising* (Golden Eagle Books, Dublin, 1949), and his posthumously published essay on Connolly in J. W. Boyle's *Leaders and Workers* (Mercier Press, Cork, n.d.). Walter Kendall's *The Revolutionary Movement in Great Britain, 1900–1921* (Weidenfeld & Nicolson, London, 1969), is based on a fantastic wealth of research, and starts, though it does not always finish, many useful lines of investigation; its bias is too sharply anti-Communist. There is no satisfactory study of the background to Connolly's Scottish career, but Bernard C. Ransom's Ph.D. thesis on Connolly in Scotland should clear up many problems when it is concluded. On Irish problems *James Larkin* by Emmet Larkin (no relation) (Routledge & Kegan Paul, London, 1965) is sound and scholarly, if unduly assertive. An introduction to the general background is available in the brilliant and comprehensive *Ireland since the Famine* by F. S. L. Lyons (Weidenfeld & Nicolson, London, 1971). Patrick O'Farrell's *Ireland's English Question* (Batsford, London, 1971) has useful insights.

On Connolly's Belfast, the best work is that by J. W. Boyle, still only available in various scholarly articles; Owen Dudley Edwards has drawn heavily on these in his own work *The Sins of Our Fathers—Roots of Conflict in Northern Ireland* (Gill & Macmillan, Dublin, 1970), whose fourth chapter ('The Breaking of the Irish Working Class'), surveys the labour conditions and movements in the Belfast of the late nineteenth and early twentieth centuries; it may be unduly sentimental about Connolly. An impressive Marxist summary covering the same topic with similar stress on recent events is Liam de Paor's *Divided Ulster* (Penguin Books, Harmondsworth, 1970). On the American side, Patrick Renshaw on the I.W.W., *The Wobblies* (Eyre & Spottiswoode, London, 1967), is lucid but not always accurate. Melvyn Dubofsky's *We Shall Be All* (Quadrangle Books, Chicago, 1969) is sounder, much more detailed, but similarly weak in assessing European links. The ideological background to the Irish-Americans among whom

Connolly worked is brilliantly assessed in Thomas N. Brown, *Irish-American Nationalism* (Lippincott, Philadelphia, 1965), but it covers only the period 1870–91. It remains fundamental for an understanding of the material with which Connolly was trying to work.